FREE WILL:
A GUIDE FOR THE PERPLEXED

FREE WILL:
A GUIDE FOR THE PERPLEXED

T. J. MAWSON

continuum

The Continuum International Publishing Group
The Tower Building   80 Maiden Lane
11 York Road   Suite 704
London SE1 7NX   New York, NY 10038

www.continuumbooks.com

Library of Congress Cataloging-in-Publication Data
Mawson, T. J.
Free will: a guide for the perplexed / T. J. Mawson.
    p. cm.
Includes bibliographical references (p.   ).
ISBN-13: 978-1-4411-9623-1 (hardcover: alk. paper)
ISBN-10: 1-4411-9623-4 (hardcover: alk. paper)
ISBN-13: 978-1-4411-0209-6 (pbk.: alk. paper)
ISBN-10: 1-4411-0209-4 (pbk.: alk. paper)
1. Free will and determinism. I. Title.

BJ1461.M39 2011
123'.5–dc22   2010030396

ISBN: HB: 978-1-4411-9623-1
       PB: 978-1-4411-0209-6

Typeset by Newgen Imaging Systems Pvt Ltd, Chennai, India

To my daughter, all of whose choices lie before her

CONTENTS

ACKNOWLEDGEMENTS

The works mentioned in the suggestions for further reading at the end of this book have been useful to me in clarifying my thoughts on this topic and thus I am grateful to their authors. I mention here a few of my greatest debts: in my treatment of the Consequence Argument and of the notion of self-forming actions, I draw heavily on the work of Bob Kane and in my treatment of agent causation I similarly draw on the work of John Bishop, Randolph Clarke and Tim O'Connor. I am also grateful for the comments of John Bishop, Randolph Clarke, Peter Kail, Bob Kane, Kevin Timpe and Richard Swinburne on my own writing, and for the comments made by the audience at the conference on free will supported by the Templeton Foundation at which I presented a version of the penultimate chapter.

Oxford, 2010

CHAPTER ONE

INTRODUCTION

WHAT IS THE PROBLEM OF FREE WILL?

If we were to read opinion pieces in our newspapers, we would find in them no shortage of worries about the levels of freedom enjoyed by institutions and individuals in our society. Most often, the worry would be that they enjoy too little freedom: for example, a favourite claim of journalists is, for obvious reasons, that there are undue restrictions on the freedom of the press. But sometimes the worry would be that a group or an individual enjoys too much freedom: if we picked up a certain type of newspaper, we would not have to search for long before we found an opinion piece designed to make us choke on our breakfast cereal by telling us in outraged tones of how the perpetrator of some terrible crime is, nevertheless, free while in prison to enjoy various pastimes of which many ordinary hardworking folk can only dream.

Sometimes our political leaders tell us that they are sending our armies into another country as they are worried about the cause of freedom. Perhaps it is our own freedom that they tell us this invasion will protect (the leader of this other country has weapons of mass destruction which directly threaten us, we may be told). Perhaps it is to the appropriately enhanced freedom of the citizens of this other country, or at least those who will be left alive after our armies have done their work, that we should look if we are to find a justification for their decision. Perhaps their real motive springs from the anticipated enhancement of our own economic freedom, once we have secured access to the natural resources of this country on our own terms. In any case, the notion of freedom does a lot of work – some reputable, some disreputable – in everyday political and social discussion and reasoning. There are certainly important issues in Political Philosophy which cluster around the concepts – concept*s*, plural, for the only thing that is certain is that there is more than one of them – of freedom as so deployed.

The issue to which this book addresses itself is deeper than any of these concerns. In order ultimately to plunge down to its depths, let me first whisk you up and away from all these worries and take you, in your imagination, to a land where you discover that the occasions for the sorts of worries sketched in the previous two paragraphs have simply disappeared: in this land, you are amazed to discover that all the problems of political and social freedom have been resolved to your complete satisfaction. Let me tell you a little bit more about this marvellous country and thus bring you to see why even here – where the reasons for all worries about political and social freedoms have evaporated – a worry about a deeper sort of freedom might yet remain.

Imagine then that you find yourself in a society which its citizens call 'The People's Republic of Freedom'. In this country, the citizens happily share the duties of agriculture; working to maintain and improve infrastructure and the environment; raising families; and caring for the sick and elderly. Their own good efforts and the technology available to them mean that they have ample time to pursue without restriction whatever religious, artistic and scientific projects they wish. You are fortunate enough to be guided around this utopia by its genial creator and are hence able to ask of him the questions that you have.

Being a lover of freedom above all else, you go looking for reasons to worry about the level of freedom enjoyed by people in this society. Early on, you read one of the newspapers and it seems, to your jaded eyes, particularly suspicious in not raising any concerns on this score whatsoever, so you inquire of the creator first what restrictions on the press are in place. To your astonishment, you learn that there are none at all. 'Ah,' you surmise, 'so that must mean that sometimes people choke on their breakfast cereal by reading of the good treatment being given to criminals.' Again, you learn, you are wrong in your presumption – this time for two reasons. First, no editor of any paper in The People's Republic of Freedom ever wishes to print anything that would interfere in this manner with the freedom of his or her readers to enjoy their breakfast uninterrupted and so, even were there such a story to be told, he or she would not choose to tell it. But, secondly and more fundamentally, there is no such story to be told *for there are no criminals.*

You are incredulous; you have passed only unlocked doors since you have arrived and have, it suddenly occurs to you, not seen a single CCTV camera (in your home country, such things now seem to sprout from every lamppost). Surely sometimes, you say, the temptations provided by this chronic lack of security-mindedness on the part of the citizens of The People's Republic of Freedom will have proved too great for one of them to resist. However, the creator benignly assures you that they have not and indeed over the next few weeks you are able to remove any cause for worry you might have on this score by experiment: try as you might, over several weeks living in this society, you cannot find a single person whom you can tempt to infringe, in even the slightest way, the laws or the freedoms of anyone else. The citizens are entirely benevolent.

Over an elongated period living amongst the citizens of The People's Republic of Freedom, you cannot find any cause to worry to any extent at all about the political and social freedoms its citizens enjoy; their society thus seems to you maximally deserving of its name. And so, being a lover of freedom above all else, you ask the creator how you might yourself apply for citizenship. He is delighted to report that the procedure for becoming a full citizen is quick, easy, and guarantees success. He himself will guide you through it over the next few minutes. Very soon you will never need to worry about suffering from a lack of freedom again, he amiably assures you.

Guided by the creator then, you are 'scanned' by a sophisticated computer, the purpose of which, the creator tells you, he will describe in just a moment; you salute the country's flag and pledge an oath of allegiance; and you drink to the dregs a large cup of the country's national beverage, Freedom Froth. This is a beverage which – it now occurs to you for the first time – you have seen being drunk by the citizens of The People's Republic of Freedom at every mealtime since you have arrived and yet had not hitherto tasted yourself. As soon as you have downed the Freedom Froth, you start to feel yourself becoming rather light-headed. 'Do sit down', the creator affably suggests, 'the drink will take a couple of minutes to work its wonders, a couple of minutes which – with your agreement – I'll happily fill by telling you a little bit more about the computer and just how it is that I have managed to eliminate any cause for worries about freedom within The People's Republic of Freedom.' The creator then goes on to tell you the following.

'I was always impressed by Mill's ideal that the state should try to grant to each citizen the maximum freedom compatible with a similar level being held by every other. But, at the same time, I was concerned that meeting that ideal by itself would not prevent there being an upper bound on the amount of freedom that each citizen could enjoy, an upper bound generated by the fact that citizens might have conflicting desires or make, as we might say, "conflicting choices". You might be familiar with the thought as expressed casually with words such as, "Your freedom to extend your arm must finish just prior to your fist hitting my nose." The presumption of such a case of course is that a citizen who chooses to extend his or her arm might find himself or herself in close proximity to a citizen who has the desire not to be hit on the nose. It thus quickly occurred to me that society could only be maximally free – this upper bound could only be removed – by eliminating conflicting desires and choices. But that, it struck me, was no physical impossibility; it was just a neurological engineering problem and I happened to have a suitable background. I thus spent several years working on three projects that, in conjunction, have enabled me to build a sustainable society of people about whose freedom no worries can legitimately be raised.' Despite now feeling rather woozy, you lean forward to make sure you hear all that the creator goes on to say; from somewhere deep within you, a sense of unease is struggling up towards your consciousness.

'The first project was a computer of such sophistication as to be infallible about what desires being had and choices being made by what citizens at what time would eliminate conflict and best enable the society to continue on in existence. The second was a transmitter capable of beaming this information in a targeted way into the heads of the relevant citizens. And the third, with which I'm particularly pleased as I was able to make it into a pleasant-tasting (even if rather gassy) beverage, was a drug which attuned people's brains to pick up on this information and necessitated that, from within five minutes of their first drinking it, they could only ever have the desires the computer legislated and make the choices the computer decreed for them. Finally, I completed these three projects and thus The People's Republic of Freedom was born, a society in which every citizen has maximal freedom – he or she can literally do whatever he or she wants or chooses – as a result of his or her being incapable of wanting or choosing anything other than whatever it is the computer tells him or her to want and choose. Your scanning by the computer is complete; your first instructions are already being transmitted; the five minutes needed for the drug you have drunk to take effect are almost up. Very soon now, you will mesh in perfectly with the rest of us, being incapable of wanting, choosing, or indeed – joy of joy! – thinking or believing anything other than what the computer determines you to want, choose, think and believe, being incapable then of having your freedom to act on your wants and beliefs as you choose frustrated by anyone or anything else.' The feeling of unease that was growing in you is now taking the shape of a more determinate thought even as you become aware that the drug is making you care less about it. With a last effort, you try to articulate it. The words are almost there, but they seem somehow stuck on your lips. The creator pauses, noticing the look on your face. 'What are you worried about?' he asks.

What you are worried about in the last moments before the drink completes its work is the problem of free will to which this book addresses itself.

CHAPTER TWO

OUR EXPERIENCE OF CHOICE

INTRODUCTION

You have to start from where you are. So in this chapter we'll start by looking at five thoughts which people ordinarily have about themselves as they first begin to reflect on their experience of themselves as – apparently – making free choices. Having treated these five thoughts in turn, we'll see how they 'lock together' into a certain view about the existence and nature of free will, the view which we'll follow tradition in calling 'Libertarianism'.[1] This, it will be argued, is the common-sense view of the subject of this book – what our everyday experience suggests to us about free will. This is the thing you feared that you were about to lose in joining The People's Republic of Freedom as discussed in Chapter One. Of course our common-sense view of ourselves might be wrong and in subsequent chapters we'll look at various arguments which suggest that various parts of it *are* wrong. But to assess the force of those arguments we need to know what they're arguments against; we need to know what the common-sense view is. And the aim of this chapter is to get that pretty well nailed down by the end.

One point before we start properly: you may have noticed that this book has a glossary of key terms at the end. I'll give a brief definition of each of these terms when they're first used in argument in the chapters between now and then, but – especially if you're new to the topic or the study of Philosophy – you might like to have a quick skim through the glossary now and fold the corner of the page down (unless you're one of those people who has a principled objection to folding page corners down), so you can find it easily again as you read on.

* * *

In everyday life, we often suppose ourselves to be free to choose between several courses of action. Shall I read a book on the nature of free will or shall I watch television? If I watch television, shall I watch the news or *The Simpsons*? Moment by moment, paths seem to be opening before us. From these paths, we seem to be picking out one route into one future and turning aside from other routes, routes which would have taken us into other futures. Once we have passed the given moment in time at which we made a particular choice, we cannot, of course, go back to travel instead one of the roads not taken, or at least we cannot go back to travel it from the start. Sometimes we can cut across, as it were, from one path to another – for example, having started reading the book, I might well put it to one side after five minutes and turn on the television instead, finding myself to have missed only an insignificant moment or two of the programme I then watch. But we can never go back, only sometimes sideways in this sense and sometimes not even that. Sometimes, by the time we find ourselves wishing that we'd chosen differently, it is too late for us to find a way across to the route we now wish we'd chosen.[2]

When we are more or less contented with the way that a section of our lives has worked out, we seldom spend much time in reflecting on how our lives would have been different had we chosen differently during that period. And no doubt this is often psychologically healthy: reflecting on what might have been can lead to dissatisfaction with what is; and, if we can no longer cut across to an alternative path, one which we realize on reflection we wish we had taken from the start, this dissatisfaction threatens to be pointless. But sometimes even reflection that is dissatisfying and pointless in this sense can be satisfying and worthwhile in another, through being educative. In realizing that, had we chosen differently, things would now be in some significant way better for ourselves or others than they are and that we cannot in this instance recover the situation, we are often enabled thereby to commit ourselves all the more wholeheartedly to making better choices in the future. And sometimes of course reflection on what might have been can lead to satisfaction and even extreme relief, as when one realizes that only by the narrowest of margins did one avoid some disaster: 'My goodness! Had I stepped out into the road then, as I almost did, I would have been hit by that bus.' And whatever its psychological effects, we certainly *can* reflect on what our lives would now be like if we had chosen another route from the one that we actually chose and we can form more or less confident counterfactual judgements concerning such things.

For example, perhaps, as I finally switch off the television having watched *The Simpsons*, I find myself thinking something like the following. 'Had I read the book, instead of watching television during that half hour, I would have learnt something about free will; had I watched the news rather than *The Simpsons*, I would have discovered more about current affairs. [Sigh.] But, then again, had I not watched *The Simpsons*, I would not have had as enjoyable a half hour as I have just had; the book would no doubt have proved boring; the news, no doubt, depressing. On balance, I wouldn't choose differently were I to have that half hour again.' And, of course, whenever we think a thought of this kind, we think that we think it truly; that is to say, we are committed to thinking that the world must be however it needs to be to make the thought true. If my thinking concerning the half hour I've just spent watching *The Simpsons* is to be true, it must really be the case that had I read the book or watched the news I would have learnt something but had a less enjoyable half hour.

Everyday reflections such as the above are necessary for us rationally to improve our judgement over time and thereby make better choices in the future than we did in the past; and, for everyday reflections such as this to be adequate reflections of reality, reality must thus be whatever way it needs to be to make thoughts such as this often true. What way is that?

The five thoughts we are looking at in this chapter are descriptions of five aspects of the answer to this question that we presuppose in everyday life. We shall deal with them in turn.

* * *

Here's the first 'everyday' thought we have about ourselves:

Sometimes I could do something other than what I actually do.

It seems that, just below the surface of our everyday decision-making and reflection on it, we believe that our world has a character such that, at certain moments, it has a number of futures greater than one possible for it. For example, in my reflections after the half hour I spent watching *The Simpsons* on television, I am committed to thinking that if I could – as is of course impossible – go back in time to the moment when I actually chose to put the book aside and spend the next half hour watching television, then it would be possible for me at that time to put the television remote control to one side instead and take up the book and, from then on, the world would go on in a slightly different fashion from the way it actually went. It would go down that path on which I end up after the half hour (unless I then subsequently switch path once more) being more informed about free will. It seems then that we believe that our universe is one in which, at least for some times, whatever it is we actually do at a given time is just one of several things that it is possible that we do at that time. We could hence call this belief our belief that the actual does not exhaust the possible; what actually happens isn't always the only thing that could happen; perhaps sometimes it is, but sometimes it is not. For obvious reasons, this assumption is sometimes called The Principle of Alternate Possibilities (though see the glossary). Let's 'unpack' this assumption a bit, first by getting a bit clearer on what it amounts to and then by looking briefly at how we would ordinarily suppose ourselves to justify particular applications of it.

First then, what exactly do we mean when we say that the actual does not exhaust the possible or that alternative futures are possible for us? There are a number of different notions of possibility available and we wish to be clear-headed as we deploy this idea hereafter, so we shall take a moment distinguishing from one another the two sorts of possibility most relevant to our discussion. The two sorts of possibility that it is most important for us to distinguish from one another at this stage are epistemic possibility and physical possibility.

Epistemic possibility is apparent possibility, relative to a set of known facts; it is, we might say, 'For all I/we know, . . .' possibility. By way of example, let us imagine a scientist investigating the issue of whether the force present in the Big Bang was sufficiently great to mean that the universe will keep on expanding forever, even if ever more gradually (the result being a 'heat death'), or whether, on the contrary, it was not great enough to produce such an effect and thus everything will eventually collapse back in on itself under gravitational attraction (ending in a 'big crunch'). She might perform a few relevant experiments and, as a result of them, report her inconclusive findings with the words, 'Either is possible', meaning that, so far, she has not been able to rule out either the hypothesis of heat death or that of big crunch on the basis of the evidence she has gathered. Were she to do so, she would be using 'possible' to refer to epistemic possibility; each hypothesis is consistent with what she knows so far; the truth of each is apparently possible given what she knows about the physical universe. However, at a later stage of investigation, the scientist we are imagining might discover something rather more startling about the way the universe is constructed, something which she also wished to report with the sentence, 'Either is possible'. With this sentence now she might be wishing to report her discovery that the force of the Big Bang was not so great as to necessitate heat death, but *neither* was it so small as to necessitate big crunch either; rather, which of these outcomes finally comes about will be brought about – she may be suggesting these new findings have led her to believe – by some not-yet-determined element. If this were the discovery she were trying to get across by saying of the heat death and the big crunch that 'either is possible', she would be using the second notion of possibility, physical possibility.

Physical possibility then is possibility relative to the initial or boundary conditions of the universe and the laws of nature that are operative on it. Remembering that epistemic possibility may be thought of as apparent possibility, we might naturally be tempted to equate physical possibility, by contrast, with *real* possibility or at least real possibility in our universe, given that its initial set-up was as it was and its laws of nature are as they are. And, having bracketed out one view for later consideration, we may indeed allow ourselves to give in to this temptation. The view we need to bracket out is the one that we have souls and that, although it is not physically possible for these souls to affect the course of nature, they nevertheless do so; they may best be thought of as performing little miracles – doing the physically *im*possible. If we put to one side for a moment those views which posit supernatural agency intruding on the natural world in this fashion, we may indeed non-problematically think of physical possibility as real possibility.[3]

If we concentrate then – in order to bracket out these views – on the sorts of issues which we suppose are non-problematically investigated by the natural sciences (for we suppose that they do not involve miracles), we may gain a useful insight into the relationship between the two sorts of possibility we're thinking about, epistemic and physical, by saying that progress in these areas is made by shrinking the epistemically possible to fit more closely the physically possible. For example, at one stage in the history of science, it was epistemically possible for the Sun to be orbiting the Earth, rather than *vice versa*; such a view was erroneous, of course, but it was widely believed on the basis of arguments that were not without intuitive appeal and science had not at that stage progressed to the stage where enough observations had been made and alternative models proposed to refute the geocentric view. Progress was however made and to such an extent that now the heliocentric system is a commonplace. Nowadays, if you asked anyone who had done even an elementary course in Astronomy whether it was possible that the geocentric view was true, they'd say that it was not. Increasing knowledge of the natural world has then, we might say, shrunk the epistemically possible in this area until it fits the physically possible. What seems to us to be possible is getting closer and closer to what really is possible; that's the nature of scientific progress.

So, to return to the thought of ours that the actual does not exhaust the possible or that there are alternative possibilities open to us: when we think that thought, is it epistemic or physical possibility that we have in mind?

It seems pretty straightforward that it is physical possibility, not – or rather not just – epistemic possibility. When I reflect on having spent the last half hour watching *The Simpsons* and think of my earlier self that, at the moment I call my moment of choice over whether or not to watch that show, it was possible both for me to end up doing what I did in fact end up doing (watching *The Simpsons*) and for me to end up doing what I did not in fact end up doing (reading a book on free will or watching the news), I am not primarily thinking of myself that at that moment I did not know which way I was going to end up spending the next half hour. That is to say that when I say, for example, 'Half an hour ago, it was possible for me to have read the book', I am not saying of myself just that half an hour ago I did not know that I was not in fact going to read the book. Similarly, *mutatis mutandis*, when we look to choices we face in the present and start to enumerate the alternative possibilities, as we might say, 'open' to us – ask yourself, 'Shall I continue reading *this* book? Shall I lay it to one side? If I lay it to one side, what shall I do instead? Is it time for *The Simpsons* yet?' – we do not think of ourselves as merely listing hypotheses about our future behaviour which as yet we have not been able to rule out as going to be true. We are asking ourselves, 'What shall I do?', not 'What will I do?' If this is so, in believing that the actual does not exhaust the possible, we are believing not simply that the actual does not exhaust the epistemically possible (though of course it does not, if only because we have not got a completed science, one in which the epistemic has been shrunk to fit perfectly the physical), but rather and primarily that the actual does not exhaust the *physically* possible (or just really possible if we ignore miracles, as mentioned earlier).

It is worth going over this ground just one more time at this stage, as attempts to rework this presumption of ours that the actual does not exhaust the physically possible as the presumption merely that the actual does not exhaust the *epistemically* possible have caused no end of confusion in the history of thought on the topic of free will, even among the most able philosophers.[4] In order to diagnose why this – false – characterization of our presumption has seemed so attractive to so many, we do well to note the logical necessity that our judgements of physical and epistemic possibility go, as we might put it, 'hand-in-hand'. We've already seen this in discussing the nature of progress in science, but let's look at it in a bit more detail.

To recap, my contention is that when we say of ourselves that, at a certain moment in time, it was possible for us to choose to do something other than whatever it is we ended up doing, we are not saying of ourselves that, at that moment which we think of as our moment of choice, we did not know what we would do. Rather we are saying that, at that moment, each of the things we were deliberating between was physically possible to us. However, despite this, it is nevertheless true, and true as a matter of *logic*, that if we supposed then and suppose now that each of the alternatives was physically possible for us, then it will also be true that we did not, at that moment, know with certainty which one we would end up doing; each would also have been epistemically possible for us.[5] Thus, we might say, judgements of epistemic possibility and physical possibility go hand in hand, and thus it is easy to conflate or confuse the two. Consider by way of an example the choice that faces you now, whether to continue reading this particular book that you have in your hands or to put it down and go and do something else instead.

It is logically impossible for you to know with certainty, in advance of deciding whether or not to continue reading this book, which of these things it is that you will end up doing. That is because if one is really to deliberate – to spend some time entertaining each option in one's mind and weighing their pros and cons relative to one another – then one must of course hold each option in one's mind *as an option*. And to hold an option in one's mind as an option is to hold it in one's mind as something one does not yet know with certainty one will not do (it will be epistemically possible for one) and thus to hold it as something which one believes one can really do (it will be believed to be physically possible for one). One cannot think of one of the 'options' before one as not really physically possible for one and yet raise of it the serious question of whether or not one might end up choosing to do it. In order to illustrate this sort of impossibility, try for a moment or two to deliberate over whether or not to fly to the moon merely by waving your hands. You will find that you cannot hold this in your mind as an option. Why? Because you realize so quickly that the so-called 'option' of flying to the moon merely by waving your hands is physically impossible for you that you immediately know with certainty that you will not end up doing it, so it is that you cannot consider trying to do it.

Because the result of a deliberation cannot be a foregone conclusion from the point of view of the person engaging in that process of deliberation, so it will always be true that the question 'What will I do?' will remain unanswered for just the time that 'What shall I do?' remains unanswered, namely until the time that one has done whatever it is one does do. And it is because physical and epistemic possibilities go together in this way that it is so important that we underscore how it is that they are nevertheless different. To yet further illustrate: let us go back to supposing that you are considering whether or not to persevere with reading this book, let's say at least to the end of this particular paragraph. Allow me to suppose further that, very early on in your deliberations over whether or not to continue reading to at least this extent, you discover that you're finding this book so fascinating that you become very confident that you will not put it down for quite a while, certainly until after completing this particular paragraph. So it is that you predict with a high degree of confidence that you will in fact decide to continue reading it until you've at least got that far. Let's really push the boat out here and say that you are as confident in this judgement of what you will decide to do as you would be confident in a judgement say that you will not seek to boil your head. Now several seconds have passed from the realization; you have continued reading during them, just as you predicted; and you are still reading now, just as you predicted. You reflect on the fact that you are doing exactly as you predicted. You will be aware – will you not? – that it seems open to you to falsify your earlier prediction that you'll continue on in this way at least until the end of this paragraph, to falsify it, if needs be, 'just out of spite' for your earlier self. And this will remain an apparent option for you until the end is reached. So it is that, by the time the epistemic uncertainty over whether or not you will indeed read at least the paragraph has diminished to zero (for you get to the end of it), then of course so will the possibility of your choosing to make your earlier prediction of your behaviour false; time will have moved on and you will face new choices.[6] Shall I read on?

*　*　*

To sum up our reflections on this first thought so far: just beneath our everyday reflecting on decisions made and decisions yet to be made, we suppose that the actual does not exhaust the possible in the sense that we suppose that a number of options greater than one is physically possible for us at moments of choice. We suppose that, at least for situations of genuine choice, everything else in the universe prior to our moment of choice remaining the same as it actually was, it is physically possible for us to do one of a number of things, that number being greater than the one we end up doing. This is a presumption not just about our knowledge of what we'll do at moments of choice, but more fundamentally about the number of options that are really available to us at moments of choice.

This presumption, when it is brought up from doing its work below the surface of our everyday thinking to the level of conscious awareness, raises an immediate worry, which we do well to say at least something about now. How, if at all, can we know that it's true? Sure, maybe we assume it in our everyday life, but is this assumption destined to remain entirely unjustified? Or perhaps even it's an assumption we have reason on reflection to think is false? This is a big issue and we shall have occasion to return to it more than once in the rest of the book (indeed a significant part of a future chapter will be devoted to looking at arguments to the effect that it's not really true and thus certainly cannot be known to be true). For now though, let us satisfy ourselves with giving an outline of one way of presenting the supposed problem and the sort of commonsensical solution to it which seems most plausible.

It is interesting that, when first presented with the issue of how one could know that what one actually does is not the only thing that it is physically or really possible for one to do, most people quickly suggest an experiment which, they suppose, *would* enable them to answer the question and which has only one drawback, albeit a significant one: it is an experiment that it is impossible to conduct. The suggested experiment would involve us somehow repeatedly 'rewinding' time to a certain moment of choice as we think of it and then playing it forward again. People suggesting this ordinarily suppose that if, over a large enough number of trials, the unfolding events repeatedly went down just the one path, that would be evidence that only that one path was physically possible and thus evidence that our presupposition that this was a moment of choice between two or more physically possible alternatives was in error. Alternatively, if in fact the unfolding events went down several different paths over different trials, that would be proof that the world is as we suppose, that different paths really are physically possible everything up to the moment of choice remaining the same.

However, *pace* this widespread intuition, such an experiment, even were we to be able to conduct it, could not, whatever its results, prove the supposition that the actual does not exhaust the possible. A sceptic could always say of the results of such an experiment, were they to show different paths being followed in different runs, 'Well, that just shows that if you rewind and replay time n times, only path p is possible (where p is whatever path followed from the moment on the nth run); if $n+1$, only path q (where q, of course, is whatever path followed from the moment on the $n+1$th run); and so on. Nothing here needs to be interpreted as showing that things are possible beyond whatever ends up being actual in any particular trial.' The fact that the sceptic could so interpret the results of even this experiment underscores the fact that there is *always* going to be a gap between what we observe, which is necessarily confined to whatever actually happens (we have a name for 'observations of things that didn't actually happen' – 'hallucinations'), and what we are having beliefs about in our presupposition that the actual does not exhaust the possible, which extends to things that remain mere possibilities. No experiment – even an impossible one such as that suggested – can close this gap. But if not even an impossible experiment could help, should we give up then on attempting to justify our presupposition that the actual does not exhaust the possible? Not at all, for all sorts of *actual* experiments may be used to justify it. We overlook them only because they lie so close to hand.

Imagine yourself going into an electrical store and telling the shop assistant that you wish to buy a new laptop computer, one capable of holding at least 500 GB of information. He draws your attention to a particular demonstration laptop on display; he types such things into it as are sufficient to get it to display the fact that it is currently holding over 500 GB of information in its memory; the price is right; you agree to purchase; and he then disappears to the back of the store, coming out again after a few moments with a computer of the same type as you have just seen in operation, boxed up and ready to go. But then a thought occurs to you, which you worriedly voice to him. Even if you both now know that the demonstration laptop is capable of holding at least 500 GB of information in its memory (which you grant you do know, as you have just witnessed that it is actually doing so), how do either of you know that the particular laptop that he is now suggesting to sell you is so capable; that it's possible for *it* to do so? The shop assistant points out that the laptop he's suggesting to sell you is exactly the same model as the one he has just demonstrated. You grant that it is, but press your worry by asking him if he has ever actually loaded this particular laptop – the one he is currently bringing out in its box – with 500 GB or more of information and he confesses he has not. And of course, even if he were to have said that, as a matter of fact, he had so tested this particular computer (the one that he's since boxed up again and is now holding before you), that testing would have been in the past. So you could still have asked him how you and he are to know that that particular computer is *still* capable of doing that which you could then grant he had shown it was capable of doing in the past. The problem you are raising of the shop assistant is obviously a particularized version of the problem that the sceptic is raising over our supposition that the actual does not exhaust the possible. How are you and the shop assistant to know that the computer that is not currently, that is actually, holding 500 GB or more of information is one that has the capacity to do so, that is, it is one for which holding that amount of information is possible? How are you to know that when you chose to read on a few moments ago, as I am supposing you actually did, you were capable of *not* reading on, that you were something for which an alternative future from the actual was at that time possible?

In response to this question, the first thing to do is to give some ground. First then, one should admit that we cannot indeed know *without any possibility of error* that an unexercised capacity is present in any particular case or that something which did not turn out to be actual was, nevertheless, possible. But, of course, we can know hardly anything without any possibility of error, perhaps indeed we can know nothing beyond the fact that we are currently thinking without any possibility of error. Some philosophers have certainly maintained that. We do not know without possibility of error that the moon is not made of cheese; that we weren't created five minutes ago with a load of false memories of experiences that in fact we've never had; that others have minds; that we're not in a virtual reality of the sort depicted in the film *The Matrix*; and so on. Nevertheless, for everyday purposes, we rightly dismiss sceptical worries about an issue based on the fact that we cannot rule out the possibility of error when reaching judgements on it. More than that is needed to ground a reasonable scepticism.

Secondly, we should insist that, insofar as we have no reason to suppose that the undemonstrated laptop is in any significant and relevant way different from the demonstrated one in its capacities, which we are taking it we don't, the worry that it *is* different in its capacities is ungrounded; and thus, if the demonstrated one is actually doing a certain thing, the undemonstrated one may reasonably be supposed to be capable of doing that thing too. Of course the possibility of error remains; you may get it home and find it does not work. But the point here is that it is unreasonable for you to expect to get it home and find it does not work until you are given positive reasons to suspect that it is in a significant and relevant way different from the demonstrated one. Similarly then, insofar as you have no reason to suppose that your current self is in any significant and relevant way different from your self of five minutes ago, the fact that you can actually put the book down now (try it now to prove that to yourself, but do pick it up again) is a reason for you to suppose that you could have put the book down five minutes ago; is a reason for you to suppose that you had that capacity then even though you were not, I am presuming, exercising it then.

In short, it seems that while we would do well to concede that we cannot know without possibility of error the truth of our presumption that we could have done something different from whatever it is that we did in fact do, we can, indeed do, have reason to suppose that it is true. We can, indeed do, have reason to suppose that our capacities, the things we could do, exceed our histories, the things we actually do. These are reasons of the sort sketched in the previous couple of paragraphs. These reasons are fallible, but they are reasons nonetheless. Without accepting that they are reasons nonetheless we should be at a loss to explain why we think that things that are not numerically identical to others that we nevertheless would ordinarily group with them are likely to be similar in their properties, including their unobserved properties and capacities.

* * *

Although, I have suggested, the belief that the actual does not exhaust the possible or, as it may be called, The Principle of Alternate Possibilities,[7] lies immediately underneath the surface of our everyday decision-making and reflection on it, it must be admitted that it is a belief that we seldom – if ever – raise to the surface of consciousness. In bringing it thus to our attention now, it is therefore not likely to strike all of us as immediately and obviously something familiar and already believed. Were we to approach the man on the Clapham omnibus[8] and demand of him that he answer, 'The actual does not exhaust the possible, wouldn't you agree? And by "possible" here, you have in mind physical or real possibility, not just epistemic, yes?', we could not guarantee that any nominal agreement we thereby garnered from him was generated by anything beyond the desire not to appear disagreeable to people who engage one in unsolicited conversations on public transport. But that is so with many of the presuppositions that undergird our everyday thinking; the principle of the uniformity of nature as it is presupposed by all inductive inferences would be another example. (That's the principle that the future will conform to the natural laws which have operated in the past.[9]) The fact that it is only after reflections of the sort that we've engaged in so far that one can elicit self-conscious and well-informed assent to such beliefs does not mean that they were not implicitly assented to and thereby doing their work prior to that explicit confession of belief being gained by our careful inquisitions.

The claim that a belief that the actual does not exhaust the possible lies beneath our everyday decisions is also not called into question by the fact, if it be a fact, that our everyday lives would continue much as they do at the moment were we to remove this presupposition. Imagine that, as you read on, you find me developing an argument that absolutely convinces you that, contrary to the tenor of what has gone heretofore, the actual *does* in fact exhaust the possible; at any moment of apparent choice between alternative futures, the appearance that more than one future is really possible is, you come firmly to believe as a result of this argument, illusory. Reflect on how you would then behave as you looked up from the armchair in which I am supposing you to have made this discovery and returned to 'the real world', that is the world of practical affairs; 'Shall I continue reading or shall I go and do something else instead?', you ask yourself once more. It is plausible to suppose – is it not? – that you would find that the discovery to which my argument had led you was entirely motivationally inert. After this discovery, you would find yourself reflecting on decisions taken and as yet ahead of you in just the same manner as you had done before it and as we characterized earlier.

This fact about you, if it be a fact about you, does not undermine the claim that this type of everyday reflection is based on the supposition that the actual does not exhaust the possible for the basis posited is a *logical* one, not a *psychological* one and this fact about you, if it be a fact about you, is a purely psychological fact. All sorts of modes of behaviour that are rational only on certain suppositions can – as a psychological matter of fact – sustain themselves once belief in those suppositions has been kicked away, but of course – unless some new supposition that supports them is quickly introduced – they cannot be sustained *rationally* in such circumstances. Thus it is indeed true that were you to become convinced that the actual did exhaust the possible, then – were you to wish to remain rational in continuing to behave in the manner that you were psychologically inclined to do in any case – you would, over time, need to find alternative ways of justifying continuing to think in these terms. And, given that you *do* have a wish to be rational about such matters (I can say this confidently as I am addressing someone who is reading a book devoted to the topic), a persistent failure to find such alternative modes of justification would plausibly lead over time – would it not? – to changes in your everyday thinking. If one gets one's motorcar up to a certain speed on flat ground, then, even if one switches off the engine, it will continue in motion just as a result of its own inertia for quite a time. But that does not mean that the motive force provided by the engine was not responsible for its getting up to that speed in the first place and – in the absence of any alternative mode of propulsion or towing – is not in fact necessary if the car is not eventually to grind to a halt.

If we believe that our universe is one such that there is more than one physically possible future open to it at various times, as I have argued we do, then we are committed to the falsity of Determinism, which – while variously defined – may be taken as stating that given the initial or boundary conditions of the universe and the laws of nature operative on it, only one future is physically possible: the state of the universe at a later time is, in every detail, causally necessitated by its state at an earlier time. Our everyday thinking then commits us to Determinism being false and thus, if we define Indeterminism simply as the thesis that Determinism is false (as indeed we shall define it), to the truth of Indeterminism.

Determinism is sometimes thought of as an obscure metaphysical thesis, about the sorts of things that might count as laws of nature, or as a principle, a regulative idea that enables us to adjudicate between empirically equivalent interpretations of quantum happenings or some such. And Indeterminism is sometimes thought of as a recent discovery, made by physicists investigating some of the most recondite sub-microscopic phenomena in nature. When presented in ways such as this, it is obviously most implausible to suggest that 'common sense' suggests Determinism is false and Indeterminism true. Who on the Clapham omnibus has opinions on metaphysical theses; regulative ideas; or Theoretical Physics? But when Determinism is presented as the thesis that only one future is possible and Indeterminism as the denial of that thesis, the considerations hitherto presented make it very plausible, indeed obvious, that we suppose Determinism to be false and Indeterminism to be true in our everyday thinking.

We have spent quite a bit of time nailing down our presumption that the actual does not exhaust the physically possible, what we have also called the Principle of Alternate Possibilities and, latterly, the thesis of Indeterminism. We have nailed it down both in the sense of articulating what it is that we understand ourselves to be committing to with it and in establishing that we do indeed presuppose it in our everyday reflections on the decisions we make. We have started to see how this presupposition might be called into question both in its nature (we have rejected the suggestion that it is really just epistemic possibility that we are thinking of in these circumstances) and as a presupposition (we have rejected the suggestion that we do not really rely on it in our everyday thinking). Even though it has been somewhat beside our main purposes at the moment, we have also done a little bit to show how we might go about justifying it as not just coherent and hence possibly true, but also as *knowable* if true, even if not knowable without the possibility of error.

This thought, which henceforth we'll just call 'Indeterminism', is the first of the five building blocks of the view of free will that we'll be following tradition and calling 'Libertarianism'. Having spent some time knocking it into shape, let's put this thought of ours to one side for a moment or two now and turn to the second building block, another thought we ordinarily have about the actions we take.

* * *

This is the second 'building block':

Sometimes I'm morally responsible for what I do.

The falsity of Determinism, that is the truth of Indeterminism, is not the only thing to which our everyday reflection on our decisions commits us. So far, we have taken as our examples of choices ones between those options all of which will have struck us as relatively trivial. There is usually very little moral significance hanging over whether one spends half an hour reading a book or watching television. But sometimes the choices we face strike us as morally significant ones and then we are often vividly aware of ourselves as morally responsible for them and for at least a part of what unfolds from them. If I choose, after calm reflection, to do what I know fully well I oughtn't to do, then I would ordinarily suppose myself to be blameworthy for that choice and for at least some of any negative consequences that flow from it. It would be possible to fill in background details in our previous example of my choosing between continuing reading the book on free will and watching *The Simpsons* so that it becomes an example of a morally significant choice; we could imagine, for example, that I have solemnly promised my wife – who is worried at my apparent laziness – that I shall not watch television during that period. But it is easier to bring things into more vivid focus if we switch to another example where the moral aspects are intrinsic to the nature of the choice at hand. Imagine me then facing the following dilemma.

I have spent a few evenings giving some private tuition on Moral Philosophy to the son of the local millionaire. As I leave his mansion after the last of these tutorials, the millionaire thus pushes – as I had expected he would – what is to me a sizeable amount of cash into my hands. I know of him that he is not going to declare this to anybody; to him, the amount is trivial and he will not give it a second thought after his large front door has closed behind me. As I crunch my way down the gravel drive past his various Rolls-Royces to the lodge gates (I have come on foot), it occurs to me that my work for the evening is not yet completed. When I get home, I must fill in my year's tax return. The walk home will take 20 minutes or so and, while I quicken my pace as it has now started to rain, I thus have time to reflect at leisure on the fact that I could omit to mention this amount when filling in the box on that form that asks one to declare all one's income during the period in question (which period includes tonight). Were I to do so, then – obviously – I would not be taxed on it. I contemplate the choice before me as I make my way home. On the one hand, I somewhat-grudgingly admit to myself, I really should declare it; a lie of omission is still a lie and so lying is what I would be doing if I omitted to mention this payment on the form. I am fully aware of the fact that I don't have any moral reason that would justify me to any extent in lying on this occasion; it is not, for example, that I face imminent financial ruin and need every penny I can get if my large body of dependents is not to be plunged into life-destroying penury. On the contrary, I am relatively well off and the additional money that I would retain were I to lie on the form would be spent by me on fripperies, perhaps a DVD box set of *The Simpsons*. On the other hand, there would be no way that this dishonesty on my part would be discovered; the practical upshot would simply be that I would end up richer by what is to me quite a sizeable amount. In fact it occurs to me that I remember reading somewhere authoritative that the 'punishment' for being discovered having omitted information such as this on one's form is simply that one is required to pay the amount owing the next year. Financially, I can't lose by omitting to mention this amount. It has now started to sleet and I am wishing I had brought a coat with me.

In constructing this example, I wish it to be clearly one involving my facing a choice between doing what I ought to do on the one hand and doing what is in some other way to my greater advantage on the other. The example will not have struck you as being of such a situation if you happen to think that all taxation is theft and should be resisted by any means; or that having any money above the bare minimum needed to survive is actually to one's *dis*advantage, as the luxuries it generates enervate the warrior spirit that is essential to any true man; or again any number of other things. But, if you have the sorts of value judgements that most have   tax evasion isn't by any means the greatest immorality one can commit, but it is in itself morally bad, and money isn't everything, but it isn't nothing either – then this example will have struck you as I had hoped it would. I also wished it to be an example which clearly met certain other criteria that we ordinarily suppose need to be fully in place for clear-cut cases of moral responsibility and which will form the focus of our fifth thought as it will be discussed later in the chapter. We'll come back to them later then, but for the moment we should note them and note that they are satisfied in this case. They are as follows.

No doubt sometimes we fail to be fully morally responsible for something we've done as we fail to realize at the moment of choice quite what it is we are doing. The situation imagined is not one of them; I am fully aware of all salient features of what I would be doing both if I filled in the form fully and if I omitted to mention this recent payment. I know that I should fill it in accurately; I know that it would be in my financial interests not to fill it in accurately. The choice I face is a well-informed one. Another closely related feature that we suppose sometimes exculpates people to some extent from moral responsibility is that the choice for which we are thinking of assessing them was rushed. Perhaps they knew all the relevant facts, but they did not have time to weigh them sufficiently for the choice they ended up making to be one which reflects on them as much as it would have done if they had had more time. Again, this is not the situation here; I have supposed that I have 20 minutes to contemplate what is a relatively simple choice: fill in the form accurately (and lose out on the money that I could otherwise have used to buy some frippery for myself) or fill it out inaccurately (and thus hold onto that money). Finally, sometimes we feel that people fail to be fully morally responsible for some choice if they are in some way coerced, a paradigm case being when a terrorist is holding a gun to the head of the person making the 'choice' and stating his intention to kill the person if he or she does not 'choose' as the terrorist instructs. Again, nothing similar pertains in this situation: it is not even that I face imminent financial ruin or some such; the extra money I would gain by being dishonest would certainly bring me benefits but is in no way essential for my well-being or for that of anyone else I care about.

Given all of this, we would think that, were I to decide to omit to mention this amount on my tax return, I would be clearly morally responsible for that choice. Given that I would have then decided to do what I knew fully well to be morally wrong, we would agree that I would thus be deserving of some blame and perhaps punishment for having made that choice, albeit regrettably a punishment which, if I am correct in my assessment of my chances of being caught, would never in fact befall me. The fact that this sort of tax evasion is perhaps best thought of as a relatively minor failing should not distract us from the fact that it is a failing. The appropriate punishment for this sort of wrongdoing would certainly not be as lengthy a stay in prison as would be appropriate had I decided in a similarly well-informed, un-rushed and un-coerced way to murder someone merely to advance my financial position. Indeed the 'authoritative' source that I remembered suggested that the law would require of me merely that I pay what I owed, which seems no punishment at all. But the fact that what I deserve by way of punishment may be relatively small doesn't make my deserving of that punishment any smaller. If I borrow ten pounds off one man and a hundred pounds off the other, then my debt to the first is a debt for an amount ten times less than is my debt to the second, and we might idiomatically express this as my having less of a debt to the first than the second or as me being less in debt to the first than to the second. But we can equally see that a truth is expressed if we say that I am no less a debtor to the first than I am a debtor to the second even though the size of the debt I owe to the first is much smaller than the size of the debt I owe to the second. I owe the first man ten pounds just as much as I owe the second a hundred.

It is worth spending a moment or two more driving home how it is that we ordinarily construe the nature of our moral responsibility for those actions of ours which obviously meet the conditions of being well-informed, un-rushed and un-coerced. Doing so will enable us to see more clearly the relationship we ordinarily suppose to exist between moral responsibility and Indeterminism, which relationship is the content of the third thought we'll look at in this chapter. So, what is the nature of this supposed moral responsibility?

* * *

Essentially the same points could be made about our assumption of moral responsibility by considering a praiseworthy action or by considering a blameworthy one. On the praiseworthy side, we could consider, for example, the bravery of the brother of one of the Masters of my College, someone who went well beyond the call of duty in the First World War by repeatedly choosing to return to no man's land so as to retrieve wounded comrades under heavy enemy fire, saving many lives as a result. As we discovered more of his story, we would no doubt become convinced that, as the *London Gazette* of the time put it, his 'courage and self-sacrifice were beyond praise' and he was thus more than deserving of the Victoria Cross, which he was unique among the many brave men who fought in that war in being awarded twice.[10] Such examples of praiseworthy acts would form an edifying subject for reflection. However, our intuitions are more easily thrown into focus if, instead of praiseworthy acts, we consider blameworthy ones and, furthermore, if we consider ones which pass beyond the realms in which we think that blame alone would suffice as appropriate response, into the territory where we think that punishment is needed. We have already considered the offence of tax evasion. To generate a more extreme example, we might consider the sort of cold-blooded and calculated murder of some innocent for financial gain that forms the basis for so many detective stories. No doubt were we to fill in the details of such an example appropriately, we would have no difficulty generating in our imagination a crime of murder which all normal people would agree clearly deserved significant punishment, perhaps imprisonment for life, perhaps – some would say – even death. But in order not to open up a whole new area of debate, let us suppose we 'fine-tune' the crime in our imagination until we are agreed that in fact 20–30 years in prison is the appropriate punishment. I take it that for some speci-fication of a crime of murder, we would reach a broad consensus on the appropriateness of a sentence of this order. How though would we justify imposing such a punishment? How in particular do we understand the 'desert' element?

Considerations which we bring to bear in order to justify punishment fall into two kinds, those which justify it due to the benefits that are supposed likely to flow from the giving of it in the future and those which justify it because of what the person to whom it is being given has done in the past. We shall consider these two sorts of justification in turn.

So, on the first hand, we might consider how imprisoning this murderer for 20–30 years would protect the law-abiding public, in whose company we no doubt number ourselves. The person we are considering has shown himself willing to murder for gain once; perhaps he has as yet shown no remorse; even if he has, we may be reasonably suspicious that his tears are crocodile ones; we cannot be at all confident that he would not kill again if he were allowed back into society. We have reason then to confine him until he is no longer a danger to the public. We might also consider the deterrent effect to other potential malefactors that this significant punishment would provide. Perhaps this man's circumstances were not unique; others, we may conclude, are probably tempted to murder in the same manner that he has done and perhaps are even now weighing in their minds the potential gains that could come to them against their potential losses. We should do our best to tip the scales in the right direction in these other people's minds by imposing a penalty which will discourage them from similar acts. Finally, we might consider the possibilities for reform that a lengthy sentence of this sort could afford. Even if keeping the murderer locked up for a long time will not in itself generate remorse and change of disposition, it will provide opportunity for other activities and interventions that might. So, for example, we might need at first to coerce this prisoner into some sort of work interior to his prison, but, within the right sort of framework, we could realistically hope that, after several decades, he would have reformed his ways until he genuinely found that earning his way through honest toil is preferable to his previous tendencies. In these ways, we, most of us, no doubt believe that the consequences of a proposed punishment are germane to its justification. But while the consequences of a proposed punishment are no doubt supposed by most of us to be relevant to its justification, we do not suppose that they alone are the *only* factors relevant to the justification of a punishment. To bring this out, we may consider an adaptation of a classic thought experiment, originally used to point to some difficulties with one form of Consequentialism.

Imagine then that you are the sheriff of a township in the Wild West in the middle of the nineteenth century. A small child has been clubbed down in a back alley with a single blow, delivered by the walking stick of the local drunk which was found lying nearby. You yourself happen to be one of only two people who knows that, despite this being the habitual sleeping place of the drunk and his walking stick being the weapon used to deliver the blow, the drunk must be innocent of the crime, as you have had him in your jail in a stupor over the period in which the attack took place. Furthermore, the other person who knows the drunk to be innocent, the township's unassuming and well-respected doctor, has just confessed to how he himself struck the child down from behind in a misguided attempt to surprise the child with a minor blow and thereby teach him a useful lesson about the dangers of wandering around in back alleys, especially those that are known to be frequented by drunks. While the injury was much more severe than the doctor had intended to cause or indeed could reasonably have guessed he'd cause, the child will make a full recovery.

The doctor is obviously deeply remorseful and ruminates on how, given that the townsfolk are an unforgiving and suspicious lot (which you must admit they are) and thus will never trust him again once they learn the truth, the many lives that he would have been able to save among them over the coming years will now be lost. As the two of you talk, a mob forms outside your jail, demanding that you search for the drunk, who they of course assume is responsible for the attack on the child and do not know you already have in custody. That you are able to announce from your porch that you already have him in your jail merely heightens their fervour and they start becoming riotous, now demanding to know why you are delaying charging him with the offence. Promising them that you will return in short order, you re-enter your jail and, going to the back room in which prisoners are kept, you find that your only prisoner, the drunk, has at last woken up with, as you predicted, no recollection at all of his behaviour over the last 24 hours; he is cursing and asking to know why you have him in your jail; what has he done?

Without answering him, you return to the front room of your jail and reflect in conversation with the doctor on the fact that, as yet, the drunk has done hardly anything. He has committed only the most minor of crimes around the township, but long years of experience enable you to know that unless something happens to shake him out of his ways and unless he can in some way be prevented from gaining access to alcohol, he will go on to much worse later. If only you could shock him by presenting him with some horrendous effect of his drinking and if only you could justify keeping him in your jail for a year or two and thus away from alcohol, he could then lead a useful and happy life. The doctor concurs; his own research into the deleterious effects of excessive alcohol on the moral character supports your conclusion. If only the drunk had committed the crime, not the doctor, then things would be so much easier and better for everyone. If only. A thought occurs to you both at once, but you are the first to voice it.

You ask the doctor if he would be willing to go along with a story whereby the drunk committed the assault rather than he. Perhaps, to make the case airtight, the doctor could testify to having witnessed the assault. This would then handily explain how the child was able to be given immediate medical treatment by him and why the doctor is now in the jail talking to you, the sheriff. Despite there being no way for this to be discovered or even suspected if you both stick to your stories, the doctor is at first reluctant, feeling too guilty already for what he has done. But, as you draw to his attention once more the many more lives he could thereby save and the beneficial effects which would fall *on the drunk himself* were you both to take this course of action, he is convinced. He commits himself to going along with the story if that is indeed what you decide to do. A brick from the mob, which is now on the verge of rioting, bounces off the front door of your jail. It is time for you to go outside and speak to them. What should you say and do?

Were you to go along with the mob's supposition of guilt, charging and no doubt gaining the conviction of the drunk (it is members of the mob who would form the jury), the consequences would be maximally beneficial. A riot would be prevented; the wider community would be better protected; an increasingly dangerous drunk would be taken out of their midst; the increasingly hardworking doctor would be left among them; and the doctor and drunk themselves would benefit as individuals, the drunk being motivated to reform himself and the doctor to work all the more tirelessly to serve his community. If we turn to consider the deterrent effect of your taking this course of action, again it is obviously better than were you to take the alternative. Drunkenness and casual violence, which we may posit are generally problems in the communities of the Wild West (it is the 'wild' west, not the 'mild' west, after all), would be usefully deterred. The study and practice of medicine, as well as availing oneself of the services of medical practitioners, which we may take it are generally beneficial, would not be deterred. And finally, if we turn to the reformative effects of this course of action, the drunk would be cured of the addiction that would otherwise have sent him spiralling down into greater and greater depths of criminality and the chastised doctor would all-the-more-wholeheartedly serve the needs of the townsfolk.

So, *if* the consequences of a punishment were the only factors relevant to its justification, we should have no hesitation at all in concluding what you as sheriff should do: you should go back out onto your porch and announce that you have charged the drunk and are even now taking a statement from a witness to the assault, the unimpeachable doctor who was first on the scene tending to the child; a conviction is assured; the mob may disperse knowing that law is upheld in their township; you are sure you speak for all present here when you thank the doctor for his good citizenship. If we hesitate in giving this course of action our endorsement and, even if we eventually do give it our endorsement, do so less than wholeheartedly, that can only be because we consider something other than the consequences of a punishment relevant to its justification. And most of us *do* hesitate in concluding that this is what you as sheriff should do. Even among those of us who do decide that, on balance, you as sheriff should do this, most fail to be wholehearted and unqualified in our endorsement of this course of action. A moment's reflection makes it obvious why we hesitate and why we cannot be wholehearted in support of your conspiring with the doctor to frame the drunk; a crucial fact which would justify punishing the drunk for assaulting the child fails to obtain. The fact is as simple as it is crucial – *the drunk didn't do it*.

Even if all the consequences of sending the drunk to jail are better than the consequences of sending the doctor to jail (and they are; the example was constructed with this end in view), we think that the fact that the drunk is innocent in itself makes doing this to him to some extent at least less good than it would have been to do it to the doctor. Opinions are divided on the importance of this condition, which we may call the 'desert' or 'retributive' condition, for the justification of punishment. Some reason that it is a necessary condition for us to be morally justified in doing something that we present as a punishment, hence concluding that as sheriff you should *not* conspire with the doctor to frame the drunk. On the contrary, such people would suggest, if you go out onto your porch and tell the truth, then even if all the consequences of your doing so turn out to be as bad as you predicted they would be – there's a riot; the doctor never works again; drunkenness and casual violence increase; respect for the medical profession declines; more people die in the town as a result of these facts; the drunk's spiral downwards into alcoholism and criminality is terminated only by an early death – you still did the right thing in going out onto your porch and telling the truth. Others take the retributive condition to be just one factor to be weighed in the balance and potentially overbalanced by others when deciding what one should do in these areas. People in this second group would then be open to the possibility that the truth might well be that, on balance, you should frame the drunk and keep him in jail nominally for this crime of assault even though he doesn't deserve it; the consequences in this case are good enough to outweigh the in-itself-bad fact that in doing this you are conspiring to send an innocent person to jail. But whether we take the retributive condition as a necessary condition or a non-necessary, albeit perhaps very important, contributory condition, we do not, if we are at all normal in our moral intuitions, regard it as irrelevant.

There is a reason why even those of us who think that the retributive condition need *not* always be met, if one is to justify interventions of a sort that are in other respects qualitatively indistinguishable from punishment, should think that it is nevertheless a necessary condition for punishment per se. This is because it is plausible to suggest that without the retributive condition being supposed to be satisfied, you as sheriff could not regard whatever you did to the drunk as a punishment. Knowing that the drunk is innocent, then, even if you decide on balance to frame him and then treat him just as you would have treated him were you to have believed him guilty (keeping him locked up in jail and so on), you would not be able any more to regard this treatment of him as giving him his just deserts; as paying him back for what he did; as a retributive act; in short, as a punishment. We might say then that even if consequentialist considerations can be sufficient to justify doing to someone whom one knows to be innocent of a particular offence what would, were they guilty of it, be appropriate punishment, these considerations are *in*sufficient for that treatment to be a punishment. For a penalty to be thought of as a punishment, the retributive condition must be supposed to be met, the person to whom this treatment is meted out must be supposed to be the person who actually committed the crime in question. If this is so, then those of us who think that in the situation we have just imagined, it is, on balance, regrettable but true that you should frame the drunk, are best presented *not* as thinking that you should punish the drunk, but rather as thinking that you should act in a way which would have been the appropriate way to punish him had he been guilty; which you even present as appropriate punishment to the outer world; but which you yourself cannot regard as punishment.

These considerations have brought out then that for *punishment* to be supposed morally justifiable, the person being punished must be supposed by the person doing the punishing to be the person who performed the action for which the punishment is being meted out. If we return to consider the case of a cold-blooded and calculated murder for financial gain and imagine that a punishment of 20–30 years would provide suitable protection to the rest of society, besides deterrence and chance for reform, then we have no hesitation in unqualifiedly thinking the actual murderer worthy of it, presuming we may identify him with certainty, and worthy of this treatment *as punishment*. He satisfies the consequentialist conditions for this type of treatment to be morally justifiable and he – in having actually been the person who performed the act of cold-blooded murder – satisfies the retributive condition necessary for this type of treatment to be a justifiable *punishment* – that's what he deserves. In the case we have just been imagining, where a child is struck down by a well-intentioned but misguided doctor, we would not wish to hold the doctor entirely morally responsible for his action, for he would not have satisfied the conditions of being well-informed and un-rushed in choosing to do what he did. He did not realize quite how hard he was hitting the child and he did not reflect adequately on the probable outcomes were he so to act. That he did not reflect adequately means that he is plausibly to some extent at least culpable for the action that he then took; he was rather negligent. That this failure to think is a lesser failure and perhaps one that we wish to excuse him of to some extent no doubt explains at least some of our reluctance to see him charged with assault and our consequent willingness at least to consider framing the innocent drunk. We think the mob of townsfolk, even when calmed down somewhat and constituted into a jury, would be likely to deal out to the doctor a punishment more severe than is his due. In the case of the sheriff example, the two conditions for fully justifiable punishment come apart – the drunk merits a punishment-like treatment on consequentialist grounds, the doctor at least some genuine punishment on retributive grounds. In the case of the cold-blooded murder for financial gain, they go together and the retributive condition is fully and non-problematically satisfied. Let us call the supposition we make that sometimes people satisfy all the conditions necessary and sufficient for fully justifiable punishment (which conditions then would not merely be that the consequences of that punishment were good, but also that they be the persons who committed the offences for which these sorts of punishment are proportionate), the supposition that sometimes people are robustly morally responsible for their actions. We shall see in a moment that it is difficult to understand the supposition of ours that people do sometimes satisfy the retributive aspect of this condition for moral responsibility without supposing that we think of them at such times as what we shall call the 'ultimate authors' of the actions for which we hold them responsible in this robust way.[11] That will be the fourth thought that we look at. But for the moment, and as a way in to this thought, let us pause and reflect on the relationship between the two thoughts we have been considering so far.

* * *

So far we have looked at two presumptions of our everyday thinking: the first, that sometimes we could do other than whatever it is we actually do (Indeterminism); the second, that sometimes we are morally responsible in a robust way for what we do (Moral Responsibility). A natural attempt to link these two thoughts would be the following hypothesis: sometimes we are morally responsible for what we do *just because* we could in those circumstances have done other than whatever it is we do. This though, cannot be the full story, as the following example brings out.[12]

Consider how you would react differently towards a dog trotting up to your front gate and relieving himself against it and towards the dog's owner coming along a moment later and doing the same. Even were you to believe, as most would, that there was nothing necessary about the dog's relieving himself against your particular gate rather than some other gate, a lamppost, or something else again, you would not hold the dog morally responsible in any way for having behaved in this fashion. (You might of course justify on consequentialist grounds treating a dog as you would were he morally responsible; you might shout 'Bad dog!' at him and so on. But these would be acts of training, not punishment.) You would not hold the dog to be morally responsible even though you suppose of him that he could have done otherwise. So we do not ordinarily suppose that being able to do otherwise is a sufficient condition for moral responsibility. However, you would hold the dog's owner morally responsible were he to behave as his dog had behaved. (If you call the dog's owner 'bad', you do so not merely as an exercise in training, but in part because you think him retributively worthy of this description.) Ability to do otherwise then is not in itself a sufficient condition for moral responsibility. The thought that it is a necessary condition is much more plausible and it is the third common-sense thought of ours that I wish us to consider in this chapter.

* * *

We might express the third thought as follows:

> *If I couldn't do other than what I actually do, then I wouldn't be morally responsible for what I do.*

In that this third thought posits an incompatibility between Determinism and moral responsibility, we may call this third thought Incompatibilism.

Most people, when this thought is first presented to them in articulate form, wish to claim it as their own.[13] But as an attempt to link the first of our two thoughts, it has less immediacy about it than either of its two components. A sizeable minority need to be brought to acknowledge that they do indeed suppose it by a more elongated process of reflection than is required to gain assent to a claim that they suppose either or indeed both of the first two thoughts. The hypothesis that we presuppose Incompatibilism in our everyday thinking is supported, however, by our reactions to certain potential large-scale discoveries that scientists might make about a universe.

Consider the following two scenarios: First, scientists tell us that they have discovered a certain universe which, at least superficially, is exactly the same as ours. There is an Earth-like planet there, with creatures on it that look exactly like us and behave exactly like us. The scientists tell us that they have also discovered that, in this universe, the initial conditions of the Big Bang and the laws of nature operative on it determine everything that happens thereafter, down to the tiniest of details. We might say then that they have discovered that the first thought that we considered in this chapter – that the actual does not exhaust the physically possible – would in fact be false if thought of this universe. This is a universe of which Determinism is true: what actually happens there is all that it is possible happen (given the initial state of the universe and its laws). As already mentioned, in this universe there are creatures superficially like us, so there are in fact creatures there who *do* think the thought that is the thesis of Indeterminism and hence who we can see – from the point of view provided us by these scientists' discoveries – are mistaken when they do so.

Reflect for a moment on your intuitions about whether you would say that the creatures in this universe are really morally responsible in the robust sense, the one that goes beyond justifying treating them for consequentialist reasons in various ways and requires of them that they be worthy sometimes of retributive punishment. Of course the creatures in this universe *believe* that they are sometimes morally responsible in this robust sense. But are they ever right? Almost everyone unaffected by the rigours of philosophical speculation on this topic inclines to think that they are not, which then supports the claim that we assume the third thought we have looked at, Incompatibilism, in our everyday thinking. When I say 'almost everyone', I report the results that I have garnered over 15 years of discussing this subject with my students though these results were not, I confess, collected with a very rigorous methodology. However, I can assuage one worry that sometimes people have with surveys of this sort (*a fortiori* informal ones such as mine). People reasonably worry that the results may be skewed by the presumptions of the person asking the question; in essence, the worry is that if an incompatibilist presents scenarios of this sort, he/she will elicit a disproportionately high number of incompatibilist intuitions; if a compatibilist does so, he/she will elicit a disproportionately high number of compatibilist ones. And of course one might expect such an effect to be all the more prominent when considering intuitions elicited from one's students, people who one might realistically hope would be aiming to impress their tutor with their level of intuitive insight into philosophical issues. In this case though such a worry would be misplaced as for the majority of those 15 years, I was a compatibilist and thus it was a source of frustration to me that almost all my pupils started off where they did. As a general – though admittedly by no means universal – truth then, I suggest that when we imagine a universe of which Determinism is true, we quickly infer from that fact alone that, whatever its residents might think, none of them is really ever robustly morally responsible, none of them ever really deserves punishment as such.[14] However, now turn to consider this second scenario.

The second scenario is like the first except that the scientists also tell us that the universe they are describing is the one you and I are in! This very universe in which you are reading this book right now is a universe of which the first thought we looked at in this chapter – that the actual does not exhaust the possible – is false. Determinism, they have discovered, *is* true of the actual world; common sense is wrong. What are your intuitions *now* about whether the people in the universe the scientists are describing – that is, this universe, that is, you – are ever morally responsible in the robust sense?

When faced with this question, opinions are more divided. The majority who at the time of being asked this question have yet to engage in philosophical speculation guided by someone holding the view that Incompatibilism is false hesitatingly report that they would then conclude that nobody was, after all, morally responsible for whatever they ended up doing, thus again supporting the hypothesis that we – or at least most of us – ordinarily presuppose Incompatibilism in our everyday thinking.[15] However, a sizeable minority – even among those who have not already been guided to believe in the falsehood of Incompatibilism – report that they would continue to regard people as nevertheless sometimes robustly morally responsible, thus, it might be suggested, supporting the claim that a sizeable minority do *not* presuppose Incompatibilism in their everyday thinking. But what is this 'minority report' really evidence of? Not much, it seems to me.

Within the group that say that were scientists to tell them that ours is a universe of which Determinism is true, they would nevertheless still say that sometimes people are morally responsible, we can conclude that – given that the first thought we examined is so well-entrenched in our everyday thinking – some say this as they are simply reporting that they would disbelieve these scientists. Obviously these people's reaction that, even were scientists to tell them this, they would still regard people as sometimes morally responsible in the robust sense is no reason at all for us to doubt that Incompatibilism is assumed in their everyday thinking. And we must also consider the fact that we made mention of earlier, that even if a presupposition which is needed for some practice to be rationally justified is kicked away by some new discovery, the behaviour based upon it can sometimes be predicted likely to continue, at least temporarily, nevertheless. So, among the people who report that they would as a matter of fact continue to regard people as robustly morally responsible were they to be told this by scientists, as well as those who are reporting that they would continue to do so simply because they would not believe the scientists, there are some who are no doubt reporting they would continue to behave this way but are not seeking to claim of this behaviour that it is reasonable. When these two 'voting blocs' are removed from the minority who report that were scientists to converge upon the truth of Determinism, they would nevertheless continue to hold people morally responsible, those who remain are very small in number and almost all of them turn out upon further questioning to be already strongly inclined, as a result of much more than ordinary exposure to the philosophical literature, to thinking Incompatibilism false. Thus we may conclude that Incompatibilism *is* generally assumed in our everyday thinking about ourselves; we might be wrong of course in this assumption, but that doesn't stop it being an assumption which we ordinarily make. If you find yourself *not* making it, then this will affect where you – quite properly, from that starting point – judge the burden of proof to lie with respect to Incompatibilism, to which point we shall return in a future chapter. But for now I shall assume you do find yourself intuitively drawn to Incompatibilism and move on to consider the fourth thought.

* * *

It will be recalled that Incompatibilism suggests that ability to do otherwise is a necessary condition for moral responsibility but not that it is a sufficient condition. For us to attribute moral responsibility to someone, it has to be the case, not just that we suppose that the person we are considering was capable of doing something other than whatever it is he or she ended up doing, but also that the fact that he or she ended up doing whatever it was he or she did was 'up to' him or her. We suppose that the agent himself or herself has to have been the ultimate author of whatever it is he or she ended up doing if we are to regard him or her as responsible for doing that thing. We might sum up this presumption so:

> *If I wasn't the ultimate author of my actions, then I wouldn't be morally responsible for them.*

This is perhaps the most elusive of our everyday suppositions about ourselves. We shall spend a whole chapter in due course examining it and what we are committed to by our belief in it. But, for the moment, in order to illustrate it in play, let us imagine the following situation.[16]

The Master of my college has done nothing but damage to it during his tenure so far; I conclude that, for the good of the college, he must die. (It never occurs to me that he could instead be coerced by senior fellows into demitting office early.) I thus formulate various plans by which I might bump him off. Finally, I settle on a scheme whereby I kidnap the Senior Tutor and implant in his head a microchip which, when activated, will allow his bodily movements to be controlled by me from my laptop computer. This having been done, I slip the trusty Webley service revolver that a previous Bursar gave to me into his pocket and then, removing his memory of this procedure, I release the Senior Tutor from my rooms and he goes back to duty, none the wiser. From now on though, if I remotely turn on the implant (as I am able to do), I can control the Senior Tutor's movements from my laptop. Thus, with the implant activated, if I move the joystick connected to my laptop to the right, the Senior Tutor will turn to his right. If I press the trigger on the joystick, then the Senior Tutor's trigger finger will depress any trigger it happens to be resting on. And, with various buttons on the keyboard of my computer, I can get the Senior Tutor to reach into his pocket and pull out whatever he finds there. I sit back and await a propitious moment.

A college meeting is called. I go along with my laptop (nominally so as to be able to read from it the agenda and papers, which are no longer routinely circulated in hardcopy [another innovation of the Master that I am keen to see reversed]). I observe that the Senior Tutor is sitting next to the Master. As the Master opens the meeting, I switch on the implant and get the Senior Tutor to pull out the revolver and – with a nifty bit of joystick waggling – point it at the Master and fire. The Master slumps forward, dead. I then switch off the implant, leaving the Senior Tutor baffled as to how he came to behave as he did. The Vice-Master, someone far more to my liking, takes over chairmanship of the meeting and finds support for his suggestion that he will in due course allow a proposal to call an ambulance to be taken under 'Any Other Business'.

I take it that, were you to come to know of the circumstances outlined in the previous two paragraphs, you would not wish to hold the Senior Tutor morally responsible for the assassination of the Master. Even though it was his finger on the trigger, there is a sense in which he was not the assassin; rather, he was the tool of the assassin, me. Just as we don't blame the gun for the assassination – guns don't kill people; people kill people[17] – so we would think we should not blame the Senior Tutor either. The gun and he were both simply tools in the literal or figurative hands of another and, behind the whole assassination, the person who had his finger on the ultimate trigger, was me. So it is I who should be blamed or indeed, were we to think the assassination morally justified, as I obviously did, perhaps praised. In any case, it is me who bears the moral responsibility for the Master's death.

This instinct to trace moral responsibility back until we find someone who we would wish to describe as the ultimate author of the action in question does not find itself dissipated, nor does it focus itself on anyone but me, if we imagine the following alteration to the procedure by which I get the Senior Tutor to shoot the Master. So, consider this second variant on the thought experiment.

Imagine again then that, as before, I kidnap the Senior Tutor and install an implant in him, before returning him none the wiser to duty with a revolver in his pocket. This time, however, the implant does not enable me to control his bodily movements directly, but it does enable me to control his thoughts directly and through them his bodily movements. For example, if I type in, 'Have strong desire to pull out that mysterious heavy lumpy object in your right hand pocket', the Senior Tutor will have a strong desire to pull out that object (the gun, of course). If I type in, 'Be unsurprised that it is a gun and weigh the pros and cons of using it to kill the Master', the Senior Tutor will do that. If I type in, 'Now – whatever the results of that process of deliberation – point it at the Master and shoot him through the head', he'll even do that. Even though we may imagine that, were the Senior Tutor so operated on, he could end up pulling the trigger after a well-informed and un-rushed mental process which he would think of as his coming to the – admittedly 'somewhat-whimsical', as he might put it – decision to shoot the Master through the head, we would still think that it was not really *his* decision. The Senior Tutor would *think* that it was he who had made the choice – it'd seem that way from the inside – but it wouldn't really be him. It would really be me again, this time (in contrast to what would have been the case had I implanted the first chip) operating in a way which shielded even from the Senior Tutor's introspective powers the fact that it was someone other than himself who was the ultimate author of 'his' actions. Even if I put a random number generator into this chip in such a way that there remained, right up until the moment the trigger was pulled, a chance that the Senior Tutor might not kill the Master (so that it was true that the Senior Tutor could have done otherwise), it'd still not be the Senior Tutor who we'd hold morally responsible for the Master's death; it would still be me who we would hold morally responsible. Again, were such a causal chain in place, the Senior Tutor would be a tool of mine, no less than the gun would be a tool of the Senior Tutor's (and thus me). Again, the moral buck stops with me. Looking back-wards in time from the moment of the shot's being fired, we can see moral responsibility for the Master's assassination passing through the intermediate cause of the Senior Tutor just as easily as it does through the intermediate cause of the gun and the bullet coming from it, right back to me, where it sticks. Unless there is someone or something standing behind me in an analogous way to the way I stand behind the Senior Tutor, I am the one who should be charged with murder (or praised for having ended a tyranny). This then is our assumption that moral responsibility requires ultimate authorship. 'Ultimate' is being used here and hereafter then to allow space, should we wish to use it, in which we might maintain that, for example, the Senior Tutor when so operated upon would still be in a non-ultimate way the author of his behaviour in such a situation.[18]

The example just discussed raises an interesting issue which it is worth bringing out even though it is a 'sidebar' to our main discussion at the moment. In the case of the second chip, the Senior Tutor, it will be noted, would have seemed to himself to be robustly morally responsible (at least unless or until the existence and nature of the chip was explained to him), because it would have seemed to him that he was the ultimate author of his choice to kill the Master; he wouldn't realize that these thoughts and the decisions 'he' took were being typed into him and caused (perhaps with a bit of randomness thrown in) by me rather than him. So we may raise the following sceptical worry: how can we know that we're not in the Senior Tutor's situation ourselves whenever it seems to us that we're morally responsible for some particular apparent choice?

At least initially, this question may be answered fairly straight-forwardly; we have reason to believe that such a chip has yet to be invented; we have no gaps in our memory corresponding to a period of time in which a chip could have been implanted; and so on. Thus, we do have a superfluity of reasons, each of us, to believe that we are not in fact in a situation like the Senior Tutor's. But the worry can be pushed at a deeper level. Were Determinism true, then – it could be argued – we would *all* be in a situation like the Senior Tutor's all the time; we would not have chips implanted in our brains for sure, but we would have equivalent structures implanted in our brains by processes stretching back in time to prior to our birth and certainly beyond our control. If there were ultimately a God or some such behind it, then there would in fact be, behind all of us, an ultimate author who thus received full moral responsibility for all that has followed and will follow from his act of creation; if not, then in fact no one would be morally responsible as no one would be an ultimate author. Either way, we – late on in the order of things – would not be morally responsible as we ordinarily take ourselves to be. In other words, it could be suggested that, if Determinism were true, it might well be that we would be determined to believe ourselves robustly morally responsible even though we could never do other than what-ever it is we did and were never the ultimate authors of our actions; we would all be significantly like the Senior Tutor in the last case we considered (minus the randomness). So, it could be argued, the fact that we believe ourselves robustly morally responsible for at least some of our actions is no reason to think Determinism false even if this sort of robust moral responsibility *is* incompatible with Determinism, as we have seen we believe it is.[19]

Such an argument parallels the argument that the fact that it seems to me that there's a desk in front of me is no reason for me to suppose that there is a desk in front of me because if I was a brain in a vat (of the right sort), it would seem to me that there was a desk in front of me even though there was not. The principle behind this argument is that until I have ruled out the brain-in-a-vat hypothesis, I cannot take what seems to me to be the case as evidence of what is the case. Similarly, the principle behind the argument of the previous paragraph is that until we have ruled out Determinism, we cannot take what seems to us to be the case with regards to our robust moral responsibility as evidence of what really is the case. But this is to put the cart before the horse; we have to take what seems to us to be the case to be evidence of what is the case in this area as in all others (bar one). If we did not do that, we could never get started on any topic in Philosophy other than the most extreme version of the Problem of Scepticism (the one).

If the only reasons to doubt that we are in fact as we seem to be are of a piece with reasons to doubt that the world beyond one's own self at the present moment exists and is more or less as it seems to be, one can 'divide through' by these reasons in the context of any investigation in Philosophy more particular than that into the most extreme version of the Problem of Scepticism. This is not to say that what seems *prima facie* to be the case in some more particular area of investigation might not be something we discover we have more reason *ultima facie* to reject than to accept. A stick might *prima facie* seem to be bent in water, but – upon investigation – this seeming might turn out to be one we had *ultima facie* reason to reject. The same thing could happen here; it *prima facie* seems to us that we are sometimes the ultimate authors of our actions, but if we were to find ourselves drawn to a general view about the nature of the universe, that is Determinism, which ruled that out as a physical possibility, then we might – depending on the strength of the reasons which took us to that general view – ultimately wish to reject as veridical this *prima facie* seeming. But that sort of worry is for later. For now, we are seeking simply to unearth the foundations of our everyday thought. We are not yet in the business either of tearing them up so that we may build elsewhere or alternatively of underpinning them. That being the case then, we may say that it certainly seems to us that we are the ultimate authors of the actions for which we are morally responsible and indeed that it is because we suppose ourselves to be the ultimate authors of these actions that we take ourselves to be morally responsible for them.

This fourth thought, the 'Ultimate Authorship' condition on moral responsibility is, as with Indeterminism, again considered by us to be a necessary but not in itself sufficient condition for moral responsibility. To see its insufficiency, consider again the situation where you are a sheriff of a township in the Wild West: the doctor was, we would ordinarily suppose, the ultimate author of his action in hitting the child; it was him, rather than anyone else, who did this (he had no brain implant or what have you controlling him). And, we would ordinarily suppose, it was possible for him not to do it – he was under no compulsion; he had, we suppose, alternative possibilities open to him. Yet, even so, we do not regard the doctor as robustly morally responsible for that action; we were worried that the mob would unfairly do so, which was why we were more sanguine than we might otherwise have been about the idea of framing the drunk. The doctor, we thought, was no doubt deserving of *some* sanction on retributive grounds for his negligence in performing this hasty act (perhaps some community service or some such), but, the striking of the child as hard as he did being a miscalculation on his part, not so much sanction as would have been the case had it been a well-informed and calculated action done from sadism or some such. These thoughts raise the questions, 'Why is the ultimate authorship condition necessary for robust moral responsibility?' and 'How does this condition relate to the condition that the person whom we're assessing must have been able to do otherwise than whatever they actually did?' We'll spend a moment or two answering these questions before we look at the fifth and final everyday thought we have about free will.

* * *

Ultimate authorship is what we take to mark off the difference between, on the one hand, mere events that occur in us or, as we might put it, processes which our bodies undergo and, on the other hand, actions which we perform using our bodies. In the case of the Senior Tutor shooting the Master, it would not be at all unnatural for us to say of him that while the action of pointing the gun at the Master and pulling the trigger was something that his body was certainly involved in, it was not something that the Senior Tutor himself was doing with his body even if, in the case of the second chip, the Senior Tutor did not realize that its status was merely that of an event he was undergoing, mistaking it for an action which he himself was performing. We would say of his situation that in fact, as *I* was the ultimate author of the movements of his body which constituted 'his' assassinating the Master, so the assassination was an action I was performing, rather than him. The Senior Tutor no more performed the action of assassinating the Master than the gun performed the action of assassinating the Master; the Senior Tutor and the gun underwent events that were components of the action which *I* was performing in assassinating the Master. But we do not need to go to improbable and inexperienced imaginary scenarios to see in play the distinction between bodily events one undergoes and actions one performs using one's body. We use the distinction in everyday situations such as the following.

You are walking across the quad. Ahead of you walks a small and rather-ridiculous-looking gentleman, already somewhat unsteady on his feet due to his wearing an over-proportioned rucksack. He steps on one end of a paving slab, which, it turns out, is loose. In stepping on his end, he depresses it and the end closest to you is raised. This causes you to trip and stumble forward slightly before righting yourself. In righting yourself, your hands shoot out instinctively and they give the gentleman in front of you a shove in the back, causing him in turn to stumble slightly before he manages to right himself. You immediately and instinctively apologize to him and no doubt feel some embarrassment and regret at what has happened. However, you do not feel any shame or remorse, as you would have done had you wilfully pushed him, mistaking him for someone you passionately disliked. So, you suppose that something different could have happened to you at that time – there was no necessity that you trip on that bit of pavement. You are to some extent sad that this different thing did not happen, because, if it had, then now you and the small gentleman in front of you would be slightly better off than you are. But, given that what has happened was not something of which you believe yourself to be the ultimate author, you do not really regard it as an action which you performed, rather than something your body underwent, and hence you do not find in it something about which you feel remorse rather than merely regret. The appropriate response for the small gentleman who you accidentally stumbled against to give when the situation is made manifest to him would be something like the following: 'Well, there's no need to apologize. It's annoying, but there's nothing you could have done about it. Don't blame yourself'. Had you instead mistaken him for someone you disliked and pushed him out of malice and he become aware of that, then the appropriate response would have along the lines of, 'Well, you should apologize. Because it's annoying and there is something you could have done about it, viz. decided not to shove me.'

Ultimate authorship then, we suppose, is what makes our actions our actions rather than somebody else's or nobody's at all and thus reduces them all to mere events.[20] And this reveals to us the connection between this supposition and another we have already discussed, Indeterminism. The world could be one in which Indeterminism was true, but we were still not the ultimate authors of any of the bodily movements that we took to be our actions. The Senior Tutor in one of the previous examples is someone of whom this is true when the implant is switched on; in a variant of the second case, as we saw, he could have done otherwise than murder the Master, because I allowed a certain amount of randomness to interpose itself between the thoughts I typed and what the Senior Tutor ultimately ended up doing, but, even so, it wouldn't be the Senior Tutor who murdered the Master, it'd be me, using him as a tool just as ordinarily people use guns as tools. So, as well as supposing we need Indeterminism to be true if moral responsibility is to be present, we suppose the ultimate authorship condition needs to be satisfied if moral responsibility is to be present. Were it not, none of those bodily movements we take to be actions would really be actions; they'd just be events that we were undergoing and some of which we mistakenly thought of as our actions. That being the case, while the world could be indeterministic without us being the ultimate authors of our actions, the world couldn't be one where we were the ultimate authors of our actions and yet not be indeterministic. If everything we did was in fact determined by factors millions of years before our birth (as would be the case were Determinism true), then we would not be the ultimate authors of any of our 'actions'. If Indeterminism was true, we might *still* not be the ultimate authors of our 'actions' – they might be brought about by mere chance, that is to say un-caused by anything whatsoever and thereby un-caused by us. So while Indeterminism might be true without our being the ultimate authors of our actions and thus without our being morally responsible for them (Indeterminism is not sufficient for robust moral responsibility), Ultimate Authorship, which is required for moral responsibility, requires Indeterminism to be true (Indeterminism is necessary for robust moral responsibility). We will return to this point in the next chapter.

For now let us to turn to the fifth and final thought we shall look at in this chapter. In the background of several of our examples so far, another thought has been operating when it came to our assessment of the moral responsibility of the protagonists; the thought has been that one escapes moral responsibility to the extent that one is not well-informed, un-rushed and un-coerced in coming to the decision in question. Let's unpack this suggestion a bit and see it in operation in a couple of cases. Then we'll be able to tie all these threads together.

* * *

The first two conditions suggested for moral responsibility here – being well-informed and un-rushed in one's decision-making – are, it seems, necessary conditions for us holding the person concerned to know enough about the action in question and be choosing it on the basis of enough reflection on that knowledge for them to be morally assessable for their choice. Imagine the following as illustrative of these two conditions in play.

In an emergency room, a doctor prescribes a certain medicine to a critically ill patient who needs immediate medical intervention if he/she were not to die. This is a medicine that would ordinarily prove life-saving to a patient in this condition. However, in this particular case, due to an extremely rare and hitherto undetected pre-existing medical condition that this particular patient suffers from, it proves poisonous. Another medicine was available and this other medicine would in fact have saved this particular patient's life, yet it would ordinarily be less effective in this sort of case, which is indeed why the doctor chose not to prescribe it. The doctor has, we may hence say, poisoned his patient when he could have saved them. But of course we do not in any way blame the doctor for his choice. He had to make a quick decision and, on the basis of the information available to him at the time, the medicine he prescribed seemed like the best medicine to prescribe. Because he was not well-informed and un-rushed, we do not regard him as at all morally responsible for poisoning his patient.

There is, it should be observed, a continuum between this sort of case and a sort of case in which the doctor *would* have been culpable for poisoning his patient. It passes through cases where, for example, the condition which makes this particular medicine poisonous is known to be relatively widespread; or where the doctor has more time to investigate the condition of this particular patient before he needs to choose what medicine to prescribe; and so on. As we move along this continuum, we would wish to say that the doctor has increasing moral responsibility for poisoning his patient, up to a point at which we would wish to say he was culpably reckless or criminally negligent in acting as he did. At this other extreme, we would naturally conclude that the doctor deserved some punishment; he should be struck off the medical register or at least suspended until he has been on a suitable re-training course. This condition for moral responsibility then admits of degrees or rather the moral responsibility that rests on it admits of degrees.

It could be suggested that sometimes we *do* wish to assess morally someone who does not in fact satisfy the conditions of being well-informed and un-rushed in coming to their choice, but here – closer inspection reveals – it is actually the choices they made earlier on for which we wish to assess them, not the choice which has brought them to our attention as someone who we may wish to assess morally. For example, the student rugby club at my college has something of a history of boorish behaviour associated with their social events and, as Dean (an office I held for a few years), I was sometimes called upon to enforce the college's regulations on its members. That being the case, I would, too often, find myself interviewing members of the rugby club several days after they had indulged in some unfortunate drunken behaviour. As these interviews progressed, I was ordinarily left with strong reason to believe that the student in question had drunk such a quantity of alcohol prior to the misbehaviour in question that he – it was uniformly a he – genuinely did not in any significant way know what it was he was doing at the time he did it. A particular member's convincing me of this though, often somewhat to his chagrin, did not prove sufficient to dissuade me from holding him morally responsible, but what I then held him morally responsible for was not the resultant behaviour but the fact that he had become so drunk earlier on in the evening while knowing fully well from his own past experience that he would probably end up doing something that infringed the college's regulations. (The same people came before me week after week.) 'I agree that by the time you chose to proposition the Master's wife, you were beyond any form of rationality; however, the fact that you had so reduced yourself is something for which you are culpable and I shall therefore be fining you/banning you from the bar for several weeks.'

So, to be fully morally responsible, one must be well-informed and un-rushed in the choices one makes. Where one approaches satisfying these conditions fully but does not quite do so, one has proportionately less moral responsibility, unless the fact that one does not more closely approach satisfying these conditions fully is itself the result of an earlier and culpable act of negligence on one's own part, in which case moral responsibility for the final action is traced back to the action which made one less capable of being well-informed and un-rushed later. These then are the first two conditions made mention of in what I am calling the fifth thought we have about ourselves in everyday life.[21]

The third necessary condition for moral responsibility made mention of here is lack of coercion; it is possible for someone to know fully well what they are doing and do it after adequate reflection, yet we still wish to exculpate them from all blame as we believe they were coerced into doing whatever it is they did. To see this in play, imagine the following scenario.

The manager of a bank is at home one evening with his family when would-be bank robbers break in; seize all present; and say that unless the bank manager assists them in robbing his bank the next morning, they will murder his wife and children. Having spent the night worriedly contemplating the alternatives, the next morning the bank manager thus takes a selection of the would-be robbers with him to his bank, leaving behind the two who are tasked with murdering his family should the bank robbery not prove successful. He ushers his group past the security guards on his authority (thus avoiding a shoot-out which would, no doubt, have claimed the lives of several, both innocent and guilty); he lets them into the safe and even helps them pack money into the bags they have brought with them. He then sees them safely off the premises and, as soon as his family calls to say that they are safe, he immediately informs the police of everything that has transpired. The bank manager then has wilfully assisted in robbing his own bank; he knew fully well what he was doing and had ample time to reflect on it, yet he is – we would say – not to any extent morally responsible. How shall we explain this?

Some would say that the bank manager in this case escapes responsibility as he is not the ultimate author of his actions; his situation is analogous to that of the Senior Tutor in our earlier examples. He has in effect become merely the unwitting tool of the bank robbers. However, this seems not quite right. The would-be bank robbers have of course set up an 'incentive structure' for him, which means that he can be relied upon to choose to do as they wish, but when he chooses to do it, it is him who chooses to do it rather than anyone else; they are not literally in control of his body. His situation is different in magnitude and moral ramifications but not fundamentally in type from those of us who face less momentous 'incentive structures' in our everyday lives. So, we should not say that it is because he escapes from being the ultimate author of his actions that he escapes moral responsibility; he does not escape from being the ultimate author of his actions. So, the bank manager could do otherwise; he is the one who is the ultimate author of what he does; and of course he knows what he is doing when he assists the robbers in robbing his bank. But nevertheless, despite meeting all these conditions, he still avoids moral responsibility. How so?

The bank manager manages to escape moral responsibility as he is not willingly assisting the robbers in robbing the bank under the description 'robbing the bank'. For this observation to be helpful, we need to spend a moment or two drawing out how one not only performs actions, but one also performs them under certain descriptions. The doctor who gave the patient the wrong medicine performed the action of poisoning him, but not under that description; he did not know when he acted that the giving of that medicine would be something that could be truly described as poisoning; if he had, he wouldn't have done it. What of the bank manager? Well, he did know that what he was doing was robbing the bank, but he did not will the action under that description. And that is the crucial factor here. If we ask ourselves, 'Did the bank manager want to do what he did?', we incline to answer, 'Yes and No', which reveals that we suppose that under one description of the action, 'doing whatever is necessary to save my family', he willingly performed the action, while under another, 'conspiring with criminals to rob my bank', he did not. It is because the bank manager did not willingly perform the action in question under the description morally salient to blame, 'robbing the bank', that he is not morally responsible for robbing the bank. The nature of coercion is getting someone to perform wilfully an action under one description by making the world such that that description fits it (e.g. its being the only way to save the lives of your family), an action which the person would not perform wilfully under a description they also know to be true of it and under which you will it to be done (e.g. its being the robbing of the bank).[22]

These three conditions on the decision-making process leading up to an action, that it be well-informed, un-rushed and un-coerced, may appear quite disparate. But they are tied together as differing aspects of a necessary condition for moral responsibility, that one wills the action under the description salient for moral assessment. Being well-informed and un-rushed are necessary for knowing the morally salient descriptions of one's action (that this drug is a poison; that this action would be boorish; that this would aid criminals in robbing a bank) and being un-coerced is necessary for one's willing it under that description. These things admit of degrees and thus moral responsibility admits of degrees. The cold blooded murderer of the classic detective story is fully morally responsible for the death he causes. The drunken rugby lout is less than fully responsible for the offence he causes. The bank manager is not at all responsible for the losses from his bank. We could hence sum up our fifth thought as follows:

To the extent that I did not will an action under the morally salient description, I am not fully morally responsible for it.

* * *

Now we have five thoughts on the table, thoughts which – we have argued – play a role in undergirding, as it were, our everyday thinking about free will. We have already started to see how they may be arranged into a mutually supporting array, and hence how they together constitute what we might say is the common-sense view about the existence and nature of free will. Let's take a moment or two looking at a frequent arrangement of these thoughts before concluding by restating as a whole what this view is.

A frequent diagnosis of our everyday thinking would have the man on the Clapham omnibus who is taking some time on his journey to reflect on the topic of this book starting off his reflections with the intuitive feeling-cum-premise that he is, sometimes at least, free in the sense necessary for a robust sort of moral responsibility, one justifying desert-based rewards and punishments, not just consequentially justified interventions. His first and most secure premise is something like, 'I am the sort of thing that is morally responsible for certain of the actions that I perform, clear cases being well-informed, un-rushed and un-coerced choices of moral significance.' It would have him then deploy something akin to an argument we've already looked at as his second and more or less equally certain premise of Incompatibilism. 'I could not be the sort of thing that is morally responsible unless the decisions for which I am in this sense responsible are ones that it is within my power to effect. Were everything determined by the initial conditions of the universe and the natural laws operative on it since then, I would not have the power to effect anything, so, my being this sort of thing is incompatible with the truth of Determinism.' Then, it would have him draw a third claim as the result of a logical inference from his first two premises, Indeterminism. 'Thus Determinism must be false.' This chapter has suggested that while these thoughts may indeed be linked in this way, robust moral responsibility and Indeterminism are independently sanctioned by common sense; we do not ordinarily need to infer the second from the first via a deployment of an argument based on Incompatibilism. The same is true for Incompatibilism itself; we believe it without basing it on an argument from something we suppose to be more fundamental than it.[23]

This common diagnosis of the everyday thinking of the man on the Clapham omnibus would then have more reflection on his part revealing to him that Determinism's being false, while necessary for him being the sort of thing he assumes he is in his first premise, is not sufficient and thus coming up with a fourth thought, that he is an ultimate cause of these actions. 'Obviously the mere possibility of doing other than whatever I ended up doing (which Indeterminism vouchsafes for me) is not sufficient for me being the morally responsible sort of thing that I am. I need in some way to be the thing that makes the difference, the ultimate author of my actions. Thus, I must satisfy the ultimate authorship condition.' Again, this is a logical order for these thoughts to occur in, but it is not the only psychological one; the supposition that we are the ultimate authors of our actions is again supported by our intuitions, independently of any arguments for it from these other thoughts. Finally, perhaps it will occur to the man that sometimes, even when one is the ultimate author of one's actions and hence could have done other than whatever it is one does, one might still escape moral responsibility through not wilfully doing what one does under the morally culpable description (e.g. cases of rushed doctors or coerced bank managers might come to mind).

My claim then is that each of these thoughts – Moral Responsibility, Incompatibilism, Indeterminism, Ultimate Authorship, and the necessity for moral responsibility that we will the action under the morally salient description – is independently licensed by common sense even if they are perhaps not licensed thereby to the same extent. Indeterminism and Moral Responsibility are perhaps licensed to the greatest extent by common sense, as they strike us in those situations which are most clearly situations of choice as, if you will, brute data: I could have behaved differently; I'm morally responsible for what I did. Incompatibilism gains less immediate support from our everyday experiences, as it is an attempt to link these two data; I'm responsible at least in part *because* I could have behaved differently. But upon reflection we do hold it; our holding it is re-enforced as we become aware of a deeper assumption we are making, that we are sometimes the ultimate authors of what we end up doing, indeed were we not so, then no apparent action of ours would really be an action of ours; all our bodily movements would in fact be mere events we were undergoing. But the assumption of Ultimate Authorship and how it entails Indeterminism are not 'brute data' of our everyday lives; they have to be elicited by reflection on thought experiments. They strike us as more speculative conclusions from our experience, not items of experience. Finally, that we are only morally responsible for those actions which we will under the morally salient descriptions again strikes us as obvious by reflection on cases such as doctors mistakenly prescribing poisons and bank managers being forced into assisting bank robbers. It is not perhaps a brute datum of experience, but it is easily drawn out from everyday experiences; the hurried doctor should not be blamed for inadvertently giving the patient a poison; the rugby lout should really be blamed for getting himself that drunk in the first place, not so much for what he went on to do when drunk; the bank manager should not be blamed for assisting the robbers in robbing his bank. These five thoughts, while independently licensed by our intuitions, 'lock together' into a view of the existence and nature of free will which we can with good reason call the common-sense view and to which philosophical reflection on the issue of free will has given a name, Libertarianism.[24]

* * *

CONCLUSION

In this chapter we have spent some time 'nailing down' five thoughts which we may reasonably suggest are presupposed by us in our everyday decision-making and our reflections on it.

- *Sometimes I could do something other than what I actually do.*
- *Sometimes I'm morally responsible for what I do.*
- *If I couldn't do other than what I actually do, then I wouldn't be morally responsible for what I do.*
- *If I wasn't the ultimate author of my actions, then I wouldn't be morally responsible for them.*
- *To the extent that I did not will an action under the morally salient description, I am not fully morally responsible for it.*

These five thoughts lock together into a view about the existence and nature of free will which we have called 'Libertarianism'. According to Libertarianism, we live in a universe where more than one future is really possible for us at moments of choice (Indeterminism). This is just as well if we are to be free, for were it not the case that we could sometimes do things other than whatever it is we end up doing, we would never really be morally responsible in a robust sense (Incompatibilism). But in fact we *are* sometimes morally responsible in a robust sense (Moral Responsibility). When we are, it is in part because we are the ultimate authors of those movements of our bodies for which we are morally responsible; they are genuinely actions which we are performing, rather than merely events which we are undergoing (Ultimate Authorship). Of course, if we did not fully know what it was we were doing when we did it, we might yet escape moral responsibility for what was nevertheless genuinely an action of ours. That is why, for moral responsibility, the action must not only be an action, but must also be a well-informed and un-rushed one. It must also be un-coerced or again one escapes moral responsibility. Only then can it be said that not only did we wilfully do a certain thing, but we wilfully did it under the description that makes it a praiseworthy/ blameworthy action (Morally salient willing). But such conditions are sometimes satisfied and, when they are satisfied, the conditions which are necessary and jointly sufficient for moral responsibility are satisfied: we freely did whatever it is we ended up doing under the morally salient description and hence we are morally assessable for it.

Given that one of the contentions that I have defended in this chapter has been that we are all already committed to thinking in the manner that this nailing down has been articulating, so I must expect that the most clear-headed of my readers will have found a good deal of what I have been saying in this chapter obvious and hence needless: 'Of course our everyday beliefs presuppose alternative possibilities are really open to us and that we can know about them. Of course we ordinarily suppose that we are morally responsible for some of our choices and that that is because we suppose that we could have done otherwise on those occasions and are thereby enabled to be the genuine authors of whatever it is we did do on those occasions. Of course, we further need to suppose that the action was willed under the morally salient description for us to attribute full moral responsibility for it and thus need the choice to be made in a sufficiently well-informed, un-rushed and un-coerced way. Why take such pains in going over all this?' These are things such people will naturally have said and asked. My answer is that even the most clear-headed among us will be grateful that have we nailed this all down so painstakingly when the storms of later chapters break over us.

We shall be particularly grateful to our earlier selves when we come in later chapters to theories of the nature of free will the proponents of which characteristically seek to establish that we never really pre-supposed all parts of this view in our everyday reflections on our decision-making in the first place.

For example, the proponents of the range of views which usually go by the name of 'compatibilist' accounts of free will (for they share the thesis that our having free will is compatible with Determinism being true) ordinarily suggest, as we shall see, that their accounts should be accepted as articulations of our common sense and every-day thinking about free will, rather than as revisions of it.[25] Similarly, those who suggest that Determinism is true often suggest that the fact that it is true is presupposed by us in our everyday thinking about the world. This type of move, we now have reason to believe, is a misguided strategy on the part of the proponents of such views. The work we have already done suggests that, on the contrary, Incompatibilism is assumed in our everyday life, as is Indeterminism. Of course, one or both of these assumptions might – for all that – not be true. But that they might not be true is in itself not a reason for us to doubt that we suppose them to be true. All of this being the case, it would be better for the proponents of these views to deny that Incompatibilism and/or Indeterminism is true yet admit that we *do* presuppose them/it in our everyday thinking and thus advance the thesis that our everyday thinking is false in these/this particular presuppositions/presupposition. They could then present their alternative accounts as *improvements* on everyday thinking, not simply expressions of it. In providing such a service to us, they could present themselves as analogous to those who displaced belief in shamanism, voodoo, and so on with belief in medical science as we would understand it today. It would not be plausible to contend that such people merely articulated more fully the underlying concepts and principles they found in the thinking of the communities they entered; rather, they replaced these concepts and principles with ones that more adequately reflected reality. Similarly then, those who argue that Incompatibilism is false or that Indeterminism is false, are – we shall in due course suggest – most plausible when they are presented as arguing not that we do not suppose the opposite in everyday life, but rather that such presuppositions, once properly thought through, can be seen to be at the least unnecessary (and perhaps even detrimental) for free will in the revisionary sense that they articulate and, once that sense is set out, we can see that it captures all or at least a significant part of the sort of free will that is worth wanting, that – when well-informed – we really care about.[26]

In the rest of this book we'll look at views which challenge elements of this common-sense view and see whether or not it can withstand challenges if this sort. The first set of views is one which challenges the incompatibilist element, compatibilist ones. These will form our focus for the next chapter.

CHAPTER THREE

INCOMPATIBILISM

INTRODUCTION

In this chapter, we'll look in more detail at a claim which links together our thoughts that sometimes we could have done otherwise than whatever it is we ended up doing (Indeterminism) and that sometimes we're morally responsible for having done whatever it is we ended up doing (Moral Responsibility). This is the claim that we numbered our third thought in the previous chapter, the claim that it is in part *because* we could have done otherwise that we are morally responsible for whatever it is we did. More precisely, the thought is that robust moral responsibility *requires* Indeterminism to be true: we couldn't be morally responsible unless Indeterminism were true. It is because then this sort of responsibility is being posited as being incompatible with Determinism that we call this third thought 'Incompatibilism'. We're going to be looking in this chapter at arguments for and against Incompatibilism. We'll look at some classic arguments in favour of it; the classic criticisms that have been levelled against these arguments; and what some contemporary authors writing in this field make of the issue.

Before we get into this though, two points deserve to be made in the introduction. The first is to do with this use of the term 'Incompatibilism', as a label for the thesis that there is an incompatibility between moral responsibility and Determinism. Sometimes you'll find in other works the name used as a label for the thesis that there is an incompatibility between *free will* and Determinism. This is in the end a mere terminological issue, but nevertheless it is one that it is as well to be clear about, especially if this is the first philosophical work on the nature of free will that you've read and you plan to go

on from it to read others. The second is a more substantive philosophical issue and indeed one at a higher level of abstraction than
any of the arguments or counterarguments we shall occupy ourselves
with in the chapter as it unfolds. It concerns where we should judge
the 'dialectical balance' to fall on the issue of Incompatibilism. Does
the incompatibilist *need* arguments of the sort we'll be considering in
favour of Incompatibilism to be successful in order to be rational in
his or her Incompatibilism; or is it rather just that he or she just needs
to be able to refute from his or her starting points counterarguments
to Incompatibilism? We shall put this colloquially as the issue of
whether Incompatibilism is most reasonably taken as guilty until
proven innocent or innocent until proven guilty. We shall consider
the first issue first.

* * *

In the literature, one will often find the term 'Incompatibilism' used
as a label for the thesis that free will and Determinism are incompatible, not used as I am using it, as a label for the thesis that moral
responsibility and Determinism are incompatible. For our purposes
it would be sufficient merely to observe this difference and move
on; we are interested in the issues, not the labels that happen to be
attached to them. However, as it provides some insight into the issues
for us to observe the rationale behind differing uses of the label
'Incompatibilism', we may linger on the topic for a moment or two
more with some hope of profiting thereby.

The majority of those authors who use 'Incompatibilism' as the
name of the thesis that free will and Determinism are incompatible
define free will as whatever it is that is necessary and sufficient for us
to be robustly moral responsible in our choices. So, in fact, the term
'Incompatibilism' as used in their works marks out exactly the same
territory as is marked out by its use in this work. Others, usually
those committed to Libertarianism, define free will as ultimate
authorship and refrain from attributing to it sufficiency for moral
responsibility on account of noting, as we have noted, that, for
example, ill-informed, rushed and coerced actions might be free in
their sense yet the agents in question escape that sort of responsibility. Nevertheless, as they posit that free will as they have defined it is
necessary for moral responsibility, so essentially the same issue of

incompatibility is being addressed in discussions of Incompatibilism in their works as in discussions of Incompatibilism in this. The only position which we might in principle shield from view by using 'Incompatibilism' to refer to the thesis that moral responsibility and Determinism are incompatible, rather than to the thesis that free will and Determinism are incompatible, is one that uses 'free will' as the label for something which is posited as unnecessary for moral responsibility. We shall consider such views under the compatibilist heading as the chapter progresses. So, in short, the discussion of Incompatibilism as we are understanding it takes in exactly the same issues as are taken in by discussions that might at first appear to understand it differently.

* * *

Secondly, before we start looking in detail at arguments for Incompatibilism as we are defining it and criticisms of them, let us briefly look at the 'meta issue' of whether or not the incompatibilist needs such arguments in order for his or her Incompatibilism to be rational. Obviously, even if certain arguments in favour of a particular position in this area fail as arguments, that is not in itself any reason to suppose that the position is false, just a reason to suppose that it cannot be shown to be true by those arguments. Even a failure of *all possible* arguments – and how could we ever know we had considered all possible arguments? – in favour of a particular position in this area would be no reason to suppose that that position was false, just reason to suppose that it cannot be shown to be true by any argument at all. And we must recall that it is intellectually respectable for each of us to hold some beliefs without being able to support them by any argument at all. This is respectable because it is inescapable. For example, each of us has fundamental beliefs about what makes for a good argument and these *cannot*, without begging the very issue these beliefs are about (something none of us regard as being a feature of a good argument), be supported by argument. More straightforwardly, none of us is able to entertain an infinite number of beliefs, so it cannot be the case that each belief we have is, as a matter of fact, based on another via an argument that we take to state that the one is a reason for the other. In short, we have to have some beliefs that are not based via argument on others; we might call them 'basic beliefs'. That being so, we cannot object to basic beliefs in principle; the only issue here can be whether the particular belief that is Incompatibilism may *properly* be held basically.[1]

It will be recalled from the previous chapter that while not an immediate 'datum' of our everyday experience, we do seem to 'start out' believing in Incompatibilism without in fact basing that belief on any argument. We saw our implicit belief in it operating in our reactions to the thought experiments involving imagining how we would wish to describe the residents of a universe that scientists had told us they had discovered which was superficially exactly as ours – with creatures superficially such as ourselves thinking thoughts such as ours – but in which Determinism was true. While we noted that we would concede that presumably many of the creatures in that universe would – given that they were like us – *think* that they were often morally responsible for certain of their decisions, we would believe of them that they were in error in this judgement. The belief in Incompatibilism springs up quickly to our conscious mind when being presented with such cases; when it is articulated for the first time, it strikes us as something we already believed unconsciously, in inarticulate form, rather than as an entirely novel implication of something we already believed. Our basic belief in Incompatibilism is then, we might say, exposed by thought experiments of this sort without these thought experiments giving us reasons to suppose that the belief is true. The thought experiments of the last chapter are not in themselves arguments for Incompatibilism. (We shall come to arguments for Incompatibilism in a moment.) They are rather ways of showing us that we already believe in Incompatibilism prior to any argument. So far then, we might say that we have reason to believe our belief in Incompatibilism is basic, that is to say it is a belief for which we have no reasons (prior to exposure to the sorts of arguments which form the focus of this chapter).[2] Having established that it is a basic belief, the question for each of us at this stage then is 'Is it *properly* basic?', that is 'Is it permissible for me to hold it without having any argument in its favour?' If it is, it might seem that we do not need to consider the sorts of arguments which form the focus of this chapter at all.

As a prelude to answering definitively the question of whether or not belief in Incompatibilism may be properly basic in this sense, we would need to establish some general criteria for propriety in this area and sadly this is no quick task; whole books are devoted to the topic of proper basicality in belief and we shall not be able to do it justice here.[3] Although then it is impossible to answer this question definitively here, I offer the following speculation for your consideration:

If Incompatibilism is true, then belief that it is true is properly basic and if Incompatibilism is false, then belief that it is false is properly basic.

This speculation might commend itself to you for the following reasons. The sorts of things which would make Incompatibilism true were it true are fundamental metaphysical relationships to do with the essence of modality and moral responsibility and, because of their fundamental nature, our beliefs about these sorts of things do not seem capable of being grounded in beliefs about anything that is in any significant way more fundamental than them and knowable with greater certainty than we know them. Thus, while it is plausible to contend that if Incompatibilism is true, it is so due to the incompatibility between ultimate authorship and Determinism, ultimate authorship itself being necessary for robust moral responsibility, our belief that ultimate authorship is necessary for robust moral responsibility is not knowable with greater certainty than Incompatibilism itself. Or again, as we shall see in our discussion in this chapter of an argument called the 'Consequence Argument', there are other principles that can be used as the premises of an argument which has Incompatibilism for its conclusion, but it is hard for even enthusiasts for such arguments to present these premises as more obvious than the conclusion they nominally support. The arguments always retain something of the air of artificiality about them. The artificiality is similar to that which one would find attending those arguments which one might advance had one found onseself arguing with someone who claimed to doubt that $1 + 1 = 2$. In such a case, one might go back to Peano's postulates (the axioms for natural numbers) to prove it from there and such a proof might be formally valid, but one could not help but worry while advancing such a proof that anyone who seriously doubted that $1 + 1 = 2$ would be unlikely to have more confidence in the truth of the postulates and the validity of the argumentation from them than they did in the conclusion. If this is so, then it seems we cannot reasonably hope to base our belief in Incompatibilism via an argument on a belief in something more basic and certain than itself and, if that is so, then if it is proper for us to have beliefs about Incompatibilism at all, it is proper for us to have them basically. Plausibly then, if Incompatibilism is true, then it is proper for us to believe that it is true basically; if it is false, then it is proper for us to believe that it is false basically. This is not to say of course that it is *im*proper to have belief in the truth or falsity of Incompatibilism non-basically. The mathematical scholar, who has believed that 1 + 1 = 2 from childhood, never basing it on any other belief until late on in her life, is not improper if she now sits down and proves it to herself by argument. The belief which she properly held basically since childhood will now have got extra justification, presuming she has reason to believe in the starting points of her proof and the validity of her argument independently of supposing the truth of its conclusion. And so even if we believe – as it was argued in the first chapter we do all (most of us at least) start by believing – that Incompatibilism is true and we now believe, as a result of considering the reasons given in this paragraph, that we may think of this belief of ours as properly basic, we might nevertheless, at the minimum, have a 'scholar's' interest in seeing whether it can also be justified. And there are two ways in which our interest in arguments in favour of Incompatibilism might be heightened beyond this 'scholarly' level.

First, the conclusion we have been left with by the considerations of the previous paragraph is that *if* it is true, then belief in Incompatibilism is properly basic, but if it is false, then belief in its being true is not properly basic. Thus, it is not possible to establish that belief in Incompatibilism either is or is not properly basic from a standpoint that is neutral with respect to the truth of Incompatibilism. And, that being so, to establish that having the belief that Incompatibilism is true is properly basic requires one to advance arguments in favour of Incompatibilism being true. Until one has done that, one cannot be reasonably confident in the proper basicality of one's belief in Incompatibilism; if one is an incompatibilist – as I have suggested in the previous chapter almost all of us are, at least initially – one has to regard one's being right, as one of course supposes one is, as, in a sense, a matter of mere good fortune prior to engaging with such arguments. If the arguments in favour of Incompatibilism work, then they may end up giving one reason to suppose that they were not needed in the first place, but one cannot know that they will work without looking at them and thus one cannot know that they are not needed until one has looked at them. This consideration then transfigures the 'scholar's' interest spoken of in the previous paragraph into a personal interest for any of us who would wish to think of ourselves as philosophers: if one is to be positively reasonable in taking one's belief in Incompatibilism as properly basic, one must have familiarized oneself with good arguments for the truth of Incompatibilism.

The second reason why paying attention to such arguments must commend itself to us as philosophers who find ourselves believing in Incompatibilism is that in fact, *pace* what has just been said, it is not that these arguments, if they work, show themselves not to be needed at all, for, as we shall see, they are plausibly needed in *defending* Incompatibilism against Compatibilism.[4] Let us go into that in a bit more detail.

It is a time-honoured principle of jurisprudence that all that is necessary for the defence counsel to be successful is that they show that the prosecution has not proved their case (either proved it beyond reasonable doubt or proved it on balance of probabilities, depending on the nature of the case). The defendant is taken to be innocent until proven guilty, not guilty until proven innocent. Something similar is the case, I have been suggesting, with our common-sense belief in Incompatibilism. We start by taking it as true; if it is true, belief in it is plausibly properly basic, so we might, in that sense, not feel more than a scholar's interest in arguments which purport to give us reasons to suppose that it is true. Such arguments might naturally strike us as 'purely academic'; we can happily go on taking it as innocent (i.e. true) until proven guilty (i.e. false) without taking any cognizance of them. Of course, as philosophers, we will have more than a 'scholar's' interest in these arguments; we will wish to give ourselves reasons to suppose that this happily going on is not a happily going on based on an illusion. But the suggestion has been that even the total failure of such arguments should not make us think that this belief of ours *is* based on an illusion, just that there is no reason to suppose that it is not, but that should not disquiet us: such is sometimes the destiny of properly basic beliefs. However, this cannot be the whole story for, to pursue the legal metaphor again, it is not that there is no case for the prosecution to be answered. So, even though we may rightly believe our client, Incompatibilism, should be taken as innocent until proven guilty, in answering the prosecution's case, we would be reckless were we not to avail ourselves of positive arguments in favour of our client's innocence should there be any. Imagine for a moment the following scenario by way of expanding the analogy.

You are a legal counsel charged with defending someone accused of murdering someone else on a particular evening. The prosecution has made their case. It has rested on circumstantial evidence: the defendant had been heard to threaten the victim the day before the murder and inherited a fortune on the victim's death. The defendant owned a gun of the calibre used in the murder, a gun which he claims he cannot now find to enable a ballistics test to establish whether or not it was the weapon used. The prosecution's case has – it seems you should concede – given the jury at least some reason to suppose the defendant guilty. However, the case against him has hardly been proven and, that being so – given 'the innocent until proven guilty' principle – you might choose to rest your case for the defence on establishing merely that all of the evidence the prosecution has presented, even when taken together, does not raise the probability of his being guilty past the threshold of proof. Once you have shown that the prosecution's case fails in this way, then you need offer no positive evidence in favour of the defendant's innocence to make it reasonable for the jury to acquit him. However, if the defendant has as a matter of fact informed you early on in your preparation of the case for the defence that, on the night of the murder, he was in a part of the country very distant indeed from that in which the murder took place, hosting a dinner party at which the local Bishop, Chief Constable, Mayor, and several other worthies were present; and if all these people stand in an ante-chamber to the courtroom, happy to be called in to testify to the fact that the defendant never left the table during the evening in question, you would be foolish not to avail yourself of their testimonies. You do not strictly need them to establish that your client has not been proved guilty by the prosecution, which is all that is required of you, but proving your client innocent is a very effective way of showing that he has not been proved guilty, so, if that way is available to you, you would be reckless were you not to take it.

Similarly then, I am suggesting that even if one starts this investigation, as I have argued in the first chapter most of those as yet untouched by philosophical speculation on the topic will start it, believing that Incompatibilism is true and even if one now believes that one's belief that it is true is properly basic, which is a reasonable belief to hold, one should *still* have more than a passing 'academic' interest in the arguments that are advanced in favour of it. Going back to our court room analogy, you will want to see whether there is in fact some positive proof of your client's innocence and the rationality of your not being swayed by the prosecution's case could turn on it. As a defence counsel who happened to have an airtight alibi for your client, if you wished, you could fail to engage altogether with the prosecution's case. You could merely present that alibi and the testimonies supporting it and rest your case there. If this alibi and the testimonies are sufficient to prove him innocent, as I am taking it we think they would be in my example, then leaving the prosecution's arguments entirely unaddressed would seem no reckless lapse on your part. Once you've proved him innocent, you don't need to go on to show in detail how the prosecution hasn't proved him guilty; it's just obvious that – some way or another – they haven't. You would not, for example, have to spend time offering alternative explanations of how it so happened that the gun used in the murder had the same calibre as the one your client claims he has now misplaced. However, had you *not* had such an alibi – had your client in fact told you that he was sitting alone at home next door to where the murder took place throughout the evening in question – then it would seem like recklessness on your part not to try to establish faults in the prosecution's arguments. Similarly then, were it merely the case that arguments for Incompatibilism failed as arguments, the balance would, nevertheless, still stay tipped over – on the innocent until proven guilty principle – on the side of its not being unreasonable for you to continue to hold Incompatibilism true (assuming as I am that Incompatibilism is indeed your starting point), for if Incompatibilism is true, then it is plausibly the sort of belief which one may hold in the absence of arguments in its favour. But, as we shall see in this chapter, in fact the prosecution – Compatibilism – has at least the makings of a good case against Incompatibilism, so, to remain reasonable in holding to Incompatibilism once one has been made aware of this case against it, one needs to defeat these 'defeaters' to one's initial belief and one must do this in at least one of two ways, either by showing flaws in these defeaters or by 'trumping' them with strong enough positive arguments in favour of Incompatibilism.

This onus to find arguments for Incompatibilism before one rests content in believing it will be all the greater to the extent that one is not in fact, as I have suggested the majority are, drawn to Incompatibilism as a starting point. Consider someone who starts off finding *Compatibilism* more plausible than Incompatibilism, as assuredly some people do. For such a person, it will be Compatibilism that is quite properly taken as 'innocent until proven guilty' by all the same principles which have led me to suggest that for the majority of us it is Incompatibilism that is so taken; he or she will not need arguments in its favour to justifiably continue on supposing Compatibilism is right (presuming an absence of any defeaters to Compatibilism, that is presuming an absence of any good arguments for Incompatibilism). Does Incompatibilism have any trumping arguments? If it does not, the burden on those of us who start off as incompatibilists to find fault in the arguments of the compatibilists will be greater than if it does. And if it does not, then for any of us – I have suggested it will be a minority, but I may be wrong about that and it will assuredly be some – who start off as compatibilists, these arguments will be *necessary*, if one is to be rational in changing one's mind. There is no general truth about where the burden of proof lies then, just particular ones for particular people, depending on their starting points. Well, let's see if Incompatibilism does have any such arguments.

* * *

First, let us recall how we stated the thesis of Incompatibilism in the previous chapter:

> *If I couldn't do other than what I actually do, then I wouldn't be morally responsible for what I do.*

That is the conclusion which we wish to investigate the possibilities of supporting by argument.

There are some who would agree with this claim yet suggest that, despite that, Determinism is not incompatible with moral responsibility, for they would maintain that Determinism does *not* suggest, as we have been assuming it does, that one could not have done other than whatever it is one actually does. In order to take these positions into view, we do better to start our discussion of Incompatibilism from a bit further back, as it were, and see what can be done first to advance the argument that Determinism does indeed imply, as we have been assuming it does, that one couldn't have done other than whatever it is one actually did. Then, secondarily, we shall turn to look at what can be done to advance the claim that Determinism is incompatible with moral responsibility, for inability to do other than what one actually does is indeed incompatible with moral responsibility. So let us first consider how we might defend this thesis:

If Determinism is true, I could not do otherwise than whatever it is I actually do.

'Straight out of the gate' as it were, this thought will seem appealing to us; we discussed it as so in the previous chapter. Determinism is the thesis that the past and the laws of nature entirely necessitate the present, that the actual exhausts the physically possible, and thus – one might think – obviously entails that nothing, including us, could ever do anything other than whatever it is that actually ends up being done. However, especially if we incline to go on from this to think that nothing we can do can ever change what is to be, there is room to question our thinking in this area, as we shall see. But first, let us see what can be done to support it.

* * *

The most articulated and discussed argument for thinking that if Determinism is true, then we cannot change anything from the way it is actually to be is usually called the Consequence Argument.[5] It has been presented in many subtly different ways by different authors over several thousand years. However, a formulation adequate for our purposes is the following:

1. We cannot change the past.
2. We cannot change the laws of nature.
3. If Determinism is true, the present, in all its details, is the necessary consequence of the past and the laws of nature.
4. If Determinism is true, we cannot change the present in any detail.

The first two premises of this argument seem undeniable. If we turn to consider the first one first, we might recall that the past extends back to billions of years before intelligent life evolved, to the initial or boundary conditions of the Big Bang. No one, it seems, would suggest that anyone *ever* had the ability to alter things occurring at these times. Of course, someone might suggest that we could in principle build a time machine and go back to change events in the past, although such people usually think of the more proximate past than that of the Big Bang when they entertain such fantasies. In any case, it could be suggested that premise one is not a necessary truth. But, even if one concedes this (which concession might in itself be ill-advised in its own terms), its not being a necessary truth does not prevent it being a truth. Given that such time machines do not in fact exist, it remains true in fact that we cannot change anything in the past. We cannot now do anything about whatever was going on in the Big Bang or whatever was going on as human life first evolved on the Earth. We cannot now do anything about what happened yesterday or even a second ago.

Matters are similar with respect to premise two. No one, it seems, would suggest that any of us have the power to change the laws of nature. Of course, again someone might suggest that we could ask God or a sufficiently powerful spirit to change the laws of nature for us, and that this super-being might agree to do so. If such a thing were to happen, then one would be able to change the laws of nature, albeit only indirectly. So, such a person might say, premise two is not a necessary truth. But again, even if one concedes this, this concession does nothing to affect the truth of premise two on the presumption that such people as say this sort of thing are pointing to a possibility that they do not suppose to be an actuality; they are not saying that in fact they are in the habit of communicating with compliant super-beings over these sorts of issues. Again then, premise two is something the truth of which we shall not seriously wish to question.

In short, while some would think that things which would render premises one and two contingent are genuine possibilities, nobody supposes that these possibilities are commonplace actualities, as commonplace as they would need to be were they to be used to explain anything about our everyday actions. That being the case, we shall not wish to raise more than minor quibbles about premises one and two. If we are going to manage to be free in our day-to-day lives, this will not be due to the services of time machines and malleable super-beings. Our attention then turns to premise three.

Premise three merely states the definition of Determinism: the events of the present are causally necessitated in all their details by those of the past in accordance with the laws of nature. The mention of 'details' here is necessary to mark off a deterministic view from an indeterministic one. An indeterminist will presumably say that the parameters within which the present must fall are the necessary consequence of the past and the laws of nature and thus be happy to concede that the present, *in its broad outlines*, is the necessary consequence of the past and the laws of nature. But the indeterminist will insist that this predetermination does not extend down to the details of the present. He or she will concede that the world may be such that, given its past and the laws of nature, only *n* possible paths are open to it at a given time, where *n* is a finite number, but, by insisting that that finite number is sometimes greater than one, the indeterminist denies that all the details of the universe are causally necessitated by its past. So, the third premise is true by definition: that's just what the thesis of Determinism is. Again then there is nothing to be argued with here. If you use 'Determinism' as a label to refer to some other thesis, then of course you can show that Determinism, so understood, is compatible with anything, including then free will and moral responsibility. But that is not cleverly evading the force of this argument; it is simply changing the topic of conversation.

So premises one, two and three look undeniable. The only hope for resisting this argument seems to rest on denying that the conclusion, proposition number four, follows from them. How could one do this?

One might in principle seek to question the link taking one through to four from one, two and three by suggesting that while we cannot change the past or the laws of nature (i.e. granting premises one and two) and we should not simply stipulate some non-standard meaning of 'Determinism' (i.e. granting premise three), perhaps we *can* change the fact that if Determinism is true, then the past and the laws of nature necessitate the present. If we could change what must be the case, then it might be true that while we couldn't change the past, the laws of nature, or the nature of Determinism, we could change what would necessarily follow from the conjunction of these. Thus we could resist the conclusion of this argument. However, the suggestion that we can change what must be the case, what is necessarily so, seems incoherent. That is what something's being necessarily the case means; that no one can change it. If someone could change it, then it would not be necessarily so, but only contingently so. While again some might suggest that a super-being like God could keep the essence of Determinism the same yet somehow change what necessarily follows from the conjunction of the first two of our premises and it, in listening to such suggestions we quickly lose confidence that they even make sense. And again, even supposing we (probably ill-advisedly) concede that such a suggestion does make sense, no one is likely to suggest that such a thing actually happens, that, whenever we freely act, God compliantly changes the validity of the principle that we cannot change a necessity. With the principle that we cannot change a necessity in place though, the conclusion that if Determinism is true, then there is nothing anyone can do to change the present in any detail seems to follow ineluctably from premises one and two. Or at least it does if we accept a rule which we may follow contemporary philosopher Peter van Inwagen in calling 'Rule Beta'.[6] ('Rule Alpha' is the name he gives to the rule that there is nothing anyone can do to change what is necessary.[7]) Rule Beta is sometimes also called the 'Transfer of Powerlessness Principle'.[8] We may state it in the following manner:

> *If there is nothing anyone can do to change a thing, X, and nothing anyone can do to change the fact that another thing, Y, is a necessary consequence of X, then there is nothing anyone can do to change Y.*

Rule Beta is a rule the truth of which will probably strike us as so obvious that, rather like Rule Alpha, we are not surprised that we did not realize the argument we have been considering relied upon it until it was drawn out for our attention. Rule Beta certainly does seem obviously true. If we try to doubt it, we can evaporate doubt faster than we can condense it by considering examples.

So, for an example of an X, let us suppose that in five minutes time the Earth will be hit by a large and fast-moving meteorite, one which will smash it into dust. Suppose further that there is nothing we can do now to change that fact. It's too late for us to send up rockets to try to blow it up or deflect its path. Whatever we now do, this meteorite is going to hit us and do this to us. Indeed nothing we could ever have done would have been able to change the fact that this meteorite was going to hit us five minutes from now; it started on the journey which led it to us many millions of years before humans evolved and we could never have developed the technology necessary to stop or deflect it. It's just too large and fast-moving. There's nothing then anyone can do to stop this meteorite hitting us (interventions of super-beings aside). That's our X. Suppose further, for our example of a Y that would plausibly follow as a necessary consequence of this X, that, when this meteorite hits us, all sentient life on the planet will be almost instantaneously extinguished. Of course it will; our planet and everything on it will be reduced to dust. There's nothing any of us can do about that consequence of the meteorite hitting us either; there's nothing we can do about the fact that *if* the planet is about to be smashed to dust by a meteorite, *then* all sentient life on it is going to be almost instantaneously extinguished. It's not as if we can change the laws of Biology within the next four minutes (by now, it's probably closer to four minutes away than five) to make ourselves the sorts of things – if such things are even possibilities – that are capable of living on atmosphere-free particles of former-planet, which will soon be the only sorts of things left exploding outwards from the position our planet is now in. So there's nothing any of us can do to change the fact that the annihilation of sentient life on the planet will follow from the planet's being shattered by this meteorite. That's our Y. It seems to follow then from our X and our Y that there's nothing any of us can do to change the fact that all sentient life on our planet is about to be destroyed. If there's nothing we can do to stop the meteorite destroying the planet (X) and nothing we can do to stop the fact that the planet's been destroyed will lead to all its sentient life's being destroyed (Y), then there's nothing we can do to stop all its sentient life being destroyed. Rule Beta seems right.[9]

Of course, we cannot prove the universal validity of a mode of inference by citing just one example where it would not have led us from truth to falsity. Indeed, while examples of this sort could be multiplied without end, one would only ever thereby get inductive support for the deductive validity of Rule Beta. That being so, there will remain a gap in the argument's defences at this point, a gap which may be shrunk by more examples but never closed up entirely. So, the person wishing to resist the conclusion of the Consequence Argument can never be compelled to abandon hope; he or she may always raise the worry that Rule Beta is not universally valid. But this hope would look increasingly desperate as examples of Rule Beta not leading us astray were multiplied. Can he or she do more than look increasingly desperate in this fashion? Yes, in principle. While one cannot prove the universal validity of a mode of inference by multiplying examples where it does not lead us astray, one can disprove it with just one example where it does. Let us see then what can be done to find an example where Rule Beta leads us astray.

* * *

Let us consider for a moment a device which we shall be able to agree is sufficiently simple and large-scale for it to be treated as effectively deterministic whether or not one is inclined to think that at bottom the universe is deterministic, a long case or 'grandfather' clock. Let us imagine that we have just had our grandfather clock serviced. We have witnessed the horologist setting it to the correct time and winding it up. And we have now seen him start it running. We observe it ticking away before us and, although it is too soon for us to tell with any confidence, a quick comparison with our wristwatches suggests that it is keeping time. Pleasingly, it passes the hour mark as we watch and strikes as we had hoped it would. All seems to be working well. We now consider the following facts about it.

The clock's hands cannot change the nature of its parts; in what relative positions these parts were initially set up by the horologist; or the laws which relate those parts to one another. Yet the nature of the parts; how they were set up; and how they relate to one another determine what time the clock says it is now. (Remember, we are, I am assuming, happy to think of the clock as effectively deterministic.) Should we then conclude that the hands cannot change what time the clock says it is? It would seem strange indeed to say simply, 'Yes' to this question, for in a perfectly natural sense of the terms the hands obviously do have the power to change what time the clock says it is; we are observing them exercising this power as they rotate slowly around in front of us, marking the passage of time and marking it, it seems from our preliminary comparison with our wristwatches, accurately. Of course, this observation might be suggested not to take us to the heart of the sort of power to change that is at issue in the debate which concerns us. But, while that is true, we do well to make this observation nonetheless, for it shows how Determinism need not lead to Fatalism and how even those who are no friends of Compatibilism do well to concede at least this point.

Fatalism may be defined as the view that we cannot affect the future. The most common argument for it might be expressed informally in a manner such as the following.

Either I'm going to get run over by a bus when I step out into the street, in which case my looking to see if one's coming will have been useless, or I'm not going to get run over by a bus when I step out into the street, in which case my looking to see if there's one coming will have been equally useless. Either way then, looking before I step into the street would be useless and wouldn't affect whether or not I'm going to get run over by a bus. That being so, I'll just close my eyes; step out like this; and . . . [Crunch]

Someone arguing along these lines would have ignored the fact that whether a particular person is going to turn out to be someone who gets run over by a bus or someone who narrowly avoids being run over by a bus can itself be caused by whether he is the sort of person who looks before stepping into the road rather than the sort of person who does not. There are deep issues raised by Fatalism and this treatment has rather glossed over them.[10] Nevertheless, what we have said has been sufficient to enable us to see that even in a deterministic system, a part of that system can be the proximate cause of some later phenomenon within it. A man's looking before he steps out into the road can be what causes him to avoid being run over. A clock's hands being in a particular position can be what causes the clock to be telling whatever time it is that it is telling at the time they are in that position.[11] If the hands then move on, so that the clock tells a different time, the changing of the hands has caused a change in the time that is being told even if the hands themselves have been caused deterministically to make this change. The fact that the hands of our clock are determined to tell whatever time it is they end up telling by the initial set up of the clock and the laws which dictate how fast the spring unwinds and so forth doesn't stop them having this ability to change. The causal chain which leads to the hands telling us that the time is whatever they are telling us it is now goes back into the past to things which have nothing to do with the hands, for sure, but in order to get to the clock's telling us that the time is now whatever they are telling us it is now, it has had to travel through the hands and, if it has travelled through the hands, then the hands of the clock have been causally responsible for the change in the time that is being told.

So, even someone who conceded that in a deterministic system we cannot change things from however they'll actually be, could maintain with justification that, in spite of that, there is a perfectly respectable sense in which we can, indeed often do, change things, for example, by reflecting on the dangers of believing in Fatalism when crossing the road, we might change from being the sort of person who is statistically more likely than average to get run over by a bus to being the sort of person who is not. To repeat: things change, that much is obvious, but it is not the case that Determinism commits us to thinking that to all these changes we are mere passive observers; for some changes, we are – in a perfectly natural sense – the bringers of change. We merely observe that it starts to rain; there is nothing we did to bring that about and nothing we can do to change it now it has started. But we ourselves can and often do put up umbrellas so as to stop ourselves getting wet; in doing that we are changing ourselves from being people who were starting to get wet to being people who are now staying dry. The compatibilist may maintain with some justification that this is one truth that the conclusion of the Consequence Argument, four, shields from us: even if Determinism is true, we can – indeed often do – change the present, change it from what it was in the past towards what it will be in the future. Even if Determinism is true and thus events in the remote past along with the laws of nature necessitated that you would be reading just this sentence at just this time, they have dictated that *you* be reading it; it is not that its being read by you has nothing to do with you. Even if Determinism is true, we are yet then, we might say, the authors of our behaviour even if not the ultimate authors, just as we might say that Deep Blue was an 'author' of the chess games it played, though not an ultimate author.[12]

While the compatibilist may make this point, in making it the compatibilist may not unfairly be accused of some obfuscation, or at least of not taking us to the heart of the issue. The sort of ability to change that it should be conceded is still – sometimes – within our power even if we live in a deterministic universe is not the sort of ability to change that the proponent of the argument really had in mind. The proponent of the argument we have been considering did not wish to suggest that in a deterministic universe people could not develop the habit of looking before they stepped into roads or of putting up umbrellas when it started to rain. The sort of ability to change that he or she had in mind was the ability to change things from whatever they actually are at the time they actually are. One might say that there was a suppressed clause in the relevant premise and the conclusion as we expressed them; more fully, the conclusion we are justified in reaching is that if Determinism is true then we cannot change the present in any of its details *from whatever it actually is*: if we are determined in the present to be actually changing – for example, putting up an umbrella and thus making ourselves dryer – and/or the cause of change in something – for example, the cause of someone near to us coming to the belief that we're putting up an umbrella – then *that* is something we cannot change. Whatever we are actually doing, or failing to do, right now, the fact that it is *that* which we are actually doing, or failing to do, right now is something which we cannot change. The sort of ability to change, which all should concede we could have even in a deterministic universe, does not get us close to having this sort of ability to change, change things from however they actually are. And that is the sort of ability which the argument has shown we cannot have in a deterministic universe. But not all compatibilists would be prepared to concede that the argument has shown even this.

* * *

Let us go back to thinking about watching our grandfather clock, it having just been set up and started off by the person who has serviced it for us. Imagine someone with us pointing to the clock at a particular moment and saying of it that, at that particular moment, the hands could not have shown any time other than whatever time it is they are actually showing. If we agreed with such a suggestion, it would likely be with some qualification to the effect of, 'Well, *given* the positions they were initially placed in and how they were connected to the mechanism; and *given* that it had been properly wound and adjusted; and *given* that it was started off at just the moment that it was, then yes, I suppose so.' That we would feel the need to make such a qualification to our 'Yes' suggests that we would agree with someone who simply contradicted this suggestion by pointing out that the hands would have shown a different time at that moment if the horologist had set them to a different initial time before starting the clock off; altered the speed at which certain crucial cogs rotated; or something along these lines. In that sense then the hands could have shown a different time right now even though they are determined by their initial set up to show whatever time it is they actually do show right now. When we say that in this sense the hands could have shown a different time, what we mean is that they would have shown a different time had they been set up differently. The only type of fact which would make us reluctant to say of the hands that in this sense they could have shown a different time from whatever time they are actually showing would be one which involved something along the lines of their being permanently disconnected from the mechanism that would in ordinary clocks be responsible for their rotation; their actually being painted onto the face of the clock in just that position; and so forth. However, if we believe that relatively minor changes to how they had been originally set up would have led to a change in the time they currently show, then we say that they could have shown a different time. In this sense we find ourselves wishing to say even of a system which we are happy to regard as deterministic that it could have been different now from how it actually is, meaning by that that it would have been different now had its initial set up been in some slight way different from the way it actually was.

To sum up: in the case of the grandfather clock, which we are happy – I am taking it – to assume is effectively deterministic, we may speak of parts of the mechanism having the power to change things – the hands of the clock have the power to change what time the clock tells (assuming they are unimpeded by grit or some such in the mechanism). And we may even speak of them having the power to do things other than whatever they actually end up doing; we say that this is true of them whenever they would have ended up doing something other than what they actually ended up doing had their initial set up been different in what strikes us as a relatively minor way. The first of these powers to change the proponent of the argument for Incompatibilism may say is 'by the by'; even so, it shows that Determinism need not lead to Fatalism. The second of these cannot be dismissed as 'by the by'. This is a sense of 'could have done otherwise' in which it seems that even things in a deterministic universe could have done otherwise than what they actually do. It thus seems to threaten the move to the conclusion of our argument for Incompatibilism. Can this second sense be used by the compatibilist then to suggest that Rule Beta is not always a valid mode of inference, and, in particular, that it is not when it comes to the crucial case of ourselves as agents?

Let us consider for an example of agency the choice you face whether or not to read the next sentence: reflect on this choice for a bit and then make your decision.

* * *

I now speak then to those who decided to read it. Given that you actually did read it, is there a sense in which – even were the universe deterministic – you could have not read it? The compatibilist has traditionally drawn on the sense of 'could have done otherwise' we have just articulated to maintain that there is. We shall call this sort of response the 'classical compatibilist' one. The classical compatibilist has maintained that, presuming there were no impediments to your stopping yourself from reading it a few seconds ago – presuming that there was, for example, no machine holding your eyelids open and the book in front of you while a neural implant forced your eyeballs to move from left to right across the page and so on – then you could have changed the fact that you read it in the sense that had you decided not to read it, then you would not in fact have done so. The classical compatibilist response to the Consequence Argument has thus been that as long as we lack impediments to doing other than whatever it is we actually do, then that is sufficient for it to be true that we could have changed what we do from what we actually do. If you would have been able to do it had you wanted or chosen to do it, then in that sense you could have done it and – the classical compatibilist has maintained – it can be true in a deterministic universe that in this sense people are sometimes, indeed quite often, capable of doing things other than whatever it is they actually do. This is sometimes called the 'hypothetical' or 'conditional analysis' of the notion of capability to do other than what one actually does; you are capable of not reading this sentence to the end just because if you decided not to read this sentence to the end but instead, let us say, break off from reading it to go for a walk, then nothing would, as a matter of fact, be in place to make you read it anyway or prevent you from going for that walk. So how, according to the classical compatibilist, does this affect the Consequence Argument we are considering?

Let us look first at whether the first two premises of our argument would come out as true or false on the understanding of us being able to change a thing just if, had we decided to change it, we would then have been free from impediments and thus succeeded in doing so. Thus we ask, is it the case that were we to decide to change the past or the laws of nature, then there would be no further impediments to our doing so? It does not seem that we would wish to answer this question in the affirmative; no one – other perhaps than those with easy access to time machines and the compliant super-beings we mentioned in passing earlier – faces no impediments to changing the past or the laws of nature other than bringing themselves to decide to do so in the first place. To suggest that we ordinarily have the power to change the past or the power to change the laws of nature would be ridiculous. (Hold on to this thought, we shall need it later.) It seems then that the classical compatibilist would be best advised to say that the first two premises of the Consequence Argument are true on the analysis which presents it as necessary and sufficient for having a capacity to change a thing that, had one decided to change it, there would then have been no further impediments to one's changing it. And this is indeed what the traditional classical compatibilist has said. (We'll look in a moment at whether they can really justify saying it.) The traditional classical compatibilist account has been that on the hypothetical analysis of what it is to be able to do something one did not actually do, nobody is in fact able to change the past or the laws of nature as nobody would in fact, were they to decide to try to change the past or the laws of nature, succeed in doing so; they would face overwhelming impediments (absent time machines and compliant super-beings). As to the third premise, this non-problematically stays true on this compatibilist reading, for we are not considering the strategy of evasion involved in tinkering with the meaning of the Determinism. So, were Rule Beta universally valid, the conclusion would come out true as well. Does it? Not according to the classical compatibilist.

According to the classical compatibilist, it simply is not true that we could not change the present in any detail, for if we wanted to change the present in at least some of its details, we would then face no further impediments to our doing so. The classical compatibilist will insist that examples abound; one would be that a minute or so ago, if you had wanted to stop reading this book and go for a walk instead, you would then have faced no impediments to your putting the book to one side and going for a walk instead. So, the classical compatibilist has traditionally suggested of the

Consequence Argument that its premises are true, yet its conclusion is false. Rule Beta can thus be shown to let us down. There is indeed nothing we can do to change the past and the laws of nature; and, if Determinism is true, these together necessitate the present in all its details. But there is nevertheless, the classical compatibilist has traditionally maintained, something we can do to change our present circumstances even if Determinism is true, because – while there are impediments to changing the past and laws of nature (there are not readily accessible time machines and compliant super-beings) – there often are no impediments to our changing at least some of the details of the present (we're not always prisoners and in chains). We have then, so the classical compatibilist maintains, counter-examples to the supposed universal validity of Rule Beta.

There is though a problem with this presented by whether the classical compatibilist can really justify holding premises one and two as true. To see this problem, we need to step back and look from a greater distance at how it is we judge of some counterfactuals that they are true, while of others we judge that they are not. When we ask what would have been the case had something happened other than what actually happened, how do we know what we should say by way of an answer? We certainly do want to say that had you chosen to try to change the past or the laws of nature a moment or two ago by praying to some super-being (as I'm assuming you did not actually do), then you would have failed; even had you made your mind up to try such a thing, as you did not actually make your mind up to do, you would have faced the additional impediment to your changing the past or the laws of nature that there are no such super-beings. To say otherwise, we suggested, was 'ridiculous'. And we certainly do want to say that, by contrast, had you decided to put this book down and go for a walk instead (as again I am assuming you did not actually do), then you would not have faced additional impediments but would have succeeded in your intention; you would have put the book down and gone for a walk. But how do we know of some counterfactuals of this sort that they are false (If you had tried to change the past, you would have succeeded) and of some that they are true (If you had tried to put the book down, you would have succeeded)? The response to this that has become standard and which we shall not question here is as follows.

We may imagine universes, 'worlds' we may call them, which differ to a greater or lesser extent from the actual world. So, in the actual world I had three cups of instant coffee this morning. I always have at least two – to get my brain working – unless the instant has run out. If the instant has run out, I then take the time to go over to the Senior Common Room and make myself enough filter coffee for two or more cups. The Common Room never runs out of filter coffee. This morning, I debated with myself whether or not to have a fourth cup of instant. In the end, I decided not to do so. We may then imagine a world which is exactly the same as the actual world except that, in that world, I did end up having a fourth cup of instant coffee this morning. That world, we would naturally say, is more similar to the actual world than is a world in which I had no instant coffee at all this morning, for it had run out, but instead had filter coffee. And a world in which I had filter coffee in turn, we would naturally say, is more similar to the actual than a world in which I had no coffee at all but instead – in a manner totally unprecedented for me (at least for that time of the day) – had mixed for myself and drunk three large gin slings, 'to get my brain working'. We can then talk of ranging possible worlds in 'logical space' by reference to their similarity to the actual world, the more similar a possible world is to the actual, the closer it gets to be to the actual in logical space. Thus the worlds in which all is as it is in the actual world except in the fact that I had an extra cup of instant coffee this morning and what follows from that[13] are closer to the actual world than is any world in which all is as it is in the actual world except in the fact that I had filter coffee this morning and what follows from that. And 'filter coffee' worlds in turn are closer than 'gin sling' worlds.

When we ask what would have been the case had something happened other than what actually happened, we look into the worlds which are closest to the actual in logical space and yet in which the hypothetical happening took place and we see there what consequences flow from the change. So, for example, in order to know what would have happened had I not had any instant coffee this morning, we look into the nearest worlds in which I did not have any instant coffee. Perhaps we want to know whether, if I had not had any instant coffee, I would have had less caffeine in my system. We see by looking into these worlds that that is not the case; I would not have had less caffeine had I not had any instant coffee. Why? Because in the nearest worlds in which I do not have any instant coffee, it is because it has run out and in those worlds I then switch to making myself filter coffee, filter coffee being a drink the caffeine content of which is very similar to that of instant coffee. (Of course some background is being presumed here, but we can easily fill this in suitably: I only ever buy caffeinated coffee; the caffeine content of filter coffee at the strength I make it is at least as great as that of instant coffee at the strength I make it; and so on.) We are not put off from the conclusion that had I not had instant coffee, I would nevertheless not have had less caffeine in my system by the fact that one of the ways in which it is logically (and indeed physically) possible I might have failed to drink any instant coffee this morning is by instead having decided to mix and drink three gin slings instead of any coffee, three gin slings being something, we may take it, which do not contain caffeine. Why does this 'not count'? Because while that is indeed one way in which I could in principle have failed to have any instant coffee this morning, it is not the way that keeps the similarities between the world in which it occurs and the actual world as close as they are kept by ways which have me having filter rather than instant coffee. This then is how we judge of some counterfactuals that they are true: had I not had any instant coffee, I would still have had caffeine in my system this morning. And it is how we judge of some of them that they are false: had I not had any instant coffee, I would have been drunk before I even started work.

So, now, with this in hand, let us go back to look at the classical compatibilist analysis of the notion that sometimes we could have done otherwise than whatever it is we do. It will be recalled that we attributed to the proponent of this view a willingness to concede the truth of premises one and two of the Consequence Argument – there is nothing we can do to change the past or the laws of nature (and three, the definition of Determinism) – but deny its conclusion, thus challenging the universal validity of Rule Beta. The traditional classical compatibilist justifies conceding the truth of premises one and two in the following fashion. Once we suppose, for example, your mind to have been different in whatever way was minimally sufficient for you to have decided to stop reading and go for a walk at the moment when in actuality you decided to continue reading rather than go for a walk, we can see by looking into the relevant possible worlds that, from that moment on, you would have stopped reading and gone for a walk; you did not actually have your eyes held open; you were not actually in leg irons; and so on. Thus when we imagine a world that is as similar as possible to the actual compatible with your mind being different from the way it actually was in this respect, we see that, in that world, nothing would have stopped you doing what you then decided to do. So, the traditional classical compatibilist maintains that it is plausible in your case to say that had some combination of neurons fired one way rather than the other, leading to the 'I'll go for a walk' thought rather than the 'I'll continue reading' thought, then you would have gone for a walk. Of course, if Determinism is true, then it was in fact physically impossible for that combination of neurons to have fired in any way other than the way it actually did, the way which actually led to the thought 'I'll continue reading', but that could be true and yet it also be true that *had* it fired differently from the way it actually did, *then* you would have behaved differently. Thus we can deny that four follows from one, two and three. Or so the traditional classical compatibilist maintains.

However, it is not at all obvious that the classical compatibilist should be allowed to concede the truth of premises one and two; a good case can be made out for saying that, by his or her lights, the compatibilist should only grant that premises one and two are true if we live in an *in*deterministic universe. Of course, one might think that showing how the classical compatibilist is in fact committed to denying the truth of the first two premises of the Consequence Argument on Determinism might in principle be held to have bolstered the classical compatibilist's position when facing that argument. If he or she should actually deny the truth of its premises on Determinism, he or she may resist its conclusion without needing to call into question Rule Beta and, as Rule Beta is intuitively plausible, this could be presented as a boon to him or her. However, as premises one and two seem even more intuitively plausible than Rule Beta and plausible regardless of whether or not we suppose the universe is deterministic, so in fact, if classical Compatibilism can be shown to be committed to their being false in a deterministic universe, this is not to render it more plausible in the light of the Consequence Argument, but rather to render it less plausible. Why then think that the classical compatibilist might find himself or herself trapped into having to say that premises one and two are false in a deterministic universe?

If we are in a deterministic universe, then *ex hypothesi* the only way we could now have been choosing to do something other than whatever it is we are actually choosing to do would be for the past to have been different from however it was or for the laws of nature to be different from however they are. That being so, our choosing to do something different from whatever it is we actually choose to do would necessitate that the past have been different from whatever it actually was or the laws of nature be different from whatever they actually are. And that being so, it seems that the classical compatibilist should in fact *deny* that premises one and two of the Consequence Argument are true in a deterministic universe. For were I, who am not actually going to do so, to try to change the past or the laws of nature (e.g. by praying to the compliant super-being who I believe exists), then, if Determinism is true, the past would have had to have been different from whatever it actually was or the laws of nature would have to have been different from whatever they actually are, in order to have led to me making this attempt. Thus in a deterministic universe – in the hypothetical sense of 'could' meaning 'would have done had I decided to' – I could change the past or the laws of nature. Were I, who am not actually going to do so, to try to change the past or the laws of nature, I would succeed in changing the past or the laws of nature. If Determinism is true, there are no impediments to me changing the past or the laws of nature once we suppose that any which have actually prevented me from trying to change the past or the laws of nature have been swept aside and in sweeping these aside we see that the past or the laws of nature would have to have been different from however they actually were or are, so I would have succeeded. Suppose for another example that Harry Houdini believed that by saying 'Abracadabra', he could change the past or the laws of nature. He never actually got around to saying 'Abracadabra' before he died, but he went to his grave believing that, were he to have done so, then the past or the laws of nature would have been different from whatever it was or they are. Well, if Harry lived in a deterministic universe, this belief which he took to his grave is true. For if Determinism is true, then had he in fact decided to do something other than what he actually decided to do during his life (had he, for example, decided to say 'Abracadabra'), then the past or the laws of nature would have had to have been different from however they actually were or are. So, if Harry Houdini lived in a deterministic universe and went to his grave never having actually uttered the word 'Abracadabra', then he went to his grave having had the power to change the past or the laws of nature simply by uttering the word 'Abracadabra'. He was able to change the past or the laws of nature in the sense that had he chosen to try to do so, he would have faced no further impediment to doing so.[14] But if the classical compatibilist is really committed to all this, then he or she is really committed to something that is obviously false, indeed earlier we called it 'ridiculous'. Even in a deterministic universe nobody can change the past or the laws of nature (time machines and compliant super-beings notwithstanding). So, what has gone wrong?

The difference between the traditional classical compatibilist treatment of premises one and two, which has them come out as true even in a deterministic universe, and the classical compatibilist treatment we have canvassed most recently, which has them come out as false in a deterministic universe, is generated by how the classical compatibilist has traditionally ranged possible worlds in logical space relative to the actual and how we have more recently been suggesting on his or her behalf they should be ranged. For premises one and two to come out as true if ours is a deterministic universe, the following has to be the case. Indeterministic worlds which are exactly like ours up until the moment I actually chose not to try to change the past or the laws of nature but at that moment different, in that in them I do choose to try to change the past or the laws of nature, are closer to the actual world in logical space than deterministic ones the past and laws of nature in which lead to me making a different choice. The classical compatibilist then who wishes to stay 'traditional', that is wishes to preserve the truth of premises one and two, must say that even if our world is deterministic, it is closely surrounded in logical space by indeterministic worlds.[15] Only thus can he or she make counterfactuals come out in the way that common sense suggests, can he or she avoid the conclusion we have called 'ridiculous'. But ranging worlds in this way will seem odd to many. Surely whether or not a world is deterministic is the sort of large-scale feature of it in virtue of which it will find itself grouped together with other worlds, not some superficial detail of it that it might turn out not to share with its close neighbours in logical space. If ours is a deterministic world, we would more naturally think, it should be ranged closer in logical space to all other deterministic worlds than it is to any indeterministic world – that was the intuition which guided our non-traditional classical compatibilist who denied that premises one and two are true if our universe is deterministic. The traditional classical compatibilist, by contrast, has to see our universe's being deterministic, if it is deterministic, as a feature of comparative unimportance when ranging possible worlds relative to the actual, so as to be able get premises one and two to come out as true yet the conclusion, four, come out as false. Let us leave this point idling for a moment to observe something scientists have in fact discovered about the actual universe which has a bearing here.

Scientists have discovered that our universe is 'fine-tuned' for life in the sense that even the tiniest of alterations in the initial conditions of universe or the laws of nature would have led to the universe not being able to contain sentient life at all. So, for example, were the force present at the Big Bang to have been even slightly greater than it was, then everything would have expanded so fast that no stars, planets, and *a fortiori* no life could ever have formed. Had it been even slightly less than it was, then everything would have collapsed back in on itself under gravitational attraction so quickly that again the same consequences would have followed: no life. So in fact, if ours is a deterministic world, it is very plausible to say that there are no other deterministic worlds in which we exist at all. The tiniest alterations in the initial or boundary conditions of the universe or the laws of nature would not lead to a world that is superficially like ours, in which we exist and are making slightly different choices from those, whatever they are, which we actually make; rather, it would lead to a universe in which we don't exist because life per se never evolves because stars and planets never form. That being so, if ours is a deterministic universe, then if we are right to think of the closest worlds to it in logical space as likewise deterministic universes, we have to go well beyond the local area before we find any other possible worlds in which we even exist. What does this observation do to the classical compatibilist analysis of premises one and two? Well, it seems to save for them the possibility of asserting of premise one that it is true even if Determinism is true, but it does not save for them the possibility of asserting of premise two that it is true if Determinism is true. I (who did not actually decide to try this) would not have succeeded in changing the past had I tried, but, if Determinism is true, I (who did not actually decide to try to do this) would have succeeded in changing the laws of nature. Let us look at this in more detail.

To investigate whether, had I decided to try to change the past or laws of nature, I would have succeeded, we need to look into the nearest worlds in which I still exist but decide to do other than what I actually did in this respect. If we are right to think that were our universe deterministic, we should range deterministic worlds closer to it in logical space than indeterministic ones, and ours is a deterministic world, then we will find that the closest worlds to the actual are deterministic, and – given fine-tuning – so I don't even exist in them. We will then have to go out to some distance to find a world in which I exist and yet decide to do something different from whatever I actually decided to do. We will need to go out all the way to indeterministic territory. Plausibly (though not undeniably), in the first such world we come to having crossed over into this territory, the history of it prior to the moment we are concentrating on is the same as the actual – that's plausibly (though not undeniably) what makes it closer to the actual than any other. If so, then premise one comes out true. For in the nearest world in which I did do something other than what I actually did, this closest indeterministic world, the past is the same up until my moment of choice. So far, so good. However, premise two comes out as false; the laws of nature in this world are different from those in the actual world, because they are indeterministic. And so in the nearest world in which I do something other than what I actually do, the laws of nature are different. That being the case, were I who will not actually try to do so, to try to change the laws of nature, I would succeed were Determinism true. And this is a part of the 'ridiculous' result that we have been trying to avoid. At the least, we still have then the ridiculous result that were Determinism true we could change the laws of nature.[16]

As well as the hypothetical or conditional analysis of our being able to do other than what we actually do implying that, if we live in a deterministic universe we are able to change the laws of nature (and possibly the past – depending *inter alia* on how fine-tuned our universe is), it has another odd implication. This is that, if we live in a fine-tuned deterministic universe and are right to range other deterministic universes close to us in logical space, almost all claims we incline to make involving what would have happened had we not done something we actually did come out as false. For example, the claim that had I not watched *The Simpsons* (as I actually did), then I would have read a book, will come out as false. For, on these assumptions, the nearest set of worlds in which it is true that I do not watch *The Simpsons* are all deterministic worlds in which the initial or boundary conditions of the universe and/or the laws of nature were different, and in those worlds – given the fine-tuning of the actual universe – the reason I don't watch *The Simpsons* is because I don't even exist. So it is not true that had I not watched *The*

Simpsons, I would have read the book. However, it remains true that had I chosen to read the book, rather than watch *The Simpsons*, I would have done so. For while to find the truth-value of the claim that 'Had I not watched *The Simpsons*, I would have read a book', we look into the closest worlds in which I don't watch *The Simpsons* and these are ones in which I don't exist so don't do anything, to find the truth-value of the claim that 'Had I decided not to watch *The Simpsons*, but instead read a book, I would have done so', we look into the closest worlds in which I exist yet choose this something else, and in those I do indeed read the book. This seems intolerable. So what should the classical compatibilist do?

It seems that the classical compatibilist is best advised to take the traditional route in dealing with the Consequence Argument, affirming that premises one and two are true even if our universe is deterministic. This avoids the 'ridiculous' claim that we have powers to change the past or the laws of nature. But in order for this to be a defensible position for him or her, he or she has to be prepared to acknowledge that worlds in which Indeterminism is true are close to us in logical space, closer indeed than some deterministic worlds even if our world is deterministic. Indeed, he or she is best advised to say that indeterministic worlds hedge the actual around on all sides. This certainly then forbids him or her from going on to say that Indeterminism doesn't make sense, is a logical or metaphysical impossibility, or some such. Indeed it commits him or her to saying that it has a high prior probability of being true, placing him or her if he or she is also a determinist under a greater onus to provide a positive argument for his or her Determinism.

* * *

Having gone into it in some detail, it seems then that the traditional classical compatibilist was right in striving to maintain that, regardless of whether or not the actual universe is deterministic, he or she may assert the truth of premises one, two and three and that he or she can do this and yet, with his or her hypothetical analysis of our ability to do other than what we do, show that four might yet be false. We have seen that doing this is, however, no effortless task; it involves the classical compatibilist admitting that indeterministic worlds hedge the actual world around on all sides, a concession that in itself raises the possibility of an argument for the falsity of

Determinism; if ours is a region of logical space in which the vast majority of worlds are indeterministic, is it not more a priori likely that the actual world will be indeterministic than deterministic? Of course Compatibilism per se is not committed to the falsity of Indeterminism, just the thesis that moral responsibility does not require its truth, but if in defending this claim the compatibilist gives us reason to suppose that Indeterminism is true anyway, the victory will seem a somewhat pyrrhic one to many compatibilists. In any case, we must ask, does any of this really constitute a success in showing that Rule Beta doesn't work? By doing all this, has the compatibilist given us reason to doubt Rule Beta or has he or she given us a reason – given that Rule Beta and the ways of ranging worlds that are more natural to us than is his or hers are obviously right – for doubting his or her compatibilist analysis of what it is to be able to do otherwise? If some analysis of 'could have done otherwise' shows that a particular person could have done otherwise than whatever it is he or she actually did even though what he or she did was causally necessitated by other things which could not have been other than what they were, is it not obvious that something has gone wrong with that analysis even before we realize that to persevere with using it and yet not give us the ability to change the past and the laws of nature, we would have to be willing to range indeterministic worlds close to the actual in logical space even were the actual world deterministic? These questions offer us a more direct line of attack on the classical compatibilist hypothetical analysis of our ability to do otherwise. We shall explore this more direct line of attack now.

* * *

There is certainly something odd about the hypothetical analysis of our ability to do otherwise, an oddness which remains and threatens to disbar it without the need for us to reflect unfavourably on the contortions the classical compatibilist must go through when ranging possible worlds if he or she is to avoid giving us the ability to change the past or the laws of nature. This oddness may be brought out by the following example.

I have something of a soft spot for puppies, especially black Labrador puppies. No doubt this is due to my sister having had one of these as I was growing up. Be that as it may, I am now so psychologically constituted that the following would be true of me were someone to approach me with the suggestion that they would like me to torture a particular small black Labrador puppy to death for their amusement and were I to take them at their word. I would react with extreme horror and, amongst the various things it would be natural for me to say in reply to them, one would be, 'I just couldn't do that'. My aversion to torturing black Labrador puppies to death is so extreme that in a situation in which it appeared that the only 'benefit' that would come from my torturing a black Labrador puppy to death would be the amusement of a sadist, I just could not bring myself to torture such a puppy to death. We may suppose, however, that the sadist persists in making his offer. 'It is simply not true that you couldn't torture the puppy to death', the sadist might say in reply, 'Here, I have a fully equipped dungeon in which a suitable puppy is already chained up; therein I have laid out for you suitable instruments of torture and a copy of "The Beginners' Guide to Puppy Torture", ready for you to consult should you need to do so. Surely then, you must concede that if you were to decide to torture the puppy to death for my amusement, there would then be no further impediments that would stop you from doing so. And, that being so, on the hypothetical analysis of what it is for you to be able to torture the puppy to death, you *are* able; you could torture the puppy to death.' That indeed I must concede the sadist's claim that were I to decide to torture the puppy to death, I would then face no further impediments to my doing so – assuming that the world is as he says it is – seems irrelevant to whether or not I persevere with my claim that I could not torture the puppy to death. Given my extreme aversion to torturing a puppy to death and that I am not even tempted to try to overcome this aversion so as to be able to facilitate this sadist's amusement, it still remains true that I could not torture the puppy to death in the circumstances I am in. Indeed it is not simply that I am not tempted to try to overcome my aversion; it is that I have a strong desire to keep that aversion or enhance it, rather than be corrupted by any suggestions that the sadist might make that I weaken it. Perhaps, if I were convinced that the sadist was the sort of person who, if not amused, would go out and murder people and I was convinced that there was no way of stopping him so acting other than by keeping him amused and no other way of amusing him than by torturing this puppy to death, then I might not be so inclined. I do have a strong affective draw towards black Labrador puppies, but I am not crippled by sentimentality in this respect; in those alternative circumstances,

I believe that I would be able to torture the puppy to death; it would still be the case that I wouldn't want to do it, or at least wouldn't want to do it under the description of amusing a sadist (I'd want to do it under the description of being the least bad way of preventing this sadist doing something worse), but I believe that I could steel myself and then do it. But the world being as it is, the sadist – we may hypothesize – telling me that nothing of the sort is the case (he just wants to have a bit of fun watching a dumb animal being tortured; if I don't torture it, he'll release it and watch 'reality television' instead), I cannot want to do it; I cannot bring myself to decide to do it; I cannot bring myself to try to do it; and thus the fact that if – *per impossibile* then in the actual circumstances – I were to decide to do it, there would then be no impediments to my doing so is an irrelevance. It doesn't detract at all from my justifications for saying simply, 'I couldn't do it.'

It seems then from this example that if we are psychologically incapable of bringing ourselves to want or decide to do something in a certain situation, then we say that we couldn't do that thing in that situation and that this remains so even if we suppose that were we – *per impossibile* – to decide to do it, there would from then on be no impediments to our doing it. In this sense most of us could not torture puppies to death merely for the amusement of sadists and our inability to torture puppies to death merely for the amusement of sadists is not diminished to any extent if we one day find ourselves in the company of a sadist who dangles in front of us the keys to his fully equipped and ready-to-go puppy-torturing dungeon. By contrast, the hypothetical analysis suggests that all of us who are reasonably able-bodied could torture puppies to death if ever we find ourselves in the company of such a sadist. As such, we have reason to reject the hypothetical analysis as capturing what we mean when we say of people that they could do things other than what they actually do. We have reason to reject it as it tells us that people could have done otherwise simply because had they wanted to or decided to do otherwise, then they would have done otherwise. This ignores the fact that for some subset at least of people who we admit could not have wanted or decided to do otherwise, we in fact do not think that their membership of that subset is changed just by there being on hand people who would have facilitated them in doing otherwise had they done what they were incapable of doing in the actual situation they were in. If this is so, then, in consistency, we should think that if in fact Determinism is true and thus the 'subset' of people who could not have wanted or decided otherwise than whatever they actually wanted or decided is in fact the set of all people at all times, then none of us could have done otherwise than whatever it is we did.

* * *

In order to resist this argument, a tempting move for the classical compatibilist to make at this juncture is to add to the conditional analysis in the following way. He or she might suggest that a better analysis than the simple hypothetical analysis of our ability to do otherwise is provided by the following account. You could have done otherwise than whatever it is you actually did just if it is true that were you to have decided to do otherwise, you would then have been able to do otherwise (the traditional 'no impediments' clause) AND you could have wanted/decided to do otherwise (an additional 'no impediments to your coming to the desire/decision' clause). It might be suggested that with the last clause, worrying examples of the sort we've just been focusing on are swept into the category that we had intuitively thought they should be in, leaving only – one might hope – non-problematic examples behind. However, within this extra clause, it will be noted, is the very thing of which we were being promised an analysis: the added clause says that 'you could have wanted/decided to do otherwise'. We may then legitimately ask the classical compatibilist 'How is *that* "could" to be analysed?' The classical compatibilist will presumably re-iterate the theme of the hypothetical analysis at this point: you could have wanted/decided to do otherwise just if, had you wanted/decided to want/decide otherwise, then you would have wanted/decided otherwise. (We might call the sorts of desires and decisions to which our focus now turns 'higher-order' desires or decisions, higher-order because they take as their object lower-order desires and decisions rather than, for example, objects exterior to the mind, the torturing of a puppy or some such.) But, with this move, the problem in the hypothetical analysis revealed by the example of my being offered the 'opportunity' to torture a puppy to death rears its head once more.

Let us return to the example; the sadist has revealed to me that, were I to refrain from torturing the puppy to death, he would simply release it and go home disappointed to watch reality television. In those circumstances, I could not want or decide to torture the puppy to death. Nor, however, could I want or decide to want or decide to torture the puppy to death. Recall, I am not just contented with myself being the sort of person who could not want/decide to torture a puppy to death in the circumstances I take myself to be in; I take pride in that fact and could not wish to change it. But this is not a crippling sentimentality on my part, for I am able to imagine a circumstance in which I would try to harden myself to torturing a puppy, for example, if I believed that it was the only way to save a group of people from equally painful deaths at the hands of this sadist. And, I think, I would succeed in those circumstances. Thus, were I to want or decide to change my lower-order wants or at least decisions, I believe I would succeed. However, that is not the circumstance that I take myself to be in; in my actual circumstances, I could not want or decide to change my lower-order wants or decisions. In the actual circumstances, not only could I not want or decide to torture the puppy to death, but I could not want or decide to want or decide to do this. Thus again, I could not do it and the fact that I am not overly sentimental and hence, were I to want or decide to want or decide to torture the puppy, I would then be able to torture the puppy is again an irrelevance. Of course, a new iteration of the hypothetical analysis could be suggested. You are capable of doing otherwise if it is true that were you to want or decide to do otherwise, you would then be able to do so AND you could want or decide to do otherwise. Analysis of the second conjunct: you could want or decide to do otherwise just if were you to want or decide to want or decide to do otherwise, you would then be able to want or decide to do otherwise AND you could want or decide to want or decide to do otherwise. Analysis of the second conjunct: You could want or decide to want or decide to want or decide to do otherwise. . . . But by now it is obvious that we have an infinite regress and thus the hypothetical analysis of our ability to do otherwise than we actually do cannot be satisfactory.

In short, it looks as if whatever psychological architecture we put in place here, there'll be some people who have a psychological aversion to wanting/deciding certain things in the circumstances that they take themselves to be in. These will be such that we wish to say of them simply that they just couldn't do those things in those circumstances. But that the hypothetical analysis will have to render them as able to do these things nonetheless for someone stands by ready to facilitate them in doing them were they – *per impossibile* then – to have chosen to do them and there are circumstances in which they would have chosen to do them. (These are, of course, circumstances which are in some significant fashion different from those they take themselves to be in.) Adding multiple epicycles of the hypothetical analysis will not eliminate these cases. I say that there will be 'some people' of whom this is true, but in fact *all* of us have aversions of the sort that I have towards torturing puppies to death for the amusement of sadists and all of us are quite proud of ourselves for having at least some of these, those which we think are proper responses to real and significant disvalues in the world. That being the case, all of us will be people who think of ourselves as unable to do things that the classical compatibilist account of having an ability to do a thing would have us able to do. As soon as a sadist offering keys to a fully equipped puppy-torturing dungeon walks by, all but the most sentimental (those who couldn't try to torture a puppy even if it was the only way to save sentient life *in toto* from an excruciatingly drawn out process of extinction), become people who could torture puppies according to the classical compatibilist.

Taking all of these considerations into account then, it appears that the best move for the compatibilist to make is *not* that made by classical compatibilists, claiming that there is a sense of 'could have done otherwise' which threatens Rule Beta. We have looked at three reasons driving us towards this conclusion. First, Rule Beta is intuitively very plausible, so very strong arguments would be needed to justify us in rejecting it. Second, generating putative counter-examples to it requires, at the least, either accepting that if the world is deterministic, then we could change the laws of nature (which is, as we put it, 'ridiculous') or that if the world is deterministic, then it is implausibly close in logical space to indeterministic worlds. While the latter route can be taken, for these reasons 'counter-examples' do not meet the high standards set by the first consideration. And thirdly and finally, the hypothetical sense of 'could have done otherwise' is, in any case, implausible in its own terms for it would render most of us capable of doing things to which we have the most extreme aversions whenever someone offers us the chance to do them. As such, Classical Compatibilism should be rejected. The compatibilist is best advised to part company with his or her tradition and accept the Consequence Argument as we have presented it. In a deterministic universe, there is no real sense in which we could ever do otherwise than whatever it is we actually do. The compatibilist game is however not 'up'. The compatibilist may move ground and attempt to block the second stage of the argument from Determinism to Incompatibilism, the stage which suggests that robust moral responsibility – the sort that allows for punishment rather than merely interventions justified purely in consequentialist terms – requires of us that we could have done otherwise. We turn to this issue next.[17]

* * *

There certainly is a type of responsibility, we might call it 'causal responsibility', which can be attributed to parts of a deterministic system. Recalling that we are happy enough to regard our grandfather clock as effectively deterministic, the answer to the question, 'What is responsible for the grandfather clock's striking?' may be given by pointing to whatever part of the clock was the proximate cause of its striking and saying, 'That bit of the mechanism there'. We suppose in supposing that the clock may be treated as effectively deterministic that, if one knew enough about its working, one would be able to trace further back in time the process which led to that part of the clock behaving as it did at that time, but the fact that we suppose that one could always in principle do this in a deterministic system (for all causes other than the first) does not stop us talking of later causes quite properly as causes, as causally responsible for later events. It would seem otiose in the extreme were one to seek to deny that the chiming mechanism was the cause of the clock's striking just because one held that it itself had been determined to do whatever it did in this regard by some other bit of the clock's mechanism. Similarly then, if we turn to the cases of agency, if we imagine ourselves as police officers investigating a series of murders and we discover Jones standing over the body of the latest victim with a smoking gun in his hand, we may hazard with some confidence (suitable background information being supposed) that he is causally responsible for the murder without presupposing anything, one way or the other, about whether or not his coming to be shooting his victims was itself the inevitable causal result of processes that preceded any of his crimes. So far, so good.

That we can certainly attribute causal responsibility in the sense outlined in the previous paragraph without presupposing the falsity of Determinism does not, it might with some justification be pointed out, seem to advance us very far towards attributing moral responsibility. Perhaps, but, in order to see what ground should be conceded to the compatibilist before we get into properly disputed areas, we should note that it does license us in making interventions which at least superficially appear similar to those we consider ourselves licensed to make when considering actions for which we hold people fully morally responsible. Consequentialist justifications for punishment-like interventions remain in play.

Suppose that my clock stops striking one day and, after the horologist has examined it, he tells me that the cause of its doing so is that a particular cog has moved out of alignment. He further tells me that the cheapest way of mending it would be for him to fix a small plate on one side of it, for this will force it back into alignment. If such a plate would produce such an effect, then his putting it into that position will be his fixing the clock. And, if it is the cheapest and most effective way of producing this result, then no doubt I shall ask him to do this for me. Similarly, if we return to consider our finding the serial killer Jones standing over the body of his latest victim, we might reasonably suppose that if we lock Jones up, that will mean that we have less murders in the future than if we let him roam free. In a deterministic universe, in other words, we may not be able to be the ultimate authors of our actions, but we can still be – we might say – the 'authors' of our behaviour and, as such, we can certainly still be causally responsible for what arises from that and thus it can still be appropriate for people to intervene so as to align our future behaviour in ways which are more in accord with standards of desirable behaviour.[18]

This much the incompatibilist does well to grant. However, he or she will surely return to the point which we made in the previous chapter, that in everyday life we distinguish between consequentialist and retributive justifications for these sorts of interventions. Only if the latter is supposed to be present do we properly think of these interventions as punishments and this is an ineliminable part of what it is for us to regard people as robustly morally responsible. Thus we justify putting serial killers who are judged to be insane into secure hospitals solely for consequentialist reasons: we wish to keep the rest of society safe from them and provide them with whatever medical care we can. We do not in any sense hold them morally responsible for what they have done, something shown by the fact that we would not be in favour of a regime which strove to make their confinement less pleasant for them than it needed to be. There will be finite resources that we can direct towards their care, but within the parameters that this fact imposes and within the realms compatible with their being held securely, we do not wish to see those who we genuinely regard as insane treated punitively in any fashion whatsoever for the offences they have committed. By contrast, when we turn to consider the treatment we would think appropriate for someone who had committed the same number of murders but solely in order to bring glory to himself as a journalist covering the story of the serial killer in question, we would think that a regime that strove to make his life in prison as comfortable as possible with the resources available was striving towards an end which it should not have. Even if Chateau Petrus was – for some reason – as cheap to provide for him as tap water, he should not be given Chateau Petrus; he does not deserve it, indeed he deserves to be denied it.

So, these are our intuitions and, given how strongly they are held, it must be admitted from the outset that the compatibilist has an uphill task in persuading us that we would wish to attribute moral responsibility to those whom we regard as unable to have done anything other than whatever it is that they have done, rather than merely treat them for consequentialist reasons in various ways which might superficially resemble the ways we would have treated them had we held them morally responsible (e.g. incarcerating them). But there have been attempts by compatibilists to do just this and we shall consider them in the rest of this chapter. First, let us return to consider the background against which these examples are deployed.

* * *

In the previous chapter, we considered a simple, two-premise, argument which seems to underlie Incompatibilism.

If I am not the ultimate author of my actions, then I am not morally responsible for them, for they are not really my actions; rather, they are merely events which I undergo. We might put it like this: moral responsibility implies ultimate authorship. That's the first premise.

But in a world where Determinism is true, what I end up doing is necessitated by things other than myself – the initial or boundary conditions of the universe and the laws of nature operative on them – so, in a world in which Determinism is true, I am never the ultimate author of the actions I take myself to perform. Ultimate authorship then necessitates that what I end up doing not be determined – necessitated – by anything other than myself. We might put it like this: ultimate authorship implies Indeterminism. That's the second premise.

Given that premise one states that moral responsibility implies ultimate authorship and premise two states that ultimate authorship in turn implies Indeterminism, and so, putting these two thoughts together then, we may conclude that moral responsibility implies Indeterminism, which is our incompatibilist conclusion: if I couldn't do otherwise than whatever it is I actually do, then I wouldn't be morally responsible for what I do.

We may note one feature of this argument straight away: it is deductively valid, which is to say that if both the premises are granted, one cannot deny the conclusion without contradiction. That being the case, the only questions we can have over the strength of this argument will be questions we have about the truth of one or both of its premises. Does moral responsibility really require ultimate authorship? Does ultimate authorship in turn really require that one not be necessitated to do as one does by anything other than oneself? If and only if one can raise significant doubts over either of these premises, can one thereby raise significant doubts over the conclusion. And so that is what we shall spend our time looking at. As an aid to doing that, let us look at what this argument suggests to us about the connection we suppose between ability to do otherwise and ultimate authorship.

Presenting the argument for Incompatibilism in this way makes it clearer than some other formulations that ability to do other than whatever one actually does is supposed by us to be a characteristic *symptom* of the sort of freedom necessary for moral responsibility, not the fundamental basis for it; the fundamental basis for that sort of freedom is, we suppose, ultimate authorship. As a symptom, ability to do otherwise can be present even when the freedom of which it is a symptom is not. We saw an example of this in an earlier imaginary case, the one where I implanted a chip in the Senior Tutor's brain that enabled me to control his thoughts yet placed a random number generator between its operations and his final bodily movements, allowing randomness to play a role in what bodily movements eventually ensued. We saw then that our inclination was to think that even if I allowed randomness to play a role in between my getting him to have some thought and the bodily movement that this thought then generated, it would still not be *him* who was freely doing whatever it is he did in fact end up doing. It would still not be him even though – with this random element – it remained true that 'he' could have done otherwise than whatever it was I typed in for him to do. And we need not go to imaginary scenarios to make this point. We see – or at least we think we see – ability to do otherwise in all sorts of inanimate objects to which we have no inclination whatsoever to attribute freedom. For example, we might say of some rotten branch that it could have snapped at any moment during a given period of stormy weather, although in fact it did so at some particular moment during it. Nevertheless we do not blame it if, in falling when it did, it damaged our car, which we had temporarily parked beneath it.[19]

If the ability to do otherwise is a symptom of freedom of the sort necessary for robust moral responsibility, not the essence of it and thus this ability could be present even when freedom of this sort is not, the incompatibilist should admit at the least that this naturally raises the question of whether freedom of this sort could be present without the symptom of ability to do otherwise. And this is the opening into which the compatibilist we are now considering directs his or her examples, so as to prise apart the notion of authorship of the sort sufficient for robust moral responsibility from a supposed ability to do otherwise than whatever it is one actually does. In order to succeed at this, the examples he or she offers then need to be ones in which we maintain a high degree of confidence in two things, first that the person being considered in the example is truly morally responsible in a robust sense (that is to say, one that goes beyond mere consequentialist justifications for interventions) for doing whatever it is he or she does and secondly that, nevertheless, there is no way in which he or she could do anything other than whatever it is he or she does.

I wish first to consider a putative case where we might wish to attribute freedom of the sort necessary for robust moral responsibility without the ability to do otherwise that I owe to Daniel Dennett.

* * *

We imagine Martin Luther, at the moment he finally declared, if our popular understanding is accurate, 'Here I stand, I can do no other.'

And we suppose of him that he was speaking the literal truth. Given the character and beliefs which Luther had fashioned for himself in dialectic with church authorities leading up to that momentous declaration, so, at the time he made it, he was incapable of making any other utterance or indeed – we *are* taking it literally, it will be recalled – of standing anywhere other than wherever it was he was standing. We may suppose then that some passing priest asked Luther if he wouldn't mind standing somewhere else – a few feet to his left – so as to facilitate this priest in setting up a stall from which he could then sell indulgences to the local populace. Luther was outraged and replied simply that he could not move from the spot he was in for such a reason; he had such an extreme aversion to the selling of indulgences that he could not bring himself to move so as to facilitate their sale. 'Here I stand, I can do no other,' he repeated. Luther's situation as we are imagining it then was somewhat akin to that in which I would find myself were I to be presented with the 'opportunity' of torturing a puppy to death for the amusement of some sadist. In the same way that I just couldn't do that, so Luther just could not move from the spot he stood on at the time he made his utterance.[20]

Of course, if we believe that the universe is indeterministic, we will think that there might well have been a possibility of randomness causing Luther to move from this spot just after having said that he could not; so be it. It remains true that nothing *Luther* could have done would have moved him from that spot even if it is true that something other than Luther could have moved him from it. 'Here I stand. I could not bring myself to do any other. Of course, randomness might intervene and make "me" do some other, but then that wouldn't really be me doing some other, would it?' Luther might say to someone pressing this point. Having eschewed the hypothetical analysis of 'could have done otherwise', as we have, we must concede to the compatibilist then that here we have an example of someone who in no real sense could have done otherwise than whatever it is he was doing at the moment he was doing it. Yet, in making his declaration, Luther certainly was not wishing to disavow responsibility for it. We may imagine for contrast someone hypnotized as part of a stage show and, once maximally suggestible, told that he was glued to the spot on which he then stood. He might then report, 'Here I stand, I can do no other.' Luther was not saying something of this sort of himself. His being rooted to the spot was not an 'in spite of myself, I cannot move from it'-rooting but rather a 'Because of myself, I cannot move from it'-rooting. And he wished to claim full moral responsibility for being the sort of person who now could not move, not just causal responsibility. He would not have been inclined to say of himself, 'Various psychological states I appear to have got into, perhaps quite unwittingly, are, it appears, keeping me rooted to this spot. So don't blame, or indeed praise, me for being here.' Rather, he would have wished to say of himself something along the lines of, 'I have wilfully put myself into states such that I cannot now move from this spot and I will myself to continue on in these states. Therefore do hold me morally responsible for being rooted here.'

In these circumstances, would we not hold Luther morally responsible for his standing where he stood? It appears that we would. Is it not the case though that he could not have stood anywhere other than where he was? It appears that he could not. Is it not then that we have found an example of a situation where we hold someone morally responsible for doing what they did even though we believe of them that at that time they could not have done anything other than what they did? Well, compatibilists would naturally conclude that we have. However, this is by no means obvious, for in fact it is by no means obvious that we *do* hold Luther to be morally responsible for his action in standing where he stood, rather than hold him morally responsible for his actions in bringing himself to the state in which he could not but have stood where he stood. In short, as we reflect on this example, we maintain a high degree of confidence that the person we are considering genuinely could not have done otherwise than do what he did at the time – stand on this spot saying this thing – but we lose this level of confidence that he is morally responsible for his action in doing that thing, rather than morally responsible for his earlier choices, choices which have led him to be doing it, earlier choices which we suppose he could have made otherwise.

While we might at first pass appear to be praising (or blaming) Luther for standing where he stood, on reflection it seems as if we are really regarding him as in a structurally similar situation to the drunken member of the rugby club who, at the moment he succumbed to rowdyism, could not but have done so (having imbibed so much alcohol earlier in the evening as to be beyond the reach of rationality). We do not hold the rugby lout responsible for propositioning the Master's wife, but rather for having drunk so much earlier in the evening that he was then incapable of reflecting on the nature of his action in propositioning the Master's wife.[21] Similarly, if we wish to praise Luther (as I shall suppose henceforth that we do), we do so for having so fashioned himself that at the time he stood where he stood he could do no other; we do not strictly praise him for his action in standing where he stood and doing no other. In that this period of 'training' culminated in this action, so the action is the natural locus of our interest, but a moment's reflection leads us backwards from it when we consider at our leisure what we are really praising Luther for having accomplished with it. We pay the builder only after he has finished the job, but we pay him for the work he put in leading up to his finishing it, not for the last few touches of paint without which we would still have considered the job completed and hence which were such that, as he was applying them, it was already true that he could not but have completed the job.

In such cases, we could call the earlier actions on which we focus our reflective tendency to appraise people morally 'self-forming actions' even though this might seem too grand a term for at least some of them. The rugby lout's drunken offence is, we may take it, an entirely unplanned and temporary hiatus in what we may suppose is at other times a very different life. In that he did not plan to form any particular 'self' for himself by his drinking (he did not drink in order to give himself some 'dutch courage' so as to do what he ended up doing, but rather for innocuous reasons) and in that the offensive 'self' which he formed he held in only the most temporary of ways (until he sobered up), we might be reluctant to talk of his earlier drinking as a self-forming action; he certainly did not reflect on it under that description. Indeed, one might even say that it is in part the fact that he did not reflect on it under that description that we are blaming him for when we blame him for having allowed himself to become as drunk as he did; he should have realized that by drinking this much he was making himself, albeit temporarily, someone whose judgement could not be trusted. In other cases though, 'self-forming actions' seems non-problematically the right sort of description. Persons who consciously and wilfully bring themselves over a period of training to the stage where they can do no other than a particular thing in a particular situation and who persist in this character trait over the rest of their lives have, by the actions which have brought them to this state, formed a 'self' for themselves and, insofar as we think of this self as laudable, we praise them for having made themselves have it; insofar as we think of this self as condemnable, we blame them for having made themselves have it. But the bad news for the compatibilist is that this sort of tracing back of our praiseworthiness or blameworthiness to self-forming actions seems to presuppose that the self-forming actions themselves were ones that the agent in question could have chosen not to perform. Were we to come to believe, for example, that Luther could not but have become the sort of person who then could not but have stood where he stood and said what he said, for, say, we come to believe that God had eternally predestined Luther to fulfil this role in the divine economy and thus determined every thought he ever had to ensure no possibility of deviance from the divine plan, then we would not wish to assess Luther at all for fulfilling his part in this plan; none of what he did was, we would think, up to him at all. Were we to come to believe that the rugby lout was being controlled by an implant similar to that which we earlier imagined me installing into the Senior Tutor, in this case being one such that he was unwittingly compelled to consume the amount of alcohol that he did, then we would not wish to blame him for his becoming drunk to the extent that he did or thus for his forming the temporary 'self' that he did while under the influence of that much alcohol. We would wish to blame whoever had installed that implant. In short, an example such as that of Luther does not seem to provide us with a case where we would wish to praise someone for an action which we suppose they could not have failed to perform.

* * *

There have been other suggestions for counter-examples to the claim that, for us to incline to attribute moral responsibility, the person being assessed must be supposed by us to be able to do otherwise than whatever they actually do. These have come to be known by the name of the person who introduced the first, as Frankfurt-style counter-examples.[22] We can construct one of these by adapting a previous example.

Let us imagine then that I have implanted a chip in the Senior Tutor which enables me in principle to do two things. The first thing it enables me to do is to read his thoughts by transmitting them to the laptop which I carry with me, on which they appear in text form. The second thing it enables me to do is to control these thoughts and thus, indirectly, his actions. For example, if I switch this part of the implant on and then type into my laptop, 'Think that it would be very nice to clap your hands together; then do it', the Senior Tutor will think for a moment that it would be very nice to clap his hands together and then clap his hands together. As yet I have switched on only that part of the implant which enables me to read the thoughts that he is having; I have not yet switched on the part that enables me to control his thoughts and indeed I only intend to switch on this second part if the first reveals that his thoughts are not to my liking. As it happens, uninitiated by me then, the Senior Tutor contemplates how nice it would be were the Master to be shot and decides himself to shoot him, a thought and decision very much to my liking. He accordingly makes his plans; steals an old service revolver from my desk; and makes sure he takes it to the next meeting at which the Master will be present. Throughout this process, I stand by, ready to activate the second part of the implant should the Senior Tutor waver in carrying out his decision to shoot the Master. As the crucial moment arrives and the Senior Tutor – my laptop tells me – is about to pull out his gun, my finger hovers over the button that will enable me not merely to observe his thoughts but to control them. Should he waver, I will instantaneously intervene and make him carry through on his earlier decision to shoot the Master. In fact however, he does not waver. He pulls out the gun and shoots the Master without my needing to do anything. Thus I never switch on that part of the implant that would have enabled me to control his thoughts; it remains inert in his brain.

Here then, we might say, we have a situation where we would wish to assess the Senior Tutor morally and, let us say, find him blame-worthy: we would wish to blame the Senior Tutor for having mur-dered the Master. Nevertheless, given that, had the Senior Tutor wavered for even a moment, I would have intervened and made him shoot the Master, he could not but have shot the Master. So, it seems, we would blame the Senior Tutor for shooting the Master in these circumstances even though, in these circumstances, he could not have failed to shoot the Master. Is this then not an example of a situation in which we hold someone morally responsible even though we are supposing of them that they could not do otherwise than the thing for which we are holding them morally responsible?

One concern one might have with this putative counter-example is that it does seem as if there is another possible course that the Senior Tutor could have taken. It may be true that he could not have got to the end of the day without having shot the Master, but he could have got to the end of the day having wavered on his way to ending up shooting him. This observation, while true, does not, it seems to me, take us to the heart of the matter or at least not straight to the heart of the matter. For, we can modify the putative counter-example so that it bypasses this sort of concern. Let us suppose, for example, that we alter the situation in this way. The implant as we now imagine it reads the brain state of the Senior Tutor and, via my laptop, tells me not just what he is currently thinking and deciding but what he will think and decide in a few moments time. Of course, if we live in an indeterministic world, such predictions cannot be infallible, but we may suppose that, even were our universe indeterministic, a rela- tively accurate set of predictions might in principle be made along these lines.[23] Let us suppose that the implant functions with whatever degree of accuracy is possible in our universe, given its level of Inde- terminism if any. I then decide that if the brain state of the Senior Tutor is such as to lead my laptop to suggest that there is a greater than 60 per cent probability of his being about to waver, I will then intervene. In fact, it never displays such a message, so I do not inter- vene; he thus – as in the first case – shoots the Master without any intervention from me. In such a modified version of the thought experiment, we may say that it was not possible for the Senior Tutor to have got to the end of the day without having unwaveringly carried out his earlier decision to shoot the Master. (In order to get this to work out, we will need to posit that this pre-waver brain-state was in itself necessary if he was later to waver; so be it; we can posit that without presupposing anything about Indeterminism.) We would still hold the Senior Tutor morally responsible for having shot the Master. So, what are we to say of this putative counter-example to Incompatibilism?

It seems to me that we would suppose the Senior Tutor to be robustly morally responsible in these circumstances, so the example works by reference to the first criterion for a successful counter- example to the thesis of Incompatibilism: our confidence in the subject's moral responsibility is maintained in it. But it seems to fail with regard to the second criterion: it does not seem to be a situation in which the person we are holding morally responsible could not have done anything other than whatever he actually did. Even though there was – *ex hypothesi* – no possibility of his getting to the end of the day without having shot the Master (or perhaps even, for the second variation on the thought experiment, without having unwaveringly shot the Master), he could have got to the end of the day without having murdered the Master; the way he could have done this would have been to have wavered (or, in the second variation, had the brain-state which was a relatively reliable indicator that he was about to waver and a necessary condition of doing so), in which case – *ex hypothesi* – I would have intervened and made him shoot the Master, but, in that case, it would not have been he who was the murderer of the Master, it would have been me. Thus, in that case, we would not have held him morally responsible for the Master's death; we would have held me morally responsible for it. Thus he could have done otherwise and, had he done otherwise, then we would not have held him morally responsible for the Master's death, which would, nevertheless, have indeed resulted. In short, the Senior Tutor could have done something different. He could have made me intervene and, if he had made me intervene, he would not have murdered the Master even though, given the nature of my intervention, 'he' would – *ex hypothesi* – still have – perhaps unwaveringly – shot him. And, of course, if I were to have made the right sort of intervention, the Senior Tutor might in fact have ended up having had apparently the same mental processes going on in him as actually went on in him; the fact that it would have been me who was behind the Master's death in these circumstances could have been obscured even from his own introspective powers. But in that situation, it would still have been me, rather than him, who was behind it. As it was, it was him, rather than me, and thus we hold him culpable; he is actually the murderer, not just the tool of the murderer.

While we have looked at only one example of a Frankfurt-style supposed counter-example, we have seen enough to see why it is that we shall not be able to construct a counter-example which is sufficient to overcome our intuitive support for Incompatibilism.[24] If, in a particular case as we are imagining it, it is obvious that there is nothing at all the person concerned could have done in even the tiniest detail different from whatever it is he or she ended up doing, then we ineluctably decline to hold the person morally responsible for doing what he or she did. And again, if the only way that he or she could have done something different was through the operations of chance, we decline to hold him or her morally responsible. This is because ultimate authorship is, we suppose, a necessary condition for moral responsibility. If we do regard someone as morally responsible for doing whatever it is he or she is being imagined actually to do, then that is because we do suppose that what he or she ended up doing was down to him or her, but, that being so, we are supposing that there is something which he or she could have done other than whatever it is he or she actually did even if that other thing is simply a small 'wavering' or the having of a pre-waver brain-state, something the doing of which would have then meant that another person or mechanism would have intervened and made the person we are considering rejoin the path that he or she had momentarily raised his or her foot as if to step from. But, it might be objected, in this latter case, are waverings not merely 'flickers of freedom'?[25] They don't seem to be the sorts of things which are robust enough to hang robust moral responsibility from. How can whether or not one is a murderer depend on something so tiny? This point can be made all the more forcefully when we move the alternative possibility earlier in time as in our second variation on the thought experiment, to prior to the moment the Senior Tutor's might waver or not and instead posit that I would have intervened had he had a brain-state which would have rendered it more than 60 per cent likely he would waver in the next few moments and one the having of which is in fact necessary if he was to have wavered. If we press this type of variation to the thought experiment, the one that makes the brain-state a necessary condition of his wavering (though not sufficient [it only renders it 60 per cent likely he'll go on to waver]), then the Senior Tutor could not even have wavered over shooting the Master. The having or not of such a pre-waver brain-state is even more obviously something which we do not ordinarily regard as the sort of thing for which the Senior Tutor is morally assessable. This is indeed so, but it misses the point that the wavering or the having of this sort of pre-waver brain-state would have had momentous consequences in the circumstances imagined, for, in these circumstances, these are the things which would have led to someone other than the Senior Tutor doing the murdering of the Master; they would have led to me doing it. So, unless we have reason to believe that the having of one brain-state rather than another is the sort of thing which could not affect whether or not one was morally responsible for the movements of one's body that resulted from it, it is not at all implausible that these sorts of things are the things off which great moral importance might hang and of course we do *not* have any reason to believe that the having of one brain-state rather than another is the sort of thing which could not affect whether or not one was morally responsible for the movements of one's body that resulted from it; just the opposite.[26]

So far then, we have not come up with an example of a situation that is of use to the compatibilist as a counter-example to Incompatibilism. Let's step back a bit to see whether there is any space within which such an example might in principle be constructed. Is this failure contingent or necessary?

* * *

It will be recalled that ultimate authorship is what we fundamentally suppose to be present when we suppose robust moral responsibility to be present and that this requires simply that oneself be the source of one's actions. It is not immediately obvious that this condition could not in principle be met while not also meeting the ability to do otherwise condition. An example we have already come across almost satisfied this description; the case of Luther. As we retold his story, we had it that he and nobody else had wilfully made himself into the sort of person who could not do otherwise than what he did at a particular moment, stand where he stood and say, 'Here I stand, I can do no other.' And even though we supposed of him at that moment that he could not have done otherwise, we did indeed *prima facie* incline to hold him morally responsible for doing what he did at that particular moment. However, on reflection, we quickly traced back what it was we were really holding him morally responsible for to certain of his earlier actions, which we called 'self-forming actions' – the ones that had made him into the person he was at the moment he stood where he stood and said what he said. He was the ultimate author of his action in standing where he did and saying what he did even though he could not, by that stage, have stood anywhere else or said anything else, but that was only because he was the ultimate author of earlier actions which made him into that sort of 'self', and we are easily persuaded that it is really those earlier actions which should form the focus for our moral assessment of him. We praise him for making himself the sort of person who could not but stand where he stood and say what he said and, once we have praised him to our satisfaction for these earlier self-forming actions, we do not feel that there is a residue of praiseworthiness hanging over the moment this process reached it's by-then-inevitable culmination as he stood where he stood and said what he said. When we look at the earlier stage, we suppose that then he could have done otherwise than have formed that self for himself, and thus the example breaks down as a counter-example to Incompatibilism. Why do we persistently look for a 'could have done otherwise condition' being met at the base of any action which we assess someone for? It is plausibly because we suppose that if one could not have done otherwise, then that must be because what one does is determined by something outside one's power and thus outside one's ultimate authorship (which is what is really essential for one to be morally assessable). But perhaps this supposition is not universally true.

To construct a viable counter-example to Incompatibilism, we need then to consider the possibility of an agent who is like Luther in that we wish to assess him or her morally (let us stick to praising him or her, as we supposed for the sake of argument we wished to praise Luther); who is like Luther in not being able to do other than he or she does in the particular choice we consider; who is like Luther in not having had his or her self formed in the sense of necessitated by anything exterior to his or her self; but who is *unlike* Luther in not having had the 'self' which then determines him or her to act in the praiseworthy way formed by actions which he or she undertook prior to the particular choice in question and which we easily suppose did meet a 'could-have-done-otherwise' condition. In making the person unlike Luther in this crucial respect, there will then be nowhere earlier in his or her history at which stage we suppose him or her to satisfy a could-have-done-otherwise condition and on which we are able to focus our inclination to praise him or her. The ideal candidate for such a counter-example then would be an agent who is by definition perfectly praiseworthy; who is by definition necessarily so (who then could not be other than perfectly praiseworthy); who is not necessitated in any way in himself or herself by anything exterior to himself or herself; and who exists outside time and thus could not, even in principle, have any part of his or her self causally determined by self-forming actions which he or she undertook in the past and which might in principle have satisfied a could-have-done-otherwise condition even if a later set of actions did not. Fortunately, it is not that the history of thought is bereft of mention of a perfectly praiseworthy, necessarily good, impassable and atemporal person; it has even – handily – given him a name, 'God'.

God is traditionally characterized as perfectly good and maximally worthy of praise, indeed worship. Furthermore, God is traditionally characterized as *of necessity* perfectly praiseworthy; it is not traditionally thought to be a contingent fact about God that he is so; it is thought to be a necessary fact about him. That being so, if we wish to do as tradition has insisted we should, praise God for the perfectly good actions he has performed, we must do this while supposing of him that he could not have performed any less praiseworthy actions than he did actually perform. That's just the sort of person God essentially is – a necessarily perfect one. Thus as an agent God satisfies the condition of being praiseworthy; we may maintain a high confidence that if we construct an example involving him acting, we may think of him as acting praiseworthily in it. God, as traditionally characterized, is also the ultimate author of all of his actions in that nothing other than himself ever necessitates that he act as he does (he is omnipotent); indeed, traditionally, he is not even affected in any significant way by anything other than himself (a property tradition has labelled 'impassability'); nor, traditionally, is there any chronology within the divine life such that an earlier self-forming stage has led to him being in these respects the sort of person he is now. So, we must focus our praise just on the action that has drawn God to our attention as it were; we cannot admit of that action that it could not have been otherwise, yet still praise God for doing it because we suppose that he earlier – when he could have done otherwise – made himself into the sort of person who couldn't have done otherwise at the moment he performed the action which, as we are putting it, drew him to our attention. Of course all aspects of this tradition have been challenged by people who maintain that they nevertheless believe in God, but the traditional picture, which we might call the classical theistic picture, undoubtedly has all these elements within it and thus it might be suggested that the God of classical theism looks like the agent who will best enable us to generate a counter-example to Incompatibilism.[27]

We need to build our example carefully however, for the God of classical theism is also traditionally supposed to have been able to do things other than whatever it is he actually did; this is because it is traditionally supposed that while it is indeed true that God can never perform any act which falls short of the moral ideal, the set of acts from which this necessitates he choose has more than one member. Thus tradition has maintained that God could have done other than what he actually does, albeit that he couldn't have done anything that was in any morally significant way different from whatever he actually does; he retains, if you will, 'wriggle room' within the domain of moral indifference amongst those options which are joint best. One might however question whether it is a necessity that God always preserve for himself 'wriggle room' in this area and, if it is not, whether, were he to choose not to do so, he would thereby really become morally un-assessable (as the incompatibilist must insist he would), for one might question whether God could not make what was morally indifferent different.

Let us use as our example God promising Moses that he will lead the Israelites out of Egypt and into the Promised Land. That promise having been made, God cannot do anything but lead the Israelites out of Egypt and into the Promised Land. The initial incompatibilist response to this, as sketched in the previous paragraph, is to point out that, by itself, this does nothing to imply that God could not have done otherwise than whatever he actually did (*ex hypothesi*, lead the Israelites out of Egypt and into the Promised Land), for there are – a quick look in an Atlas reveals – a variety of routes from Egypt to the Promised Land by which Israelites might have been led. God's promise – which, of course, he could not help but keep – did not determine every detail of the manner of his keeping it. Having promised to lead them out of Egypt, God could not lead the Israelites in big circles that kept them interior to Egypt or lead them out of Egypt but into the Sahara and leave them there. But he could have led them out of Egypt into the Promised Land by crossing over the Red Sea in boats, or by going around the Red Sea, or – as we are told actually happened – through a miraculously parted Red Sea. These different modes of getting past the Red Sea were all, we may posit with some confidence, morally indifferent, and thus his moral perfection left him wriggle room over which mode to utilize. This response, however, invites the thought that surely God *could* have specified the *precise* manner in which his promise to lead the Israelites out of Egypt and into the Promised Land would be fulfilled. Had he done that, he would have shrunk his wriggle room to zero, by making one of the ways of getting past the Red Sea that would otherwise have been morally indifferent relative to the others morally different from them through being morally preferable,

preferable as it would have been the way he would have then specified he'd use to enable the Israelites to pass that particular obstacle. Of course, an exhaustive specification of exactly how it was that God was to lead the Israelites into the Promised Land – detailing, for example, exactly what each water molecule in the parting Red Sea would do as he parted it – would have taken multiple lifetimes to convey to finite minds such as those of the Israelites, if indeed it could be conveyed to such minds at all, but that would have been no barrier to God's promising to behave in that fashion to finite minds such as theirs. God could have said something like the following, 'I hereby promise you, Moses, that I shall lead the Israelites out of Egypt and into the Promised Land in precisely the way that is exhaustively specified in a certain proposition, which I hold before my omniscient mind. Of course, being so large and complex, I shall not seek to convey this proposition to you and, frankly, you'd find a good deal of it tedious in the extreme were I to do so. (What do you care about the exact distance "Red Sea Water Molecule three billion, five hundred and sixty four" moves?) Rather, I simply refer to the proposition in this manner. Nevertheless, rest assured that reference to a particular proposition which exhaustively describes the relevant section of the history of the universe is determinately secured and thus what we might call a "meticulous" promise has been entered into by my promising that you'll get to the Promised Land in just the manner that this proposition specifies. And of course, rest assured, I shall keep this promise, as I keep all my promises – I am, after all, morally perfect, even if I say so myself.'

Were God to make such a meticulous promise, it seems that we would wish to say of him that he was yet perfectly praiseworthy for having then followed it through; we would wish to say this despite the fact that we would need to suppose that he could not have done otherwise than follow it through in precisely the manner that he did, for the precise manner of his following it through was specified in the promise itself; that's what made it a meticulous promise. So is Incompatibilism threatened by this example? No, none of this ultimately threatens Incompatibilism, for manoeuvring in the manner of the previous paragraph re-introduces stages to the divine life, which allows us to think of the divine life as divided up in a structurally similar manner to the way we viewed Luther's life as divided up into an earlier self-forming stage and a later stage. The stages in the divine life need not perhaps be construed as temporal stages, but nevertheless they are there and discrete and thus sufficient for the incompatibilist to point out that at one stage in the divine life God could have done otherwise than what he did *apropos* of leading the Israelites out of Egypt and into the Promised Land even if at another he could not. We may say that once God has made a meticulous promise, then he does indeed have to keep it or, to put it in atemporal mode, if it is eternally the case that he makes a meticulous promise in this area, then it is eternally the case that he keeps it meticulously. But it remains true that he could have done otherwise than make and keep a meticulous promise in this area; he could have made a non-meticulous promise and kept that (in a variety of ways) or made some other meticulous promise and kept that in whatever way was necessary. So, the wriggle room still survives. Not even God can be used to construct a counter-example to Incompatibilism.

* * *

CONCLUSION

We have seen that the Consequence Argument supports Incompatibilism, through supporting the claim that Determinism is incompatible with us having an ability to do other than what we do. The classical compatibilist response to this argument relies on advancing a sense of 'could have done otherwise' in which, even in a deterministic universe, people sometimes could have done otherwise than whatever it is they actually did. This response was found to be lacking for three reasons. First, Rule Beta, which the classical compatibilist is forced to reject, is intuitively very plausible. Examples of its apparently working can be multiplied without end. Second, putative counter-examples to it require of us, if we are to accept them as counter-examples, that we either accept that if the world is deterministic, then we could change at least the laws of nature (and possibly the past) or accept that if the world is deterministic, then it is implausibly close in logical space to indeterministic worlds. Third, the hypothetical sense of 'could have done otherwise' is implausible in its own terms, for it would render most of us capable of doing things to which we have the most extreme aversions just whenever someone offers us the chance to do them.

As we saw, this though was just the first stage of the argument for Incompatibilism. The non-classical compatibilist accepts with the Consequence Argument that Determinism does indeed entail an inability to do other than whatever one actually does, but denies that ability to do other than what one actually does is necessary for moral responsibility. In order to find support for such a contention, he or she needs effective counter-examples to Incompatibilism, that is to say situations which maintain our confidence both that the person we are considering is morally assessable for the action in question and that the person we are considering could not have done other than whatever it is he or she actually did.

In looking for such counter-examples, we first looked at a somewhat-imaginary re-telling of the story of Martin Luther's famous declaration, 'Here I stand; I can do no other.' Here we concluded that while we did indeed wish to assess Luther morally and yet admit that at the time he made this declaration he could not have done other than make it, what we really wished to assess him for was not his action in making this declaration; that was simply the action which drew him to our moral attention. Rather we wished to assess him for his earlier 'self-forming' actions, those by which he made a 'self' for himself such that at that moment he was then unable to do other than stand where he stood and say what he said. And when we turn our attention to these earlier actions, on which our praise (we assumed it would be praise when we told the story) is really focused, we suppose that when doing them he did satisfy a robust 'could have done otherwise' condition. Luther then is not, on reflection, a counter-example to Incompatibilism. We then considered Frankfurt-style putative counter-examples to Incompatibilism. But we found that while again our confidence in the moral responsibility of the person concerned for the action in question could be maintained, in each of the putative counter-examples the person concerned could in fact have done something other than whatever it is they actually did, even if these other options could be reduced to being momentary 'flickers of freedom'. As we saw, on some such flickers things of great moral significance could depend, for in the relevant variants of the Frankfurt-style examples, the identity of the ultimate author of the resultant action is dependent on whether or not they occur. It's one person's action if they don't and another's if they do. Frankfurt-style putative counter-examples to Incompatibilism were thereby also judged failures. Finally, we turned to consider the case of God and concluded that even an action of his in fulfilling what we called a meticulous promise would not provide a counterexample to Incompatibilism.

Overall then, our third common-sense thought that Determinism is incompatible with robust moral responsibility has emerged from the considerations presented in this chapter, especially the Consequence Argument, with more support, rather than less. It is important to note that the argument of this chapter does not by itself imply that if the universe is indeterministic, then we *do* have free will, for – as we have seen – other things are usually supposed by us to be necessary for free will, specifically that we be the ultimate authors of our actions and, for us to be morally responsible for them, that we will these actions under morally salient descriptions. The argument of this chapter just gives us reason to suppose that only if the universe is indeterministic can we have free will. Or, as we might put it, it gives us reason to suppose that Indeterminism is a necessary, even though not sufficient, condition for free will of the sort necessary for moral responsibility. Naturally then, our attention now turns to the issue of whether or not our universe is indeterministic. Is this condition in fact satisfied? This is the question we shall look at next.

CHAPTER FOUR

INDETERMINISM

INTRODUCTION

In Chapter Two we articulated the view that we called 'Libertarianism'. Libertarianism is a view about the nature and existence of free will that is itself built from various elements, one of which we labelled 'Incompatibilism', the thesis that a necessary condition of us being morally responsible for a particular action is that we could have done other than whatever it is we actually did in doing that action. In the last chapter we looked at some arguments in favour of Incompatibilism, in particular the Consequence Argument. And we looked at some counterarguments to it, those of both the classical compatibilist (who maintained there was a sense of 'could have done otherwise' in which we could have done otherwise even if the universe is deterministic) and the non-classical compatibilist (who maintained that while Determinism does indeed entail that we could not have done otherwise, ability to do otherwise is not in fact necessary for moral responsibility). We found faults with all forms of Compatibilism and thus concluded that the incompatibilist component of our common-sense view is true. We cannot be free in the sense necessary for moral responsibility if we live in a deterministic universe. For us to be free in this way, we need Indeterminism to be true. In this chapter, we thus turn to consider whether our universe is one in which Indeterminism is true. As we saw in Chapter Two, we do ordinarily suppose that ours is an indeterministic universe but what, if anything, is science telling us on this front? Is it supporting common sense or giving us reasons to doubt it? On the one hand, over the last hundred or so years, Indeterminism has come to rule as the dominant paradigm of interpretation for Physics, but, on the other hand, what we might think of as the advance from folk psychology to neuroscience has pushed many of the practitioners of brain science in the other direction. And are there not experimental results (the famous Libet experiments) that suggest that the feeling we have of making choices is illusory? We'll look at these issues in this chapter.

Before we do so, let us do as we did at the start of the last chapter, and briefly make a point about the 'meta-issue' of where the dialectical balance should be judged to fall. Paralleling the point we made at the start of Chapter Three, we should first underscore the fact that, given our starting points as suggested in Chapter Two, we *need* an argument for Determinism if we are rationally to believe in it. Just as Incompatibilism was 'innocent until proven guilty'[1] and thus would have emerged vindicated at the end of the last chapter – even absent the Consequence Argument – when arguments against it were found wanting, so Indeterminism is 'innocent until proven guilty' and thus will emerge vindicated at the end of this chapter just if the arguments for Determinism are found to be wanting. Secondly, we may see that these arguments will need to meet a high standard of proof if they are to prove it guilty. We can see this by considering how resolutely we hold to Indeterminism. Consider the following belief, which I hazard you hold with a greater certainty than you'll be able to muster for the premises and validity of any argument which has Determinism as its conclusion. It was physically possible for you to have put this book down a few moments ago, even though – I am supposing – you did not actually try to do so. Contrast that belief with the following, which I hazard you also hold. It was not physically possible for you to fly to the moon simply by waving your arms a few moments ago, even though – I am supposing – you did not actually try to do that either. If Determinism were true, then each of these actions that you did not actually try to do would be as impossible as the other (given the initial condition of the universe and its laws). On Determinism, given that you actually tried to do neither, you were no more able to put the book down five minutes ago than you were able to fly to the moon by waving your hands five minutes ago. 'This is a hard teaching. Who can accept it?'[2] We have seen that the determinist cannot weaken our common-sense aversion to conceding such a claim simply by pointing out that if we lived in a deterministic universe it might well be that we would have the illusion that we could have done things other than whatever it is we actually did. That was the way of the hyperbolic sceptic, which we – surely rightly – eschew in all cases other than those where we have positive reason to believe that our common-sense views are illusory. And we have seen that we can justify to various extents the common-sense beliefs we have about our unexercised capacities. If someone were to ask you why you believe that you were capable of putting this book down five minutes ago even though in fact you did not do so, you would not be at a loss to answer them or unable to perform experiments that, presuming the results turned out to be as you would expect them, you would think gave them reason to agree with you. Insofar as you are not in any significant and relevant way different from your earlier self and you are now able to demonstrate your capacity for putting the book down, that is a reason to think that your earlier self was similarly capable. So we start with a strong and, we suppose, well-grounded belief that we could often do otherwise than whatever it is we end up doing. To overcome this, determinists will need very strong arguments. Let's see if they have any.

* * *

Determinism is the view that, given the initial or boundary conditions of the universe and the laws of nature operative on it, only one history is physically possible, or, as we put it in the second chapter, Determinism is the view that the actual exhausts the possible: what actually happens is the only thing that it is possible to happen.[3] One striking way of picturing one of the implications of Determinism's being true is to imagine a super-being, one who is not himself or herself a part of the universe but looks down on it from outside; who is omniscient about it as it is at a particular moment; and who is able to perform calculative tasks of any degree of complexity. If we imagine such a being looking at our universe at the moment of the Big Bang and then looking away, we may say that, if our universe were deterministic, then, with his or her super powers, he or she would be able to work out where everything would be five minutes from then, five years, five billion years and so on. Were there such a being and were our universe deterministic, then he or she would not need to look back at our universe to discover that, several billion years after he or she had first looked at it, you were born or that you are reading this sentence right now; he or she could work out all this and everything else that's true of the universe from the knowledge of events at the Big Bang and knowledge of the laws of nature.

This suggestion was perhaps most memorably endorsed by a French mathematician, Laplace.

We ought to regard the present state of the universe as the effect of its antecedent state and as the cause of the state that is to follow. An intelligence knowing all the forces acting in nature at a given instant, as well as the momentary positions of all things in the universe, would be able to comprehend in one single formula the motions of the largest bodies as well as the lightest atoms in the world, provided that its intellect were sufficiently powerful to subject all data to analysis; to it nothing would be uncertain, the future as well as the past would be present to its eyes.

Of course, many people have believed that such a being is no mere philosophical whimsy; there is a God who has meticulously predestined every detail of His unfolding creation so that he is omniscient about its future in just this way. Whether or not we subscribe to this view, it is important for its deployment, even in our imagination, that we conceive of this super-being as *outside* the universe, as there are good arguments to the effect that the computing power necessary to predict the future of our universe could not itself be accommodated within our universe. And thus we see that while 'perfect predictability for an extra-universal super-being of the right sort' is indeed a necessary feature of a deterministic universe, predictability to any particular extent by any of us need not be supposed to be so. It is worth dwelling on this for a moment or two before we move on, for it will help us sweep from the table some bad arguments.

* * *

On the one hand, the world could be highly predictable yet indeterministic. For example, the indeterminist will probably say of rolls of a fair die or choices over what drink to order at a bar that they are indeterministic, yet he or she would do well to concede (and it is certainly not incompatible with his or her Indeterminism for him or her to concede) that these sorts of things might well turn out to be predictable. One can predict that, as one repeatedly rolls a fair die, the proportion of sixes one gets will increasingly converge on one-sixth. One might well predict that someone who one knows has certain general preferences will order one sort of drink rather than another at a bar. None of this predictability need be denied by the indeterminist. For the roll of a die to be indeterministic, all that is needed is just that the face which ends up on top on any particular roll not be causally *necessitated* by its preceding state and how one throws it, not that over a large enough number of runs one will not be able to predict the proportion of times a particular face will show uppermost. For a person's particular choice of which drink to order to be indeterministic, all that is needed is that he or she not be necessitated to choose one way rather than another by subliminal advertising or other factors in the physical universe that precede the moment when he or she decides to say 'A glass of the house red', 'A pint of bitter', 'A Singapore Gin Sling', or whatever it is he or she does end up saying.

On the other hand, it is also the case that the world might be deterministic but highly *un*predictable. We are now all familiar with the notion of a chaotic system, one the later development of which can be radically affected by even the tiniest of changes to its initial conditions, and we are happy to suppose of some chaotic systems that they may be viewed as effectively deterministic. A computer running a 'virtual snooker' game might be conceded to be something that may be regarded as effectively deterministic even by someone who believes that the universe is indeterministic at its most fundamental level. As he or she looks into the details of how the programme runs, he or she might discover in the programming that in its virtual space, its virtual balls are governed by Newton's laws of motion, which are fully deterministic. Yet, that having been conceded, determinist and indeterminist alike should concede that it might well be that if one were to be playing the game and hit a ball with a known force and direction into a set of other balls of known virtual mass and so on; and then immediately close one's eyes, one would not be able to predict with any reasonable confidence where the balls it would then go on to hit would be when one reopened one's eyes in a few seconds time. There might even be an 'unpredictability in principle' to be had in some such cases (though not this one), cases where a computer that could predict a certain outcome couldn't work faster than the physical process it was attempting to model.

So, given the points made in the previous two paragraphs, we may see that two popular arguments, each of which relies on mistakenly tying Determinism to perfect predictability by us, are confused. The first confused argument is this: if Determinism were true, then human actions would be entirely predictable, but humans sometimes do unpredictable things, so Determinism can't be true. The second is this: if Indeterminism were true, human actions would be entirely *un*predictable, but humans generally don't do unpredictable things, so Indeterminism is false. Both these arguments are equally unsound. 'Perfect predictability for an extra-universal super-being of the right sort' is the only sort of predictability entailed by Determinism. 'Predictability without possibility of error' is the only sort of predictability the absence of which is entailed by Indeterminism. That being so, we need not get into ill-defined and fruitless disputes about just how predictable or unpredictable we find human behaviour. Any answer one gives to this question – 'Very', 'Hardly at all', 'Somewhat' – will be compatible both with Determinism and with Indeterminism, and will not form a premise from which one can advance an argument for either.

We have already seen that Determinism does not entail Fatalism, Fatalism being the view that humans cannot in any sense affect the future. And just as Determinism's not entailing perfect predictability by us puts paid to two popular arguments in this area, so Determinism's not entailing Fatalism puts paid to two others. The first one is this: because there's nothing I can do to change a particular future happening, let's say whether the Earth is about to be hit by a meteorite, so whether or not the Earth will be hit by a meteorite must be determined. The second one is this: because there *are* things I can do to change the future, let's say whether I'll be hit by a bus when I next step into the road, so Determinism is false. As we have seen, whether or not our universe is deterministic, some things in the future are affected by us – whether we are likely to be hit by a bus in crossing the road is affected by whether we look before we step into the road – and some things are not – whether our planet is about to be hit by a meteorite is plausibly something than we, individually and collectively, can do nothing about. The indeterminist is not suggesting that we can affect *all* aspects of the world's future; there are no doubt some things in the future that we can do nothing about even if Indeterminism is true; the determinist is not suggesting that there is nothing at all we can do to affect the world's future; there are no doubt some things we can do something about even if Determinism is true. Again, there is no ground here then from which one may advance an argument either for Indeterminism or for Determinism.[4]

So, from what basis might one advance an argument for Indeterminism or for Determinism? In thinking about how to answer this question, let us first look at a point which is not an argument in favour of either, but is rather an argument that there cannot be conclusive arguments in favour of either. The truth of Determinism, we shall see, is not in fact something that could be shown to be true (even if it is true) or shown to be false (if it is false), or at least not shown decisively.

* * *

Determinism is in principle irrefutable as failing to find a necessitating cause for some particular event, say some sub-microscopic quantum happening, is always going to remain compatible with the hypothesis that there is a necessitating cause but that one's own powers of investigation are not up to the task of uncovering it in this case. We can perhaps see this most clearly if we imagine ourselves at a stage of development in the natural sciences that those inclined towards Indeterminism would have no hesitation in describing as bringing science to its completion. At such a time, let us suppose that it is discovered that there are a certain number of fundamental particles and that they behave in ways that these sciences can only describe statistically.[5] At such a point, those inclined towards Determinism may, if all else fails, posit tiny mechanisms interior to each particle, pieces of clockwork so tiny that they will forever elude the microscopes and so on of scientists; these tiny mechanisms, they may suggest, deterministically produce the behaviour of each particle. The person inclined to Determinism may maintain such a thesis without fear of refutation. Not all hidden variable interpretations of submicroscopic phenomena will commit one to action at a distance or to information travelling faster than light and of course even those that do commit one to these things may be endorsed by people who would rather commit themselves to these things than relinquish Determinism. This is all to say that because Indeterminism is an interpretation of the findings of science, not itself one of the findings of science, so Determinism as a different interpretation is always going to remain a viable interpretation of anything that the person more inclined to Indeterminism will incline to think of as an undetermined event. Thus, in short, Determinism is irrefutable. This point is often made. The point that the same can be said, *mutatis mutandis*, of Indeterminism is less often made.

Indeterminism is in principle irrefutable, as the discovery of what someone who inclined towards Determinism might happily label a necessitating cause for some particular event, say some sub-microscopic quantum happening, is always going to remain compatible with the hypothesis that it was a non-necessitating cause of that happening. After all, all that one will have observed is that the happening did in fact happen after whatever it is the determinist is saying necessitated that it happen, not that the happening *had* to happen after that. An indeterminist might assert that while, say, particle a's being in that position and moving at that speed at that time is what did indeed cause particle b to be in the position it was a moment later and moving as it was, that does not mean that b could not have gone off in another direction even had particle a been just as it was; all that it means is that it did not as a matter of fact go off in that other direction. Indeterministic interpretations of phenomena, even if they might seem increasingly unsupported, are never going to be ruled out by such discoveries. So Indeterminism is as irrefutable by scientific discoveries as Determinism. We can take a step back and see the common reason why both positions are irrefutable.

In the cases both of Determinism and Indeterminism, what is being asserted is a modal claim, that is to say a claim that transcends what merely happens and talks about what must happen or need not happen. That is why no observation of what actually happens can force either the determinist or the indeterminist to relinquish his or her position.

It might be argued that Determinism is in something of a weaker position than Indeterminism to withstand the future shocks that Science might deliver for the following reason. While the determinist is committed to saying of everything that happens that – given the initial conditions and the laws of nature – it could not have happened in any other way, the indeterminist is not committed to saying of everything that happens that – given the initial conditions and the laws of nature – it could have happened another way. And this makes for a difference. The determinist cannot allow that there are local indeterministic subsystems within his or her universe, for even the slightest amount of Indeterminism is incompatible with his or her theory. The indeterminist by contrast can allow that there are some local deterministic subsystems within his or her universe, for Indeterminism just asserts that not everything is deterministic, not that nothing is. This is indeed true, but in itself it guarantees nothing; were the indeterminist to concede more and more areas to his or her deterministic rival, his or her claim that he or she would not need to concede all areas would look increasingly desperate. The person who claims that all swans are white is, by making such a claim, opening themselves to greater danger of refutation than the person who claims that at least one swan is black. But that does not make us favour the hypothesis that at least one swan is black from the start and does not mean that, as we see more and more white swans, we don't dispense with it in relatively short order.

All this having been said, while scientific developments cannot be strictly incompatible with either Determinism or Indeterminism, they might in principle be more 'congenial' to one of these views rather than the other. So, if, search as we might, we cannot find anything that strikes us as a necessitating cause of a particular happening and we find that positing a hidden necessitating cause requires of us that we suppose tiny unobserved mechanisms that we would have no reason to posit were it not that they are needed by Determinism or we posit that there can be action at a distance or information travelling faster than the speed of light, things which again we would have no reason to posit were it not that it was needed by Determinism, that could reasonably be suggested to be good reason for us to relinquish Determinism. On the other hand, if, search as we might, we cannot find a situation in which a particle moving in one way hits another in a particular state and does not cause it to move in the precise way that the second always does, then while that is not strictly speaking proof that the first sort of happening causally necessitates the second sort of happening, it may reasonably be taken as evidence that it does, for to maintain that it merely inclines the second particle to move in that fashion and that we've merely yet to see an occasion where this inclination did not in fact result in the second sort of happening will seem increasingly extravagant. So, while we should not say that scientific findings can ever finally prove Determinism true or false (Indeterminism false or true), they could in principle – when combined with our preference for believing the simplest theory that accommodates the data – give us a reason to prefer one of these views over the other. Are the most recent findings of science giving us such a reason, one way or the other? We may say, cautiously, that they are.

* * *

For Determinism to be true, two conditions need to be satisfied by the universe. The first is that there needs to be a determinate way that the world is at any given time. A given fundamental particle or what have you needs to be in a definite location; moving at a definite speed; accelerating or decelerating at a definite rate; or what have you.[6] The second condition on Determinism's being true is that there need to be laws of nature of a universal and deterministic sort concerning how the universe can evolve from its state at any given time. Laws entirely adequate to explain every happening in the universe have to have a form such that if a given fundamental entity is in such and such a state at a given time and it interacts in such and such a way with another, then it must be in such and such a state at a later time. That the actual universe satisfied both these conditions was the consensus view of scientists from at least the days of Newton until the end of the nineteenth century. The twin pillars of Determinism were – it appeared for generations – securely grounded by the success of Newtonian mechanics in explaining – it appeared for generations – *everything* in a way that lent itself to deterministic interpretation. This was sufficient to make a deterministic paradigm of interpretation universal amongst scientists. Indeed so fixed did it become that when certain astronomical observations could not be accommodated by Newtonian mechanics, their mere incompatibility proved sufficient for the majority of scientists to dismiss them as inaccurate observations. Rather than saying of such observations that they disproved the favoured theory, they said of them that they were themselves disproved by the favoured theory. However, the twentieth century revolution in Physics which we call Quantum Theory has brought down both pillars of Determinism.

Under the most widely held – Copenhagen – interpretation of Quantum Mechanics, there is uncertainty and indeterminacy which goes deeper than mere epistemic uncertainty and indeterminacy; it goes down to the ontological basis of the universe. We do, of course, face many obstacles on the path of knowing what is going on at sub-microscopic levels, but the consensus view now is that not even a super-being of the sort Laplace imagined could know the exact positions and motions of these fundamental entities, for they do not have exact positions and motions at the same time (the Heisenberg uncertainty principle). Nor is it that they have determinate properties of another sort. The fullest description that may be given to them, and that may be given to them even by a Laplace-style super-being, leaves their exact state indeterminate. And even were we to insist on claiming that they have exact states at any given time (not though ones that can be specified with notions of position and motion), the consensus is that there are in any case no deterministic rules that ensure that the universe can only evolve in one particular way from whatever state it is in at a given time. As we enter the twenty-first century, the indeterministic paradigm is now as dominant as the deterministic one was in the nineteenth century. Of course, as we have already observed, neither Determinism nor Indeterminism can be forced on one by the results of any experiment. It is a general truth of the Philosophy of Science that no unique interpretation can be forced on one by any results; we are always facing the problem of underdetermination of theory by data. And that general truth applies here as elsewhere. But, nevertheless, at the start of the twenty-first century, the simplest and sufficient interpretation of the findings of scientists working in the field of fundamental Physics is widely held to be indeterministic.

What weight may we put on any of this? Two considerations suggest that it is not much. The first is that the one thing we know with more certainty than we know anything else about the current state of research in Quantum Physics is that it is not the whole story. Current Quantum Theory cannot be squared with Relativistic Physics, which lends itself non-problematically to deterministic interpretation. A 'grand unified theory', one which brings these two branches of the discipline together, could, it might thus seem, lend itself more naturally to either an indeterministic or a deterministic interpretation. Uncontroversially, we are not at the stage of having a completed science. Only slightly more controversially, we are not at the stage of knowing that a completed science is possible (and we shall later see arguments to the effect that we can know that it is impossible if we build into our criteria for completion unification). To return to uncontroversial territory, even if a completed science is possible, we do not know how close we are to being at the stage of having a completed science. The least controversial of these claims alone means that we should not extrapolate confidently from current fashions of interpretation within one branch of it. Secondly, the very fact that the consensus has surged one way and then the other over the last few hundred years should make one wary of placing weight on whichever opinion is currently in vogue; fashion in this area is, it appears, fickle. Modern Physics does give us more reason to suppose that Indeterminism is true than did the Physics of Newton's day. But the dramatic nature of the change of opinion in itself gives us reason to pause; once the pendulum has swung one way, it could very well swing back. There are already interpretations of Quantum Mechanics which are deterministic – they are not popular, but they are or may be made experimentally adequate. We cannot know how future science will develop (if we did, it wouldn't be future science) and thus we cannot know whether in a grand unified theory, let alone a completed science, these deterministic interpretations will be judged to have been closer to the truth after all. The position is rather as if we have seen two runners racing one another over the first couple of hundred yards of a race which we know has – at the least – hundreds more yards to it, the end post indeed being out of sight. We have observed that one runner was in a comfortable lead for the first hundred yards and that the other then overtook him and has maintained an equally comfortable lead for the next hundred. 'Which one will win?', we are then asked. Plausibly, if we have now to put our money on one of the runners to win, we should put it on the one who is currently in the lead, but we would not be reasonable in feeling confident that we would win this bet having made it.[7]

So far then, we might sum up our findings in one rather-dispiriting word, 'inconclusive'. We have come upon no arguments which should lead us either to suppose of our belief in Indeterminism that it is true, or to suppose of it that it is false and the world is deterministic after all. The current vogue in the interpretation of fundamental physics is indeterministic, and we may indeed draw some comfort from that, in the manner of the person who has already placed a bet on the runner who is currently in the lead in a race drawing comfort from the fact that he is currently in the lead. However, as this is a race the finishing line of which is not in sight and the other runner in which has been in the lead before, so we cannot start counting our winnings quite yet. Of course, given the 'innocent until proven guilty' point that we made at the start, the fact that Indeterminism has not been proved guilty is in itself is a weak form of vindication for it. But it is not more than that; it is not the more that we got when considering Incompatibilism in the previous chapter. There we were able, not merely to find fault in the compatibilist's arguments, but also to advance arguments in favour of Incompatibilism. Here we have not been able to do that.

Perhaps we can make more progress by shifting our focus from considering what science is telling us about the sub-microscopic world of quantum phenomena, up to the level of what it is telling us about the medium-sized (as we will think of it) world of human brains and bodies. Some have suggested that, once we do so, we can see that we have reason to suppose Determinism true or, as we might better put it, 'effectively true' however the Indeterminism/Determinism dispute is to be resolved at the lower level. We'll look at their arguments next.

* * *

One move that is sometimes made in this debate is to suggest that even were Indeterminism to reign at the sub-microscopic level of elementary particles-cum-waves, these indeterministic effects may be judged to be insignificant at the relatively macro-level of human brains and bodies. They will 'cancel out' at this higher level and we may thus think of Determinism as 'effectively true' for the sorts of things that concern us in this work, most fundamentally our limbs moving in the ways that constitute our most basic actions.[8] We have already seen an example of an object towards which we incline to hold this attitude; in considering how we might think about the workings of a grandfather clock, whether we were in general inclined to be indeterminists or determinists, we were happy to treat it as 'effectively deterministic'; if its hands were in a particular position at a particular time, then, we supposed, some other part of the mechanism must have necessitated their being in that position at that time; their being there was not, we supposed, in any sense a matter of chance. By way of another example, consider the chair on which I suppose you to be sitting as you read this. Perhaps, according to the dominant paradigm of interpretation of Quantum Physics, it is not physically impossible for any atom which presently constitutes this chair to disappear from its current location and reappear a few feet to your left; it is just very unlikely that it will do so. Perhaps we may also take it that the chair is just the aggregate of all the atoms that constitute it and thus that, according to the dominant paradigm, it is not impossible that they will all disappear from their current location at the same moment and reappear a few feet to your left in precisely the same arrangement they currently have relative to one another. Such a happening is so unlikely that in the whole history of the universe (were the chair and yourself somehow to be preserved over such a long period), its chances of happening would be negligible, but perhaps, according to the dominant paradigm of interpretation of fundamental physics, the chances of its happening would not be technically zero and thus, in that sense, it could happen. In a respectable sense, the chair could disappear from under you and reappear a few feet to your left without the intervention of a puerile ghost or some such being responsible for its doing so. Be all that as it may, the right answer to the question of whether the chair could suddenly disappear from under you and reappear to your left without such an intervention is surely 'No'. In general, objects of the size of grandfather clocks and chairs may be treated as effectively deterministic whatever we may say of the quarks or what have you that constitute them. So, having ceded this ground to the determinist with respect to grandfather clocks and chairs, can the indeterminist consistently fail to cede the same ground with regard to objects of a not-entirely-dissimilar size, ourselves? The determinist might claim that they cannot.

This must strike us as an attractive move dialectically as it seems to enable us to sidestep the issue of Indeterminism at the most fundamental level. However, sadly, it will not work. While there are some systems which we may treat as deterministic even supposing that we live in a universe that is at bottom indeterministic – plausibly grandfather clocks and chairs are indeed examples of such – it is by no means clear that we are to be counted amongst them. All depends on whether we are, as we suppose grandfather clocks and chairs are, things in which indeterministic effects at the sub-microscopic level *are* cancelled or dampened out at higher levels; there is no necessity that they *always* be cancelled or dampened out. There may be things in which these effects are preserved at more macroscopic levels or even, as we may put it, 'cascaded'. And we may be things of this latter sort even if grandfather clocks and chairs are, we suppose, things of the former sort. With the emergence of the science of chaotic systems, we have learnt that very small changes in the initial conditions of a system can lead to large changes in its subsequent state. The brain certainly does contain structures that seem to exhibit this sort of chaotic nature, so it is not at all implausible to suggest that in the brain there might be similar cascade effects, amplifying, rather than dampening out, the results of even the tiniest amount of quantum indeterminacy at the sub-microscopic level. And we do not need to hinge the point that we might not be able to be safely subsumed into the same category as grandfather clocks and chairs on the claim that the brain is as finely balanced a chaotic system as our comments so far might seem to suggest. Suppose that neuroscience were to discover that a large number of molecules, let's say several thousand, were responsible for the transmission of information over crucial synapses in the brain and that were a large proportion of these molecules not to behave as they do in a particular case, the net effect would be no different at a higher level. Such a discovery could certainly be made and one can easily imagine someone inclined towards interpreting us as effectively deterministic suggesting that it would show that even if, from the moment a synapse fires, a cascade effect might take over and magnify the effect of its firing, getting a synapse to fire in the first instance would require much more than just one happening at the quantum level, and thus we may, after all, be treated as effectively deterministic at this 'mid-level'. However, in fact, even this discovery would not mean that we could conclude that quantum indeterminacy is damped out in the relevant operation of the brain. That would only follow were we to posit that the relevant quantum happenings could only be brought about a small number of times in the region to which we are confining ourselves and there is no need for us to believe that; perhaps several thousand quantum happenings are affected at once and the cascade effect takes over from there. In short, presumably some brain-states lead to the macroscopic happenings that are our actions and presumably these brain-states are made up at the sub-microscopic level of many quantum happenings; perhaps we cause our actions by operating simultaneously on a number of disparate tiny locations, any one of which is perhaps not sufficient (or perhaps even necessary) for the event that is our resultant action to occur, but which then jointly cause it to occur. Or perhaps the brain is more finely-balanced than that, so less is required of us to generate a cascade effect at a higher level. Either way, we have no reason to suppose that the brain may be treated in the manner of grandfather clocks and chairs as 'effectively deterministic', for we have no reason to suppose that happenings at lower levels within it are dampened out rather than amplified at higher levels. So there is no support for the determinist here either.

There have, however, been a series of experiments that have seemed to some to threaten our freedom in another way in that they have seemed to some to suggest, not that the brain may be treated as effectively deterministic, but that the apparent efficacy of our decisions is illusory. Let us look at these.

* * *

In a series of experiments first conducted by a scientist called Benjamin Libet in the 1980s, the participants had electrodes fitted to their scalps and were sat in front of an 'oscilloscope' timer, resembling a clock face with rapidly rotating hands. They were asked to carry out a simple action, such as pushing a button, at a moment or moments of their choosing within a given time frame, and they were instructed to note the position of the dot on the oscilloscope timer when they first became aware of the 'wish or urge' to act. Pressing the button resulted in the position of the dot being recorded and so the experimenter had two times which could be compared, the time reported as the time the participants first felt the 'wish or urge' to push the button and the time at which the button was pushed. In the original series of experiments it was discovered that on average 200 milliseconds elapsed between the time participants reported of themselves that they were first consciousness of their wish or urge to press the button and their act of pressing it. So far, so unremarkable. But now we come to a third time. Researchers were also able to analyse the data coming via the electrodes attached to the participants' scalps to time a third happening; they discovered that brain activity primarily centred in the secondary motor cortex occurred, on average, 500 milliseconds before the pushing of the button more or less whenever the button was going to be pressed (more on the 'more or less' in a moment). That is to say, it appeared that 300 milliseconds before the time that participants reported of themselves that they first became aware of a wish or urge to push the button, there was a build-up of activity in this part of the brain which was strongly positively correlated with the fact that they were about to form a wish or urge. This came to be called 'readiness potential'.

It is worth starting by observing that almost every aspect of these original results has been thrown into doubt by subsequent experiments.

In particular, the extent to which this correlation is 'more or less' established is currently under dispute. Some Libet-style experiments have found the correlation to be rather weak; others to be rather strong. Amongst those which find that a marked readiness potential almost always precedes a formation of a 'wish or urge' to perform the task, it is not clear to what extent – if any – it is absent when the wish or urge ends up not being acted on, leaving open the question then of whether even if this readiness potential determines something, it is not the decision to push the button it determines, but just the raising in one's mind of the possibility of pushing the button at that stage rather than some other.[9] There are also other worries one might have with fixing the timings of the events under consideration, even before one goes on to then speculate as to what these events happening at these times means for the presence or otherwise of free will. So, for example, Libet asked participants to memorize the position of the dot on the oscilloscope at the moment at which they first became aware of a felt urge or wish to push the button. Did they get it right? We cannot just assume that they did. First, the most popular explanation of the phenomenon of déjà vu draws on the supposition that the mind 'mis-files' under the wrong time index certain mental happenings, giving consciousness the illusion that it remembers experiencing something like this before when in fact it is experiencing it for the first time. Perhaps, something similar goes on here. Second, even if we push this concern to one side, we surely cannot assume – as those conducting these experiments characteristically do assume – that it takes participants no time whatsoever to note the position of the dot on the oscilloscope and thus that the time at which they say they first became aware of a wish or urge to act really is the same as the time at which they first felt a wish or urge to act. Rather, given the instructions that they must in fact be supposed to be following (for otherwise we could not interpret the results they provide as indicative of anything relevant), participants have first to feel the wish or desire and then to decide to note the position of the dot at the time they first felt it, which process would itself surely take some time and, indeed, presumably be preceded by the having of another readiness potential accompanying (preceding?) the feeling of a wish to follow the instructions the experimenter has given them, unless, that is, this decision is one that the participants manage to make without such. But then are readiness potentials not necessary for every decision after all?

While worries of the sort sketched in the previous paragraph are cogent ones to have about many Libet-style experiments, I shall not pursue them further here for some of them have been made moot by post-Libet developments. In the past 30 years, scientists have attached increasingly sophisticated machines to scalps and, on the basis of what they have been able to read off from them, predicted with a degree of accuracy that is markedly better than they would have got by chance when the subjects of their experiments will perform whatever simple task they have been assigned to do. Sometimes these scientists are able to get their predictions right in way that is markedly better than chance from their observations of brain-states which occur *seven or so seconds* in advance of the time that their subjects first suggest they were aware of being about to decide to perform the task. Let us then imagine, for the sake of argument, that scientists discover a certain brain-state always and only occurs several seconds prior to the desire or wish to perform the set task, which desire or wish is then universally acted upon. This, it should be underscored, is *not* something scientists have discovered; we are only *imagining* for the purposes of argument that they have. But it is worth while considering what, if anything, would follow from it for the defensibility of our views concerning free will were it to be discovered, for if the answer is 'nothing', then we may safely infer that nothing follows from the more sketchy and minimal correlations that have in fact been discovered.

Let us suppose then that scientists perform a series of experiments that enable them to locate a brain-state which uncontroversially occurs several seconds before the first conscious awareness of an urge or wish to perform the task of pushing a button, an urge or wish which is then always acted upon. When the urge or wish to push the button is going to be formed but *not* acted upon, when one is going to exercise one's power of 'veto', another subtly different brain-state is observed to arise. These experiments are repeated many times and give rise to the same results. Were all this to happen, one might suggest that this particular Libet-style experiment would imply that unconscious processes in the brain were the true determiners of the participants' apparent decisions to push the button whenever they did push it and hence that this apparent-decision-making was not in fact what initiated their performing the task then rather than at any other time or not at all. One might say that if one's brain is already in a state such that it will inevitably cause one's finger to depress a button at a particular time several seconds prior to one's forming any conscious urge or wish to depress the button at that time, then one's forming that urge or wish thereafter and one's subsequently apparently choosing not to veto it on this particular occasion is not what actually initiates the performing of the task. This would seem to be the right interpretation. And from it one would have to infer that participants' feeling that they were able to do otherwise than push the button at the moment they actually went ahead and pushed it, their feeling that they were able to do otherwise everything else in the universe prior to that moment remaining the same, was illusory. And this would, it *prima facie* seems, be a remarkable discovery, one that would, it *prima facie* seems, undercut our common-sense belief in Indeterminism and thus free will. But first appearances can be deceptive. Such a discovery would not *ultima facie* be that remarkable, not a discovery the like of which we have yet to encounter; and it would not be a discovery that would have implications for Indeterminism and free will.

When one is being taught to drive, one is sometimes put into a car with dual controls, that is to say one in which the instructor sitting in the passenger seat has his or her own steering wheel and other controls, the input from which would trump that from one's own controls were the instructor to activate and operate it. If driving such a car, it would obviously be quite possible for the instructor to switch on his or her controls surreptitiously and take over the driving of the car. Were the road to bend to the left, then both the instructor and oneself (assuming one's already mastered the essentials of driving) would naturally turn the two steering wheels accordingly and the car would turn to the left; one would assume it had done so because of what one had done with one's own wheel and thus that, had one not turned one's wheel, the car would have not turned as it did, but in fact one would be in error; the instructor would have been in control of the movement of the car and one's own controls would have been entirely disconnected from the process determining where it then moved. Several minutes might elapse with the instructor really driving the car and oneself just believing that one was doing so before one realized what was happening, before one realized that the car was not actually being driven by oneself any more. Similarly then, were an experiment of the sort just sketched to be conducted, one might expect the participants at first not to believe that what they would at first continue to call 'their' decision to push the button at whatever time they did end up pushing it was in fact determined (or at least 'effectively determined') by unconscious factors which preceded their apparent experience of choice by several seconds. It would, after all, still have felt to them that they were in control and could have done otherwise right up until the last moment. However, by exposing them to the evidence, we could reasonably expect them to overcome this disbelief, just as we might overcome our disbelief in the hypothesis that we had not been in control of a car for the last several miles of its journey were our driving instructor to tell us that for the last few miles he or she had been operating the dual controls. Such an experiment then, were it to be conducted, would show that our feeling of apparent 'could-have-done-otherwise' choice is not infallible when it comes to judging of its presence. For in the circumstances imagined, the participants would have the feeling of apparent choice over whether or not to push the button when they did in fact push it (which we have observed relies on their supposing that they could do other than push it everything else in the physical universe up to the moment of choice remaining the same) when in fact they were already determined by preceding unconscious states to push the button then. But it would be rash in the extreme to conclude from this that the feeling is always illusory. Sitting in a car with dual controls and one's driving instructor surreptitiously switching them on and operating them can prove to one that one's feeling of being in control of the movement of a car can be sometimes illusory, but we hardly suppose from this that this feeling is *always* illusory, that nobody ever drives their own cars.

In his original experiments, Libet asked his participants to allow the urge or wish to push the button to 'appear on its own at any time without any pre-planning or concentration on when to act' and of course the urge in question was one the acting on which was known to the participants to be of no moral import; it would result in pushing a button which they believed to be connected only to a timer which would record the moment at which it was pressed. Nobody supposes that whimsical actions, the fruits of processes which one seeks to allow to arise spontaneously from one's unconscious and which pertain to matters of known moral indifference, are paradigms of the sort of free choices for which we are morally assessable. Indeed, they lie at the opposite end of the spectrum from such paradigms. So, were it to be shown that one could – by allowing an urge or wish pertaining to a matter of known moral indifference to arise spontaneously from one's unconscious – get oneself to have the appearance of free choice while in fact it was absent, that would have no direct bearing at all on whether when one forms and decides to act on a wish or desire after conscious deliberation and perform an action which has, one supposes, moral significance, the feeling that one could have done otherwise is there similarly illusory. We are already familiar with stage magicians 'forcing' cards onto people, that is utilizing various powers of suggestion to ensure that people apparently freely 'choose' the card that the magician wishes them to choose. These tricks can be very impressive, to none more so than the people on whom they are performed. They show that we are sometimes not as free as we feel ourselves at those times to be. But they do not show that we are never – at any other times – as free as we ordinarily suppose ourselves to be. They raise in our minds the possibility that we are not as free in everyday life as we ordinarily suppose ourselves to be, but, I suggest, they do not raise the *probability* of our being not as free in everyday life as we ordinarily suppose ourselves to be precisely because the circumstances in which we observe we are able to generate the *prima facie* appearance of freedom in a situation in which we *ultima facie* wish to say it was absent are so far removed from the circumstances of everyday life; from paradigmatic examples of free choice, and from examples of morally significant choice.

As well as the indeterminist not being committed to the proposition that every apparently free choice is really a free choice, we must remember that, as stated at the start of this chapter, the indeterminist is not committed to saying of really free choices that they cannot be predicted by us with a greater probability of our getting these predictions right than chance alone would secure for us. On the contrary, he or she may allow that human behaviour may be highly predictable, and – no doubt – in conditions artfully constructed for the very purpose of making it predictable over choices that maximally lend themselves to accurate prediction, human behaviour will prove to be very predictable indeed. So, even if the results of new generations of Libet-style experiments confirm and advance the sorts of correlations that might initially seem most worrying for the claim that we have free will of the sort we ordinarily suppose, on reflection they can be seen to be irrelevant to it.

We have suggested then that experiments of the Libet sort cannot do anything to undermine Indeterminism. But this is not to say that there could not even in principle be experiences which would go beyond what they achieve and raise in our minds not merely the possibility that our experience of choice is generally illusory but raise the *probability* that our experience of choice is generally illusory.

* * *

Consider the following: At a fun fair you visit the tent of the fortune teller. After having crossed her palm with silver, she informs you that, despite this, she is not about to speak to you about your future. Somewhat chagrined, you are about to ask for your money back when she pulls out from under her table a large book with your name inscribed upon it; today's date; a hyphen; and then a date five years hence. She tells you that, being such a good fortune teller, she knew in advance of your arrival at her tent that you would find this book far more intriguing than any predictions she might make orally. She has written down in this book, so she tells you, all the significant things that will happen to you and all the significant decisions that you will make over the next five years; it is a 'complete and unabridged diary of your future', she says. As you reach to open it, she snatches it back, telling you that she will not permit you to read it before the next five years have elapsed, but – if you like – she will go with you to a solicitor of your choice and make arrangements for the book to be kept locked in his or her safe until the five years are up, after which you may read it and retrospectively test the accuracy of her predictions. You agree to this plan; the book is locked away in the safe of a trusted solicitor; and the next five years of your life unfold. At the end of the five years, you return to the solicitor who assures you that nobody has touched the book in the meantime; the safe is unlocked; and you read in the book a complete history of the five years that have just elapsed. To your astonishment, it is correct in every detail, including every detail of the various internal struggles you went through prior to reaching the various significant decisions that you have made over the last five years.

Were this to happen, it would be evidence that the appearance of free will that you had over those five years was generally illusory (over those five years). It would not be, as a Libet-style experiment turning out a particular result would be, evidence that in certain carefully controlled and unusual situations skilled scientists can generate an illusory appearance of free will; it would be evidence that in everyday circumstances – for such, I am assuming, will be what made up the majority of your last five years – reality is such as to generate an illusory appearance of free will. It would be evidence of this because an explanation of the fortune teller's ability to predict your future (an ability of which we may take it the book provides ample evidence) would be that your future was determined by factors which preceded your moments of apparent choice during that five-year spell, indeed preceded your going into her tent at the funfair five years earlier. This would be an obvious explanation of what you had just experienced and as such your experience would naturally lead you to consider it favourably. But, it must be admitted, it is not the only possible explanation of your experience, so your experience would not be conclusive evidence in favour of Determinism's being true.

An alternative explanation of the experiences we are imagining you to have had over the five years and then in reading this book would be that the hitherto-trustworthy solicitor and fortune-teller have been in cahoots, putting an initially blank book in the safe; spying on you; and then writing up the details of their investigations in the book after the events. However, insofar as you have no reason to suspect hypotheses such as this to be true until the moment you find yourself reading the book, then reading this book is – despite the availability of these alternative hypotheses – now giving you at least *some reason* to suppose Determinism is true. As we have told the story at the moment, it is plausible to contend that the disjunction of all the other possible explanations of the book's being as it now is which do not suppose Determinism to be true outweighs in probability the explanations of it that have Determinism being true. If so, then in the situation as we have so far described it, you would not be rational, on balance, in believing Determinism to be true on the basis of your experience. But we can adjust details of the situation we are imagining so that this is no longer the case. We can imagine, for example, increasing the improbability of the solicitor's being in cahoots with the fortune teller by positing that other, apparently independent parties, have been continuously observing him, the fortune teller, and the safe over the period in question, and so on. Such adaptations can never eliminate the possibility of alternative non-deterministic explanations of what you observe for, after all, if all else fails, one could simply posit that the book started out entirely blank but had a magical and hitherto un-instanced property of being able to be written on directly 'by one's actions', as it were, over the five years in question. But such hypotheses will look increasingly implausible in themselves and, as they increase in implausibility, so – I take it – eventually Determinism, however implausible it starts off being, will become the most plausible explanation of what you observe in a variation of this thought experiment (at least absent background knowledge of moral responsibility, of which more in a moment).

So, Determinism could be true; we could in principle get reasons for supposing it to be true; but we have yet to come upon any such reasons. Furthermore, we have seen that we cannot reasonably expect to come upon them; even an experience as striking as that provided by a fortune teller of the sort we have most recently imagined would need careful detailing to make reasons in favour of a deterministic interpretation strong enough to overcome the availability of a hoard of alternative non-deterministic explanations of what one had experienced. If this was the end of the story, we might hence conclude that Indeterminism wins by default, on the 'innocent until proven guilty' principle as discussed in the introduction. We may dismiss the case against it while admitting that new evidence could in principle come to light in the future, for example, if we encountered the right sort of fortune teller, which would rationally lead us to demand a 'retrial' – to re-investigate the issue as we might wish to reverse our verdict. But we should not finish our consideration of the arguments for and against Indeterminism without considering the resources which are provided to us by the discoveries of the previous chapter, for they seem to offer us the possibility not merely of showing that Indeterminism has not yet been proved guilty, but that we may prove it innocent.

* * *

We established in the previous chapter that if Determinism were true, then we could not be morally responsible for any of our choices, the thesis we have been calling Incompatibilism. But, given Incompatibilism, if we have reason to believe we are morally responsible for at least some of our choices, then we thereby have reason to believe that Determinism is not true. And surely we do have reason to believe we are morally responsible for at least some of our choices and thus surely we do have reasons to believe Determinism false and thus Indeterminism true. This is a simple argument; we believe its premises; it is valid; and it gives us reason to suppose that Indeterminism is true. What could be said against it?

We saw in Chapter Two that we do in fact regard ourselves as morally responsible for a certain subset of our actions, those which we perform while willing them under the morally salient description. But that we do in fact do this is arguably no reason to suppose that we are right when we do it. That being so, we may say that even if we add to Incompatibilism – which, post-Chapter Two, is something we do have reason to suppose we are right in assuming – the premise that we are sometimes morally responsible, we do not thereby generate an argument which gives us a reason to suppose we are right in believing in Indeterminism. Of course if one adds the premise p to the premise 'If p, then q', one has a valid argument for q, but that valid argument is not giving one a reason to believe that q is true unless one has a reason to believe that p is true as well as to believe that 'If p, then q' is true. So, before we can think of this argument as giving us a reason to believe Determinism is true, we must return to consider our assumption that we are morally responsible for some of our actions. Can it be justified?

As we have seen, when we look to justify a belief of ours, we must look to find something that (a) is more obviously correct than it is, and that (b) lends some sort of evidential or logical support to the belief we are trying to justify. That this is the inescapable nature of justification presents problems for our belief that we are sometimes morally responsible for our actions, for that belief is so fundamental to our everyday lives that there does not seem to be anything that would be more obviously correct and more fundamental than it in the way that it would need to be were it to be able to provide evidential or logical support. We have reached, one might say, the bedrock. We can of course easily find examples of particular applications of the general thought, and these will strike us as more vivid in virtue of their particularity than the general thought. I might tell you – in graphic and bloody detail – the story of a cold-blooded mobster, who tortured several of his victims to death for his amusement. With enough details ladled on top, you would then have no hesitation in saying of the mobster that he should be locked up for life, perhaps even executed, and so on. You would regard it as absurd were someone to accept that this particular mobster had behaved in the way I had described yet suggest, by contrast, that he should be regarded as no more morally culpable than a virus which just so happened to produce symptoms which were equally painful to its victims and also to produce very similar social effects. The mobster is obviously morally responsible; the virus, which might be equally undesirable in the effects it produces, is obviously not morally responsible. By the use of such examples I could no doubt drive home the fact that we all believe that sometimes we are morally responsible for our actions.[10]

Despite all this, the person who is canvassing the opinion that we are mistaken in our assumption that we are sometimes morally responsible for our actions is not going to be put off by examples of cases where we cannot resist holding people morally responsible. He or she may concede that we ordinarily *suppose* of paradigmatic examples of evil actions, such as those of the mobster, that the criminals in question should be punished, because we ordinarily suppose that they are morally responsible, but that general supposition may well be false; if it is, then of course all its particular manifestations in our everyday moral lives are false too. Multiplying examples of cases where we are strongly drawn to make moral judgements does nothing to establish that any of these judgements are ever right. The objector may say that we may compare the situation that faces us here with other beliefs that might well once have been widespread, but that we now realize to have been fundamentally confused, for example the belief that there are witches.

One could imagine a culture arising in a certain village in the colonies in the seventeenth century, a culture wherein it was universally accepted as an assumption of everyday life that some people were witches; they habitually used magical spells and potions in order to try to bring bad fortune on upright and God-fearing folk. One day someone arises in the midst of this culture and tells the villagers that there are no witches. This is not the suggestion that, as it happens, at the moment there are no witches in the community, though of course there have been some in the past and may yet be more in the future. It is not the suggestion that the folk have come upon before, that all of those accused in the latest witch-hunt are in fact innocent. The villagers are familiar with people who have maintained such things. And they have constructed mechanisms which have enabled them to settle these disputes to their general satisfaction; for example, they tie putative witches up and throw them into the village pond; if they sink, they are innocent; if they float, they are guilty. Sometimes they even manage to extract an innocent person from the pond before she drowns, in which case, all the better. But the suggestion that is now before the villagers for the first time is that that nobody, not even those who float when put to this test, has been, is, or ever will be a witch. Witches don't actually exist at all; they never have; they never will do. The villagers will naturally be perplexed by such a radical view the first time they hear it. As it has always seemed so obvious to them that some people are witches – even if not at present, then in the past and potentially in the future – they will not know how to deal with the outrageous suggestion that in fact none ever are. They will perhaps fall back on what they take to be paradigm examples of witches. 'That wizened old lady who cackled a lot; had a black cauldron into which she was spotted dropping spiders, toads, and so on while pronouncing incantations; and who in fact herself said, "Yes, I am a witch; I plead guilty as charged" when arrested, surely *she* was a witch', they will say. But the person pressing the claim that there are no witches is surely not going to be put off by this. Even if this poor unfortunate of whom they now speak believed of herself that she was a witch, she herself was wrong.

On the 'innocent until proven guilty' principle (not perhaps that this principle is one to which we can realistically expect the villagers in our story will warm), given where they are starting from, the villagers are in fact *reasonable* in persisting in their belief that there are witches unless or until they are presented with reasons for abandoning that belief. Someone's merely telling them that it is false is not that person's articulating a reason to suppose it is false, so they are in fact reasonable in continuing on as they have done in the past unless other reasons to suppose that there are no witches lie to hand. In fact in the case of witchcraft we, of course, suppose that they must already be in possession of these reasons prior to the interventions of the first sceptic, which is why our sympathies are on the side of the sceptic from the start in this case. Be that as it may, the sceptic can no doubt – if the villagers are open-minded enough not to start treating her as a witch – draw these reasons to their attention for the villagers do, we suppose, have reasons to abandon their belief in witchcraft and they are not, we suppose, so cognitively dysfunctional that they will not be able to recognize them. Even if the villagers do not realize that they are reasons, then that is so much the worse for the villagers (and especially those accused of witchcraft); we realize that they are reasons and thus that the villagers are unreasonable in continuing on in their belief in witchcraft. That belief may be innocent until proven guilty, but it has in fact been proven guilty by the facts, which is why we have in fact abandoned it and, we suppose, the villagers should do likewise and are probably capable of doing likewise. The analogous point cannot be made apropos of our abandoning our belief in moral responsibility. We who believe in it are obviously not going to take our belief in it as analogous to the belief in witches that was prevalent in the society we have just imagined; we will rather take it as analogous to our belief in something that we take ourselves to have no good reason to reject the existence of, for example, our belief that at least some people are accountants. So we will reject the would-be analogy outright. We reach an impasse.

All of that being so, we must say that it is in fact impossible for us to justify the premise that we really are morally responsible for at least some of our choices or indeed undermine it. This, it must be underscored, is not to say that we have any reason to suppose that this premise is false or indeed true, just to say that because of its fundamental nature we cannot justify either accepting or rejecting it by reference to anything more fundamental than itself. If we grant that it is true, we can use it in conjunction with Incompatibilism to argue for the falsity of Determinism. But the determinist, of course, may simply deny that it is true. We will say that believing that people are sometimes morally responsible is analogous to believing that some of them are accountants; he or she will say that is it analogous to believing that some of them are witches. And we'll have to leave it there.

CONCLUSION

In this chapter we have looked at the debate between Indeterminism and Determinism. We have seen that it is in principle impossible to prove either correct from a scientific basis: hidden variable interpretations of phenomena that indeterminists are happy to treat as chance may always be advanced by the determinist and indeterministic interpretations may in principle always be advanced to explain phenomena that determinists would be happy to treat as necessitating causes. Despite this, science could in principle, in conjunction with our preference for simplicity, provide one with reasons to favour one or the other of Indeterminism and Determinism. At the moment it gives us reason to favour Indeterminism. As brought out in our consideration of Libet-style experiments, it will be impossible to construct an experiment which shows that our appearance of being able to choose something other than what we actually do is generally illusory, rather than illusory in very artificially constructed and controlled conditions, for respectable scientific experiments of their essence require artificially constructed and controlled conditions. Nevertheless, experience – such as that we imagined with a fortune teller – could in principle give one reasons to suppose that this appearance was generally illusory. Pending such experiences however, we should operate on the 'innocent until proven guilty' principle and continue to believe in Indeterminism.

After making these points, we looked at what would indeed be a valid argument in favour of Indeterminism, building on our work in the previous chapter. If it is the case that we are morally responsible, as we do of course suppose we are in everyday life, and it is the case that if we are morally responsible then Indeterminism must be true, as we saw we had reason to believe in the last chapter, then it must be the case that Indeterminism is true. However one premise which we need reasons to suppose is true (if we are to have reasons to believe this argument is not just valid but sound) is the premise that we are in fact morally responsible. We do indeed assume this in everyday life, but what reason is there to suppose this assumption true? We saw that the assumption is so fundamental to our everyday reasoning that we cannot in fact find independent reasons to suppose it true. But nor can we find reasons to suppose it false. So this argument, despite its validity, is destined to remain of questionable soundness and thus not be of use to us in proving Indeterminism innocent to anyone who's already decided that it's guilty. The determinist convinced of Incompatibilism will fairly accuse anyone advancing it of begging the question against him or her. So be it. A point which has been made before is that one has to start from wherever one is and we in fact start by believing true the premise of moral responsibility that, Compatibilism being shown to be untenable in the previous chapter, Determinism may now be seen to require us to reject. That being so, our judgement must be that the argument is sound as well as valid.

So where does all this leave us? We have a view, Indeterminism, to which we are intuitively drawn and which cannot be disproved; it is also the view that currently happens to be favoured by scientists. But the intuitive support for the view is based on a feeling of being able to choose otherwise in certain situations and this is a feeling which scientists have been able to show can be present even when, on reflection, we do not believe that the ability to choose otherwise was really present. As observed, we did not need in fact to wait for scientists to show us this via Libet-style experiments; stage magicians have been 'forcing' cards and the like on people since time immemorial. This does not by any means prove that the feeling is always illusory, but it raises the possibility that it might be in our mind. We cannot find any more basic truth or principle on which we can construct an argument for Indeterminism that we may reasonably expect will be accepted as both valid and sound by all parties to this debate, for even the valid one that proceeds via Incompatibilism from our moral responsibility to Indeterminism will not strike as sound those determinists who are convinced of Incompatibilism (as we argued in the previous chapter they all should be). Of course not, given that they are determinists, they will take it as a *reductio* of our being morally responsible. If we had in Indeterminism a view that could not be more ultimately justified, we might yet justifiably continue to believe in it nonetheless, for all our most fundamental beliefs will – their being our most fundamental beliefs – have this feature and thus we might appropriately deploy the 'innocent until proven guilty' principle and rest content with that. As it is, we do have available to us an argument in favour of its innocence that must strike us as both valid and sound, the argument that, given Incompatibilism and our moral responsibility, Indeterminism must be right. So, while this of course assumes the soundness of the argument of the previous chapter as well as of our intuition that we are sometimes morally responsible, Indeterminism emerges vindicated at the end of this chapter as did Incompatibilism at the end of Chapter Three.

CHAPTER FIVE

ULTIMATE AUTHORSHIP

INTRODUCTION

We have now looked in some detail at all but one of the ideas which we listed in the second chapter as constitutive of Libertarianism, the view which we claimed was the common-sense view of the existence and nature of free will. We have looked in most detail in the last two chapters at Incompatibilism and Indeterminism. Free will of the sort necessary for moral responsibility in the robust sense – the sense that justifies genuine punishment, in addition to the sorts of interventions that might be justified solely on consequentialist grounds – requires our pre-reflective belief in Indeterminism to be right. But this requirement in itself need be no cause for concern. Not only do we have no reason to suppose that Indeterminism is wrong, we have at least some reason to suppose that it is right, especially if we allow ourselves to use the argument which takes us to it from our supposition that we are morally responsible (via that supposition's incompatibility with Determinism), which argument we cannot resist thinking sound. However, as we have already observed on several occasions, the mere falsity of Determinism, while necessary for us being free is not by itself sufficient.

If we are drawn to Indeterminism, we shall probably regard the breaking of a rotten branch in the wind as something indeterministic; it could have happened in a different manner; at a different time; or not at all. But, even if we do think of it this way, we do not hold the branch morally responsible if, by breaking as and when it did, it fell on and damaged our car, which we happened to have parked temporarily beneath it. Similarly, that a particular movement of a person's body not be determined in all its details by preceding

physical events that stretch back in time to those which are uncontroversially now beyond his or her control and to facts that are always
beyond his or her control (the Big Bang and the laws of nature) is
not sufficient for that movement to be an action which he or she
is performing using his or her body, rather than merely an event
which his or her body is undergoing. If we are drawn to Indeterminism, we shall probably regard the movements that characteristically accompany certain medical conditions, palsies and the like, as
brought about by factors which include a certain amount of randomness and thus which are undetermined in at least some of their details.
But we hardly regard a person's arm flying up as a result of a nervous
disorder of this sort as that person's raising his or her arm. We do not
do so even if – coincidentally – by flying up as it does it happens to
fulfil an occurring intention of the agent in question; or even if it
happens to be caused by that occurring intention.[1]

What is necessary for a bodily movement to be an action is not
that it be uncaused, but rather that it be caused, but caused by the
agent in question – rather than solely by things external to him
or her.[2] Of course, things outside the agent's control may be – and
usually are – partial causes of what the agent ends up doing, for, if
nothing else, they causally explain why he or she faces the choices
that he or she does, his or her capacities – what futures are physically
possible for him or her and what are not. But, for the resulting choice
to be a genuine choice, it has to be the case that if anything necessitates the choice being made the way it is actually made, then it is the
agent and nothing outside of the agent that necessitates it being made
the way it is actually made. In any case, for a genuinely free choice,
the agent himself or herself must give to the world some causal
'oomph', as we might put it. This is the 'ultimate authorship' condition for free action, which will form the focus of our attention for
this chapter.[3]

* * *

It is important to start by taking some time to underscore the fact of
which we have just made mention in passing: ultimate authorship
does *not* require that nothing other than the agent himself or herself
play any causal role whatsoever in his or her coming to do whatever
it is he or she does. On the contrary, such things will always play a
causal role and their doing so need not undermine to any extent the

freedom of the action that the agent eventually performs or its status as an action. Most obviously and immediately, events in the agent's mental life will be partial causes of his or her coming to do whatever it is he or she does come to do. But extra-mental events may also – a moment's reflection reveals – be partial causes; why the agent is wherever he or she is and facing whatever choices he or she now faces will be due in part to causes beyond the agent's mental life and many of these causes will be beyond his or her control in even the loosest sense of 'control'. An example for all agents reading this would be the fact that he or she is on the surface of the Earth, rather than some other planet. It would be folly to insist that to be the ultimate author of one's actions one must be 'free' of any causal influence either from one's interior mental life or from anything originating outside of oneself. Rather, if we are to be the ultimate authors of our actions, then ultimate authorship must be compatible with causal influences of this sort and, as we shall see, it is.[4]

To see all this in more detail, let us return to consider the example of my choosing whether to declare a cash-in-hand payment on my tax return, as I know I ought to do, or whether to lie by omission, so as to be able to spend the money that I would otherwise have paid in tax on some frippery for myself.

It will be recalled that we are to imagine me deliberating for the 20 minutes or so that it takes me to walk home, prior to the moment that I need to fill in the form. In this time I reflect on the reasons I have in favour of each alternative: tell the truth and I will end up doing what I know I ought to do; lie and I'll get to buy myself some pleasant frippery. Let us suppose that I take the full 20 minutes to reach my final decision, but that, in the end, the decision is to tell the truth on the form. I get home; give it one last moment's consideration; and then clearly declare the cash-in-hand payment; pop the form in an envelope; and post it off. Now someone asks for as complete a causal explanation as can be provided of my doing this. What may the person who believes that in this circumstance I am the ultimate author of my action in writing down the truth say in response to this request? Certainly not that nothing other than myself at the moment of making my choice causally influenced my choice.

One factor which needs to be mentioned in answering the question is the reflections that I engaged in during the 20-minute period of walking home that led up to my moment of choice. These reflections are events in my mental life and are, we would ordinarily suppose, not causally irrelevant to my ending up doing what it is I end up doing. Of course they *might* be causally irrelevant; I might have ended up writing the truth as a result of a whim – entirely forgetting the reasons I had in favour of telling the truth as I had reflected on them during my walk home. But that sort of thing is unusual. So, let us imagine that it is not the case here. Let us instead imagine that the fact is that I forced myself while walking home to linger for several minutes in my imagination on how guilty I would feel were I to lie and realized by doing so that this would be very guilty indeed and that the fact that I did so linger and so realize is a cause of my ending up telling the truth rather than lying. As I finally decide, I recall these reasons rather than forget them and act on whim. Assuming that I live in an indeterministic world and that the particular situation I am in is as we are supposing it is – one of genuine choice right up until I write on the form as I do – then there will have remained, at the end of these 20 minutes, a non-zero physical (not just epistemic) probability that I would lie nevertheless, despite my having lingered in my imagination on how guilty I would feel were I to do so. That being so, the events in my mental life which constituted this reflection did not causally necessitate that I tell the truth. But they did causally incline me to do so; my engaging in this sort of reflection raised the probability that I would tell the truth. Indeed, I may well have engaged in this sort of reflection precisely because I thought that doing so would raise the probability of my telling the truth, deliberately steeling myself during the walk home against later temptation by focusing at length on how bad I would feel were I to give in to it. In that case, the reflection would itself be an act I performed, rather than merely an event that I underwent. And it would in itself be morally assessable, in this case, presumably, as praiseworthy: trying to get myself into a state so that later, when I spend merely a moment or two filling in the form, I do not find myself as tempted to lie as I would otherwise have been is in itself to be applauded as a certain type of self-forming action. On the other hand, if the reflections had popped up unbidden by me and continued on to the extent that they did and in the manner that they did without any direction by myself, then they would be mere events that I was undergoing and as such I would not be morally assessable for them.[5] But, in either case, if we suppose that the situation after I had engaged in this sort of reflection remained one of choice – rather than becoming through my so reflecting one where I was then determined to act as I did (randomness notwithstanding), in the manner of Martin Luther as we imagined him earlier – then we must suppose that there was, right up until the time I made my final decision, a non-zero probability that I would lie (and of course a non-zero probability that I would tell the truth). The probability that I would lie might have been shrunk from its starting value by my reflecting in this way, indeed we suppose that is has been (we are not, after all, considering a case where I then bypassed the results of my reflections and acted on a whim). But we suppose – assuming as we are doing that the situation remained one of genuine choice – that it was not shrunk to zero. The general point then is that events in our mental lives during periods of reflection on decisions yet to be taken raise the physical probabilities of some outcomes and lower the physical probabilities of others; they causally incline us to act in some ways and disincline us from acting in others. They incline; they do not *always* fully *necessitate* what we end up doing.[6]

We must also consider what the probabilities of the various outcomes were even prior to my 20 minutes of conscious reflection on the reasons I had in favour of each. What values these probabilities took at the start of this period of reflection was itself plausibly not something entirely causally independent of things which had occurred prior to then. If we suppose, for example, that I have been brought up in a very 'traditional' fashion, one in which a strong emphasis has been placed on instinctual truthfulness, then, even prior to my starting to reflect on the choice at hand, the probability of my ending up choosing to tell the truth will be much higher than it would have been had I been brought up by people who espoused an 'All taxation is theft' view or a 'Constantly calculate how you can maximize your own personal utility over time when deciding how to act' decision theory. So, as well as factors interior to my mental life over the 20 minutes I took deliberating on what choice to make, factors outside my conscious mental life and prior to then – my upbringing and resultant unthinking assumptions and character traits – were causing me to act as I did. But again, insofar as we suppose the situation remained one of genuine choice for me, we suppose again that these things inclined me to tell the truth but did not necessitate it. We may say then that, as well as events in my mental life being used to explain (to some extent) why I ended up telling the truth, these other inclining causes may be used to explain (to some extent) why I ended up telling the truth. It is to some extent (but only some extent) 'down to them' that I ended up both thinking as I did during the 20 minutes in question and then doing what I did at the end of it.

In summary, we should say that my background, my character, and events in my mental life during the 20-minute period in which I was reflecting on how to fill in the form increased the physical probability of my filling it in as I did (relative to how it would have stood had I had a different background, a different character, or spent those 20 minutes differently). They then should be adverted to in giving as full an explanation as can be given of why it is that I ended up telling the truth. It is not that these things were causally irrelevant to the final outcome (though several of them could have been; whimsical actions do occur). But we should remember when mentioning them that the fact that they had a causal influence on me does not imply that they causally necessitated me; they didn't; they left it open to me to do what I did do or to do something else (assuming – as we are assuming – that the situation really was and remained one of genuine choice right up until the moment I finally chose to write down the truth).

* * *

As a slight aside, we may observe that we see the same sort of probabilistic explanation playing a role in our explaining happenings in other areas that we regard as indeterministic. For example, I take it that we would suppose of an ordinary die that which number ended up displayed uppermost once it was thrown could be something undetermined by the manner in which it was thrown on a particular occasion. Let's call such a situation one in which a fair die is fairly thrown. If a die of this sort was so thrown and it failed to show a six, we would then no doubt advert to probabilities were we to be asked for an explanation of why it was that a six had not been thrown. The probability of a six coming up was only one-sixth (in that there was only one way that it could happen out of the six outcomes that could have happened), whereas the probability of a number other than six coming up was five-sixths (in that there were five ways that a number other than six could be shown).[7] So, a six was a less likely outcome than a number other than six and the fact that it was less likely explains to some extent – and indeed the greatest extent that this phenomenon can be explained if we suppose it is indeterministic and the die a fair one fairly thrown – why the die did not end up showing a six. Of course this explanation in terms of the relative probability of various outcomes is not a 'complete explanation' of the event which is constituted by this particular die coming up showing whichever face it has come up showing, in the sense that it doesn't explain why the number that did come up was whatever it was, rather than six; it just explains to the extent that it can be explained why it wasn't six. The explanation of its not being six in terms of its being much more likely not to be six than to be six doesn't explain why it was in fact that, let us say, a four came up rather than a three, for example; it doesn't explain it in a manner that shows how no outcome other than a four coming up was possible. Indeed it does not, but a 'complete explanation' of this sort is precisely what cannot be given if Indeterminism is true and this is an indeterministic system, for it is simply not true that no outcome other than four being thrown was possible; a six being thrown was equally probable and it is just that – as it happens – four was actual. If someone were to insist on asking what explains why four, rather than six, was thrown (not merely why some number other than six was thrown), we would have to say that the answer is 'nothing', nothing explains that. In an indeterministic universe, there are some happenings which are not causally necessitated by preceding events and some which are not even causally inclined and this (four rather than six) is, we suppose, one of them. Rolling a fair die in a fair fashion causally inclines it to come up showing a number other than six with a greater probability than it causally inclines it to come up showing six, but it does not causally incline it to come up showing four with a greater probability than six; nothing, we suppose, causally inclines four to be any more probable than six at the time such a die is so thrown.

The situation with my choice to fill in my tax return truthfully is similar, similar but not exactly the same. It is very important that it is not exactly the same, as assimilation to a 'mere chance' event is one of the things which threaten Libertarianism. Nevertheless, we shall concentrate first on the similarity before turning to the dissimilarities. If someone asks why I told the truth, rather than lied, then the fact that the probability of my telling the truth was high (both before I started reflecting on my walk home and all the more so afterwards) does in part explain why I did so. We will surely not be able to put as exact a figure to these probabilities as we are able to do in the case of the die coming up a number other than six,[8] but we may well say that by the time I finished my walk it was very much greater than 50 per cent likely that I would tell the truth and correspondingly very much less than 50 per cent likely that I would lie. However, in contrast to the case of the die, once we have given the relative probabilities of the various outcomes to whatever degree of specificity we can give them, 'nothing' is not the right answer to the question of whether there is anything else to which we can refer in explaining why the form got filled out truthfully rather than not. In this case we must mention another happening which while not causally necessitated by preceding events was, as we have seen, causally inclined by them, the happening which was me choosing to fill in the form truthfully. When we ask if anything in addition to my character and the events of which we have already made mention contributed to this happening, the correct answer is yes, *I* did.

When considering my having chosen[9] to tell the truth on my tax form, while again there is no 'complete explanation' of my having done so in that there is no explanation which shows how no outcome other than my doing so was possible,[10] in contrast to the die example, the fact that I ended up telling the truth *does* have an explanation that goes beyond its merely being quite probable that I would given my upbringing and the events going on my mind prior to my moment of choice; it goes beyond it to me. Given all the prior conditions, it was open to me to tell the truth and open to me to tell a lie and what in fact made it the case that I told the truth was me; *I* caused the truth to be written. So, for as complete an explanation as one could give of the fact that a truth ends up being written on the form, one would need to mention this as well.

When agents cause something, they are able to do so in virtue of possessing at the time that they cause things certain properties, those properties which ground their powers to cause the things that they do cause. So, for example, when I cause the truth to get written on the form, I do so in part because I have – amongst other things – the property of being able to write legibly on the form at that time. However, this is not the same as accepting that when as an agent I am the cause of something, it is, after all, an event in me that is the cause of it – the event of myself having whatever properties it is that I have at the time that I choose. My having those properties at that time explains why this is indeed *one* of the actions that is open to me. But it does not fully explain why it is the one that I ended up doing. Had I not been able to write legibly, then there would indeed have been no way for me to write the truth on the form. But what explains why I *do* write the truth on the form is not simply the properties I have at the moment I make the choice; what explains it is that I – with the properties I have, undergoing the events that I do at that time – cause my hand to write a truthful claim in the relevant box under the description of it as a truthful claim.

In summary, for as complete an explanation as can be given of my free choice to write down the truth on the form, one would need to mention prior events in my upbringing – they have a role to play in the causal story that leads to this outcome – as well as prior events more generally – one would need to mention how it was that I got into the position where I faced that particular choice in the first place. One would need to mention my character, that I have developed the virtue of truthfulness. And one would need to mention particular events in my mental life during the period in which I was coming to my decision, for example that I reflected at length on the guilt that I'd feel were I to lie. This would, *in toto*, set the background to my choice and would, we are supposing, not leave what choice I made a matter of causal indifference; taken together these factors would strongly incline me towards truthfulness, make the chances of my telling the truth considerably higher than 50/50. In addition – unlike the case with the fair throwing of a fair die – one would need to mention an agent – me and what I did, choose to tell the truth. Someone who pointed out merely that, given my upbringing, character, and mental life, it was quite probable that I'd end up telling the truth would *not* have offered as complete an explanation as could be offered for the happening that was my telling the truth; to offer as complete an explanation as could be offered for that sort of happening (an action in contrast to a mere event), he or she would have to add mention of the agency of the agent – of the fact that I ended up choosing to tell the truth, that I provided my own bit of causal 'oomph' as we might put it.

The mention of this additional thing, me, is needed to make it clear that what was always quite likely to do happen anyway (the truth's getting written down) was in this particular instance neither uncaused by anything other than the events preceding it, nor causally necessitated by something exterior to me. This, I am suggesting, is what makes the difference between its being my action rather than an event I underwent or the action of someone else. If there had been no cause in addition to those that inclined me to write the truth, so that the fact that 'I' ended up writing the truth was similar to the fact that the branch ended up breaking when it did or a number other than six ended up being thrown, then 'my' writing the truth would not have been genuinely an action that I performed, rather than merely an event that I underwent; *I* would not have written the truth; the truth would just have ended up being written, and written by 'me' only in the attenuated sense that its getting onto the page involved a causal chain that went through my body and mind. (Thus we use scare quotation marks around 'me', 'I', and so on in such cases.) Had that been the case, then of course no moral credit would have ended up coming to me for the truthfulness of the entry on the form (unless a relevant self-forming action had taken place earlier, which self-forming action would itself, I suggest, have had to have fitted this model of agency). Ultimate authorship then is a necessary condition for moral responsibility, because without it our bodily movements cease to be our actions.

Harder to imagine than 'my' telling the truth's being uncaused in this fashion is a case where something external to me causally necessitated that 'I' tell the truth. But we can construct such a case by imagining a scenario where someone implants in my brain a chip of a sort similar to that which we have previously imagined such that he or she could control without possibility of error (later randomness notwithstanding) what movements my body made, right down to the details of how 'I' moved a pen on a form and thus what 'I' ended up writing on a form. Let us in this case imagine the person responsible for the implantation of the chip is a tax official who has been secretly observing me and wishes to ensure simply that my form gets filled out correctly. He operates the chip and thus makes 'me' write down the truth on the form. I meanwhile have decided to write the truth down and, as I observe my body moving in accordance with my will, I take myself to be doing so. But – rather as in the case of the driving student who has not realized that the instructor has taken over the control of the car – I am in fact mistaken when I think of myself as having written down the truth (in anything other than the attenuated sense that it is through my bodily movements that the truth has arrived on the form). I think that I've provided some causal oomph to the world and that it's in part as a result of that that the truth got written, but in actuality either I've failed to provide any oomph or the oomph that I have provided hasn't causally contributed to the truth being written down. In either case, I am of course unaware that it is not in any part as a causal result of my will being as it is that my body moves as it does; my body acts in accordance with my will but it is not following my will. Thus it is not, strictly speaking, me who has been truthful. Such would be a scenario where things would look very similar from both the outside and the inside to the way things look in the example as initially imagined. But in such a scenario, unbeknownst perhaps to everyone but the tax official, the fact that 'I' would have ended up doing that which it was always quite probable I'd end up doing – telling the truth – would not have been down to me; it would have been down to the tax official. Again, I would fail to be morally responsible for the truth being written down on the form through its failing to be an action I was performing.[11]

These two sorts of case – 'uncausedness' by anything but prior events (and thus 'uncausedness' by me [unless I caused these prior events with a self-forming action]) and causal necessitation by an exterior agent or body (and thus 'uncausedness' by me), however, are different from the ordinary and in particular from the situation as we originally imagined it. We suppose in our example that there was indeed something, or rather someone, which made the truth get told. This was someone who was above and beyond the factors which causally inclined me to do what I did and was someone who made that which may well have been likely to happen 'by chance' – that is, on balance of probabilities – anyway happen not as a result of chance. We suppose that that someone was not a tax official exterior to me, but rather that that someone was me. And thus we need to make mention of this supposition, the supposition that I have added some causal oomph, if we are to give as full an explanation as we think we can give of why I told the truth on my form, indeed explain at all why it is that *I* told the truth rather than merely that the truth got told. When I chose to tell the truth, that decision was caused in part by my background, my character and my being aware of the reasons that favoured it (certain events in my mind); these together might have brought it about that 'I' told the truth even had I – the agent – not chosen as I did; they might have inclined me in that direction and I not done anything about it, just passively letting the events unfold that way; or they might have inclined a tax official to operate a chip that then necessitated that 'I' do as I did. But in fact neither of these things happened (we suppose); the totality of events was not, as it happens, the only thing that brought about my writing the truth; I was in fact a part cause of its happening: I superadded to all of this causal commerce at the moment of choice. And thus the writing of the truth was an action that I performed.

So, for me to be the ultimate author of my action of writing the truth down on the form, it is not necessary that nothing outside of myself would have proved causally sufficient for the truth to be written down by 'me' on the form. It could be the case that the inclining causes would have proved sufficient to bring about that the truth be written down in conjunction with the right sort of intervention-prone tax-official (one who would have intervened if he'd detected the right sort of pre-waver brain state). But, were that to have in fact obtained, then the truth's being written down, while it would be an event that would have been brought about by my body, would not have been me bringing about the event, would not have been me acting: it would have been brought about by the events that were these inclining causes and the action of the intervening tax-official. The answer to the question, 'Was anything outside of my control causally sufficient for a particular outcome, the truth's getting written down on the form?' might then be 'Yes' even when we consider a situation in which that same outcome has in fact been brought about by me acting. We should not then seek to identify the nature of ultimate authorship by supposing that where it is present the person's choosing is *necessary* for the particular outcome that it actually brought about; it might not have been necessary.[12] Rather then, the essence of ultimate authorship is that, where it is present, I in fact cause (even if other things would have caused had I not) whatever it is I do, in this case, the truth's getting told on the form. For this to be the case, it has to be true that nothing outside of me causally necessitated that 'I' do whatever it is I do, but not that nothing outside of me causally inclined me to do whatever it is I do, nor even then – as we have just seen – that nothing outside of me would have proved sufficient to make 'me' do whatever it is I do if I hadn't done it myself. It just has to be the case that in fact one of its causes was me. If I add my own causal oomph to the world in this way, the resulting movements of my body and the outcomes that they bring about are actions that I am performing using my body, rather than merely events that my body is undergoing.

Not all actions are free. As we have seen in our discussion of the thought we numbered our 'fifth', if we act in ignorance of the nature of our actions or in rushed circumstances (like the doctor who inadvertently poisons his patient) or if we are coerced (like the bank manager whose family are threatened with death if he does not assist in the robbing of his bank), we are not properly regarded as free in the sense necessary for moral responsibility even though we are not rendered by ignorance, rush or coercion non-agents; these sorts of difficulties do not reduce our bodily movements to mere events. So, for an action to be free in the sense necessary for moral responsibility, not only does it need to satisfy the ultimate authorship condition and thereby get to be an action, but it also needs to satisfy the condition that its agent will what he or she does 'under the morally salient description', as we have put it. The doctor did poison his patient, but when he administered the drug to his patient he did not will the action under this description; we know that for certain as we know he didn't even believe that description to be true of what he was doing. This being the case, we say of his action in poisoning his patient that it was not free. He performed the action that was his poisoning of his patient, but – willing that action under the description 'healing my patient' – he non-freely performed the action. Given that it was also the case that he was not negligent in not knowing of the drug he administered that it was a poison, we do not, therefore, think he is to be negatively morally assessed. The bank manager did know that the description 'robbing my bank' was true of his action in assisting the bank robbers, but he too was not acting freely when he performed the action that was robbing his bank; he was not acting freely as he willed his action under an entirely different (and indeed again morally laudable) description ('doing the least bad thing necessary to save the lives of my family'); thus again he non-freely performed an action and thus is not to be negatively morally assessed for it. But some of our actions *are* free; we do them in full awareness of their moral status and without coercion. And for these we are morally responsible.

* * *

There are various views of the nature of causation and of the sorts of things that can be causes; some maintain that only events may cause; others that only substances may do so.[13] We have allowed that events and agents, a particular type of substance, may do so. On the account we have been developing, one true substitution for 'x' in 'x causes y' is an agent whenever the outcome, y, is genuinely an action rather than merely an event. When it is a free action, the substitution is a well-informed, un-rushed and un-coerced agent. It is profitable to ask at this stage whether agents are the sorts of things that themselves can feature as effects, as *y*s, in the causal relationship. There is one – and only one – context in which it appears that they can. It seems natural to say that parents cause the agents that are their offspring to come into existence and we may perhaps express this fact without its sounding too unnatural as their 'causing agents'. Be that as it may, once an agent is in existence, the only thing that other agents and events can cause with respect to him or her is for him or her to undergo events; once an agent has started existing, he or she cannot in any way himself or herself be caused, be the effect of other substances, actions and events (although of course other agents and events can cause him or her to cause something else, through, for example, inclining him or her towards a particular outcome by presenting him or her with reasons to favour that outcome). That being the case, once we are considering an already-existing agent, we may say of him or her that nothing can cause him or her; he or she cannot himself or herself be the effect of anything preceding him or her. And that being the case, if he or she then goes on to cause some effect, that effect *must* be undetermined by preceding events – because it was caused by him or her and he or she was undetermined by preceding events.[14] It is this then that explains most directly why it is that genuine actions cannot be determined: genuine actions require agent-causal oomph and the event that is the agent providing agent-causal oomph has as its initiator – obviously – a pre-existing agent, a pre-existing agent being the sort of thing that by its nature cannot itself be the effect of any cause.[15]

While, as we have seen, there can be actions that are not free (if they are done in ignorance, a rush or coerced), an alteration being made to the world in such a way that an agent who would otherwise have stood at the start of a chain that led to some causal oomph entering the event-causal chain is bypassed and a similar causal oomph is provided by some other agent or mere events, would not lead to a non-free action being performed by that first agent, but rather to his or her performing no action at all (though the fact that it is a not his or her action might in principle be obscure even to that first now-former agent); thus we have used scare quotation marks around the relevant terms when talking about such cases. Were Determinism true then, we wouldn't really perform any actions at all; all we would actually do is participate in events. But, of course, as we have already seen, we have no reason to suppose Determinism is true; indeed we have just given ourselves one more reason to suppose it is false; agents 'disappear' from a deterministic universe.[16] Were Indeterminism true, we might still not perform any actions; we'd just perhaps mistakenly think that we did when all that was really happening was events causing others in an indeterministic fashion, in which case again agents would 'disappear', although perhaps we'd not realize it. It is in this latter connection that the need to posit agent causation (in addition to indeterministic event causation) may be made most obvious by considering what has come to be known as the problem of 'luck', a problem which – I suggest – needs the non-disappearing agent we have been discussing for its solution.[17] First, let us state the problem; then we can see how the theory of agency that posits ineliminable agent causation can solve it in a way that the theory that posits that agent causation may be reduced to event causation cannot.[18]

If the other beliefs we have about ourselves that we have seen vindicated in this book really are true, then we could – right up until the last moment – choose differently from the way that we actually do in situations of genuine choice, however unlikely our doing so may have been rendered in particular cases by events that preceded that moment, for example in cases where we realized that we had overwhelming reason to choose the way that we did. One way of presenting this fact is by imagining another possible world in which our correlates *do* choose differently from the way that we actually choose. So, in the actual world, 'Timmy One' as we may call him chose to type that last sentence rather than – as it suddenly occurred to him he could do – give up on being a philosopher altogether and live off his wife's earnings for the rest of his life, lazing around the house watching *The Simpsons*. In a near possible world, everything up until the moment at which I continued to write the book remaining the same then (that's plausibly – though not unarguably – what makes it so near), my correlate – 'Timmy Two', we may call him – chose to give up on being a philosopher in order so to dissipate himself. No events were different in these universes prior to these choices being made differently by Timmy One and Timmy Two, so, someone might say, it is just a matter of luck that the book wasn't left incomplete. I then cannot take any credit for its being finished; I cannot take any credit for the actual world containing philosopher Timmy One, rather than wastrel Timmy Two.

I concede that this 'luck objection' would indeed be pressing were there merely to be event causation, because it is indeed true that there would then be nothing other than events to which one might turn to avoid the charge of luck and – in that the events preceding the choice were, *ex hypothesi*, exactly the same in the two worlds – so indeed it would have been true that we just got lucky in getting Timmy One, a feature of the world which is then hardly to my credit.[19] But that is definitively *not* the case on the model we have been suggesting. On this model, there is something in addition to events to which we may turn: me. In the actual world, I chose to try to complete the book, rather than give up and waste my life in front of the television. It is simply not true that this was me 'getting lucky'; it was me 'making my own luck', if you will, in that it was me choosing to finish the book rather than go along with the fleeting desire to give up on all strenuous activity and dissipate myself. But this is not really luck at all. Unlike on the pure event causation model, there is something to which we can apportion the credit for the actual world going the way it does (rather than the way it does in the world in which Timmy Two lives); that thing is me. It's down to me that the actual world ends up being a world which contains philosopher Timmy One rather than wastrel Timmy Two, in which this book gets completed rather than not.[20]

* * *

These then are arguments in favour of the view. We have in addition, I suggest, direct experience of its truth, of our providing the agent-causal oomph of which it speaks.[21] Obviously we most clearly experience the causal oomph we provide *qua* agents in cases in which other causal influences are as absent as they can be. So, in a moment, I'm going to call upon you to imagine with me a case where other causal influences are stripped away as much as possible and, then, while an ineliminable residue of event-causation will remain, we shall, I suggest, be able to see the contribution made in addition by agent causation. I shall suggest that if you reflect on yourself as you were when you last made a choice between options that you regarded as genuinely indifferent and ask yourself what it was that in the end made you do whatever it was you actually ended up doing, you will most probably recall an experience of your giving the world an oomph, not simply that of the event that was your deciding to do whatever it was you did decide following on from the oomph provided by the thought of yours that immediately preceded your decision. Of course, this sort of self-reflection can be deceptive. Perhaps, what you mistake for agent-causal oomph is only event-causal oomph bubbling up from your subconscious. We know that in some cases this sort of self-reflection is certainly deceptive in just this way. If we asked the person who had had a stage magician 'force' a particular card on him or her whether he or she felt himself or herself to have added a particular oomph of his or her own along the way to picking out the card that he or she did pick out, the person would reply that he or she had indeed felt himself or herself to do so. But we know that such a feeling in that case is illusory; there, we know, events entirely prior to the moment the person concerned considers (falsely) to be his or her moment of choice are responsible for the particular card being picked. But we cannot in general take the fact that an experience of a certain sort can – in, note, contrived circumstances – be illusory as a reason to suppose that it is generally illusory. So the mere possibility that this impression of our providing an agent-causal oomph to the event-causal chain is illusory should not make us reflect on it as any less evidence that we do generally add agent-causal oomph where it seems to us that we do.

Allow me to imagine then your facing a choice between what strike you as two indifferent options. You ask for a pint of beer at the bar and are offered a choice by the barman of a straight glass or one with a handle. Nothing in your upbringing inclines you one way or the other; you have no cogent character trait or beliefs; in considering the reasons for and against each option, you quickly realize that you have no reason to choose either way. However, not wishing to be like Buridan's ass and not wishing to throw the decision back onto the barman (as you think that would simply delay matters unnecessarily), you say arbitrarily, 'A straight one, please'. In this case, while background factors will be relevant to explaining why it was that you faced the choice that you did – had you been brought up by members of the temperance movement, you might have been unlikely to have asked for this type of drink in the first place – nothing other than you explains why you asked for a straight glass rather than a handled one. It will of course still have been the case, during the moment or two that you took between being asked the question and answering it as you did, that mental events were going on in you – your thinking 'I don't want to be like Buridan's ass. I don't want any unnecessary delay in getting my beer.' So, even in a situation where an agent chooses between two options that are entirely indifferent to him or her, the sort of causal oomph provided by agent causation will occur alongside that provided by event causation. But we can, I suggest, disentangle them by introspection and we can see in the mental happening that is your deciding to ask for a straight glass (so as to move beyond a Buridan's-ass impasse and get your drink as expeditiously as possible), the oomph provided by the agent entering the event-causal world.[22]

Of course, if we suppose that there is event-causal oomph (as I have been supposing there is), then it is simpler to suppose that there is only event-causal oomph, rather that to suppose that there is, in addition, agent-causal oomph. But – to ascend momentarily to the more abstract heights of the philosophical topic of causation – it is not at all clear that we cannot reduce event causation to substance causation and see agent causation as merely a subspecies of the latter; it is certainly no clearer that this cannot be accomplished than it is that the reduction of agent causation to event causation can be accomplished. And if a reduction of event causation to substance causation could be accomplished, then that would level the playing field once more when it came to simplicity.[23] But even if it could not; even if by positing agent-causal oomph in addition to event-causal oomph one is positing a more complex structure to reality than the person positing that there is merely event-causal oomph, that in itself is only slight reason to suppose to be false the view that I am arguing for, slight when compared to the reason we have to suppose it to be true provided by our everyday experience of free action, which experience would have to be discarded as unreliable were we not really to be the ultimate authors of our actions in the way that it vouchsafes for us.

The temptation to eliminate agent causation from one's account in favour of pure event causation arises in part, I think, because at the moment that the agent causalist, as we may call him or her, suggests the agent adds his or her oomph to the world, we always have the mental event of the agent's choosing to do whatever it is he or she intends to do in his or her action. So, the most immediate effect of the agent cause – where the oomph enters – is an event, the event of the agent's choosing to perform the relevant action under some description or other.[24] So, the agent causalist will have to accede to the person who we may call the 'pure event causalist' that a 'je n'ai pas eu besoin de cette hypothèse'-response will always be tempting and indeed may concede (if he or she is not too hopeful about the prospects of reducing event causation to substance causation) that such a response posits a simpler metaphysic.[25] But temptations should in some cases be resisted. And this, I am suggesting, is one such case.

We may also consider the issue 'negatively', by recalling situations in our lives where this experience was noticeably absent – where 'we' ended up doing something without providing this additional agent-causal oomph.

So, for example, I am at the moment regularly awakened in the middle of the night by my wife, who in turn has been awakened by our newborn child starting to stir in the Moses basket next to the bed. I am sent downstairs to get some milk. I make the decision not to allow myself to wake up more than is minimally necessary for 'me' to get the process right (as I wish to get back to sleep as quickly as possible after the feed). In my bleary state of semi-consciousness, 'I' thus perform the relatively complex task of sterilizing a bottle and teat; putting milk from the fridge into the bottle; warming it; and then returning upstairs. Despite not consciously willing myself to perform any of the sub-tasks that make up the overall task of getting the milk, 'I' end up doing – if all goes well – exactly what I would have done had I splashed cold water in my face; done five minutes calisthenics; had a couple of strong coffees; and then closely read and followed detailed written instructions concerning each sub-task, so as to be fully conscious and alert to all the possibilities and then will each part of the process under a cogent and full description. As it is, I am dimly aware of myself doing each of these sub-tasks under the relevant descriptions; 'Here "I" am sterilizing a bottle', 'Here "I" am getting the milk'. But I do not actively will myself to do them under these descriptions; I am more a spectator to my body's movements than an agent using my body. In the case either of my actively willing each stage of the process under its description or 'my' getting the milk from semi-conscious habit, the same outcome – we may thus suppose – obtains; the milk gets upstairs. But, I am suggesting, in the case of 'my' bringing it upstairs out of semi-conscious habit, 'my' bringing it upstairs is less of an action that I am performing and more of an event I am undergoing. It is not, assuredly, merely an event I am undergoing – as when in complete unconsciousness my body turns itself in bed. For I am not completely unconscious, non-cognizant of the descriptions of my sub-tasks, let alone entirely and in every sense unwilling as I do what I do (I wilfully put myself into this state of semi-consciousness in the first place, it will be recalled). When 'I act' in this way, I am in a sort of 'half-way' house between complete unconsciousness behaving and fully willed, conscious and cognizant acting. But, in this half-way house, I am less in control of my behaviour; the sub-tasks 'I' do, 'I' do without consciously choosing to do them having reflected on their nature and willed them under a description. My only conscious choice and thus full action was really the choice and action to put myself into 'auto pilot' when getting the milk, so that 'I' then performed these other sub-tasks semi-consciously and thus not fully as actions – a particular sort of self-forming action. If I now wake up the next morning and reflect on what it was like during the semi-conscious period – while I was, for example, sterilizing the bottle and teat – it strikes me as not at all unnatural for me to say of myself then that I was not in some sense fully present in my body during it; I was not providing the agent-causal oomph that I would have been providing had I gone about the task by having splashed cold water in my face; done the calisthenics; and so on. At the time I was not conscious of the absence of this agent-causal oomph (of course I wasn't; I wasn't conscious of much), but now, on reflection, I can see that it was absent.[26]

* * *

The person who maintains that we have ultimate authorship of our actions[27] maintains then (unless he or she holds that event causation may be reduced to substance causation) that there are two types of cause: agents and events. Only *agents* can cause *actions*.[28] They characteristically do so because they believe themselves to have reasons and their beliefs that they have reasons are events happening in them, but the causal oomph that they provide transcends that of the events that they undergo, including that of the mental events which are their believing themselves to have whatever reasons they believe themselves to have. So, agents outstrip the causal powers of the parts that make them up; they produce events directly (at the minimum the events of their deciding to do whatever it is they decide to do under the description they decide to will it under), events which are not in fact solely caused (even though in all cases other than entirely whimsical choices they will be partially caused) by preceding events.

This analysis carries with it then certain metaphysical commitments, which we must look at in a little bit more detail before closing this chapter. Specifically, through believing in ultimate authorship, we are committed to believing that there is a certain type of existent – agents – the causal potency of which cannot be reduced to the causal potency of the events that this type of existent undergoes. If we do not think that event causation may be reduced to substance causation (and I have offered no argument that should lead us to think this), we will say then that the *relata* of the causal relationship – the values for x and y in propositions of the general form, 'x causes y' – may be agents, which are a particular type of substance, as well as events, which are not. Whatever its ontological extravagances when considered alongside a view which posits that only events may cause, this is not, it will be observed, to posit some fundamentally new sort of causation (the *relation* in 'x causes y' stays the same whether the x is an event or an agent).[29] All it posits is that agents – not merely events – have causal power. Agents can initiate causal chains, not merely be participants in them through being the things in which events occur; they can, as we have been putting it, add their own causal oomph to the world.[30] (Of course the view commits one to the falsity of certain philosophical analyses of causation, those which would make it a priori that agents cannot cause.)[31]

So, what sort of thing is this substance the causal efficacy of which cannot be reduced to the causal efficacy of the events that it undergoes? A traditional answer has been that it is a non-physical substance, a soul. But, while that may be the right answer, it is not at all clear that the person who believes in agent-causation need believe in souls, as it is quite possible for someone to maintain that physical substances such as ordinary human beings have causal powers which are independent of the powers of the things out of which they are constituted. In short, souls would do the job, but are not needed to do it.[32]

To bring this out, let us imagine a particular pointillist painting. Obviously, at some level of description, the painting consists of a series of patches of colour – as of course do all paintings, but the pointillist style makes the fact more obvious than some. These patches of colour have various causal powers, for example the power to reflect light of certain wavelengths and absorb light of other wavelengths.

The picture that emerges if one stands back and looks at the canvass from a distance has other causal powers; for example, it may have the power to make one realize that it depicts people relaxing on a riverbank. We may say of the higher-level entity, the picture, that it has causal powers which the lower-level entities that constitute it, the patches of colour, do not have. Similarly, we may suggest that humans *qua* agents are higher-level entities with causal powers that exceed the causal powers of the component molecules or what have you which constitute humans *qua* collections of cells. It must be conceded that there is a natural inclination to think that higher-level entities cannot have causal powers that are genuinely independent to any extent of, or in any manner exceed, the causal powers of the lower-level entities that constitute them; they couldn't have been different or indeed have been exercised differently without a change in the causal powers of the lower-level entities or their exercise. That is to say, if the painting has the power to cause the average viewer to realize that it is a depiction of people relaxing on a riverbank, then it only has it in virtue of the patches of colour having the powers to appear the colours that they do to the average viewer and if you had wanted to paint a different painting, there'd have been no way of doing it other than by putting the dots in different places. And this is a natural inclination which the believer in agent causation cannot give in to in the case of agents (at least if he or she is to continue to locate the agent entirely in the natural world, rather than go down the soul route).

According to the agent causalist who locates agents in the natural world, when the particular sort of higher-level substance that is a human agent causes an event, he or she does not have the causal efficacy that he or she does solely in virtue of the casual efficacy of the lower-level entities that constitute him or her at that time; the agent himself or herself can cause something without the efficacy of his or her doing so simply being the efficacy of his or her parts doing whatever it is they are doing. His or her parts doing something may of course be allowed to be necessary for the agent's doing something; it just has to be the case that their doing whatever it is they are doing does not necessitate that the agent does whatever it is he or she does. It just has to be the case that, *qua* substance, he or she adds his or her own bit of causal oomph to that which is being provided by his or her body parts and events. Indeed, when it comes to the higher-level entity that is the human agent, that he or she have brain-cells and that his or her brain-cells be doing certain things is very plausibly causally necessary for him or her to make the choice that he or she does end up making (at least in the ordinary run of things – agents not having their minds 'uploaded' into computers and the like). The believer in agent causation is not committed to denying this (even the believer in souls is not committed to denying this); he or she is just committed to the claim that the causal powers of these lower-level entities do not in themselves exhaust or determine the causal powers of the higher-level entity, the agent, and how they are exercised; thus the space within which the agent *qua* agent makes a difference.

We are now in a position to see that believers in agent causation within the physical world are committed to the actuality and irreducibility of what we may call 'top-down causation'; they are committed to the falsity of the claim that there can be no difference in a higher-level property without a difference in lower-level property through being committed to the claim that the higher-level is not in fact determined by the lower. We all believe in bottom-up causation; that's plausibly the story to tell about how we are caused to see a picture of people relaxing on a riverbank by the light reflected by thousands of tiny dots of colour from a painting. And we can probably be made to believe in top-down causation without much difficulty, at least as a useful story to tell in everyday life. That's the story to tell about how, having enjoyed looking at this particular painting, I end up buying a postcard of it from the gift shop on the way out, and thus why it is that the particles that constitute that particular postcard, rather than those that constitute some other, move with me out of the gallery when I leave. But *irreducible* top-down causation and the claim that there can be a difference in a higher-level property without its being determined by a difference in a lower are much more controversial notions.[33] At this stage we cannot do more than point out that, however controversial they might be, there is nothing incomprehensible about them. Just as agent causation per se does not posit a new relation of causation, just that – in addition to events (unless event causation can be reduced to substance causation) – substances can stand in for xs, the first term in the causal relation, so the person who posits irreducible and non-dependent top-down causation is not positing a new relation of causation either, just that the familiar everyday notion operates from the higher-level down in a way which is not just a story – shorthand for lower-level entities producing epiphenomenal higher-level effects; in fact, there can be changes in higher-level properties which are not determined by changes in lower. The assertion that causation can go in this direction is no less comprehensible than the assertion that it cannot.[34]

If we do wish to use souls as the point of origin for our agent-causal oomph, we may of course insert them at this stage non-problematically instead of irreducible top-down causation of the sort we've been discussing and, from then on, the story will be the same. Positing souls interacting in this way with physical substances and events is, it will be observed, in stark contrast to the sort of interaction posited by the view that we bracketed out earlier. In contrast to that view, souls interacting here would be providing causal oomph that was quite compatible with the laws of nature (of course, the physical universe would have to be acceded not to be a closed system). So, we may say that, roughly, if you think it more likely that there would be souls than that there would be irreducible top-down causation of the sort we've been discussing, you should conclude from the fact that we have free will that we probably have souls.

So, the naturalist (i.e. the person who does not wish to explain our agency by drawing on the operations of souls) must see agents as emergent entities the causal potency of which exceeds and is not determined by the causal potency of the lower-level material out of which they are created and the events they and their parts undergo. It would be an implication of our being these sorts of things that the sciences dealing with higher-level agent-involving phenomena were not reducible to fundamental Physics. A quick inspection of Sociology, Economics, Politics, Anthropology and the like suggests that the subject matter of their discussion is not reducible to that of Biology; in turn, a quick inspection of Biology suggests that it is not reducible to Chemistry; and in turn a quick inspection of Chemistry suggests it is not reducible to Physics. Yet all these reductions would have to be possible if causation always goes bottom-up.[35] Of course, someone who has hopes for total reductionism will be able to point to the fact that these are early days and say that the fact the project of unifying the sciences has not yet been accomplished is not conclusive reason to suppose that it will never be accomplished. And they are of course right when they say this, but while not being conclusive reason, it may yet be some reason to be sceptical of the chances of success for total reductionism. That it has not yet been accomplished is certainly no reason blithely to assume that it can be accomplished, especially given that assuming that it can be accomplished is incompatible with an assumption that is already and obviously known to be right, indeed is something that we know with greater immediacy than anything else, that we are agents.[36]

CONCLUSION

In this chapter we have looked at the nature of ultimate authorship, what it is that constitutes our being the authors of our actions. We have seen that it is quite compatible with our being the authors of our actions that events outside our control causally incline us to do whatever it is we end up doing (or indeed incline us not to do whatever it is we end up doing); incline, but not necessitate. We have also seen that it is not necessary that nothing other than oneself as agent would have proved causally sufficient to produce the particular effect that one produced with one's action had one not produced it oneself. (Randomness or brain-chip operators might have taken over had one not chosen to do a particular thing and resulted in one's body nevertheless moving just as it did one's having chosen to do that thing.) The nature of ultimate authorship then is not that one's choice is the only cause of what one ends up doing, nor that nothing other than oneself would have caused 'one' to do what it is that one ended up doing had one not caused it oneself, but just that in fact one *did* cause it oneself, one provided – as we put it – a bit of causal oomph to the chain of events going on in and around one. This causal oomph – though its most immediate effect is an event (the event of one's choosing to perform whatever action it is one chooses to perform under whatever description one chooses to perform it) – is caused by oneself *qua* agent, *not* caused solely by prior events within oneself. The causal potency of oneself *qua* agent cannot then be reduced to the causal potency of one's parts or of the events that one undergoes or one's parts undergo. To the extent that one is informed, un-rushed and un-coerced in coming to will one's action under whatever description one wills it, one's action is free and one is then morally responsible for it.

Unless event causation may be reduced to substance causation, we may say then that being an agent causalist, as we dubbed the position to which our reflections must inevitably draw us, commits us to a more pluralistic picture of the *relata* of causation – though not the relation itself – than the person we dubbed a 'pure event causalist'.

Even so, this is no great reason to doubt that the view is right, especially when we reflect on situations which, it was argued, provide us with direct experience of our providing agent-causal oomph (most vividly situations where we move ourselves out of Buridan's ass impasses by acts of the will) and situations in which, in retrospect, we note the absence of such oomph (situations where we went through some routine task on 'auto pilot', as we put it).[37] Another reason one might have to doubt that we have this power would be provided by reflecting on the fact that suggesting that we do commits one either to positing that we have souls or to positing that even though we are at one level of description entirely physical and may thus be described in the terms of Physics, at another level we *qua* human agents gain causal powers which are not reducible to or determined by the causal powers of the parts that make us up or the events we or any of our parts undergo. The commitment to irreducible top-down causation of this sort however, as we also saw, is no great reason to doubt the view, though it does entail (as would the soul view) the impossibility of 'unifying the Sciences'. But then again, the claim that all of Anthropology, Economics, Sociology, Politics and so on can be reduced to Physics is a promissory note issued by some philosophers which we have no reason to think the universe will honour, especially no reason when we realize that for it to do so would be for it to show that we were not free agents in the sense that, if this chapter has been right, we are more immediately aware of ourselves being than we are aware of ourselves being – or rather doing – anything.

CHAPTER SIX

CONCLUSION

We started this book by listing five of the common-sense thoughts we have about ourselves as free agents. They were as follows:-

- *Sometimes I could do something other than what I actually do.*
- *Sometimes I'm morally responsible for what I do.*
- *If I couldn't do other than what I actually do, then I wouldn't be morally responsible for what I do.*
- *If I wasn't the ultimate author of my actions, then I wouldn't be morally responsible for them.*
- *To the extent that I did not will an action under the morally salient description, I am not fully morally responsible for it.*

As we started by observing, these thoughts 'lock together' into a theory of free will, which we labelled Libertarianism. Over the course of the book, we've seen that we have only slight reasons to doubt elements of the Libertarian view and more than slight reasons to endorse each element. We may say in conclusion then that common sense has been vindicated. We are in fact as we suppose ourselves to be, the sorts of things that could do other than whatever it is we actually do; that are hence enabled to be morally responsible for whatever it is we do, enabled when what it is that we end up doing we end up doing in part because it was ultimately us who chose to do that thing and we chose to do it under the morally salient description. When we as agents enter into the world of events, starting off causal chains in this way, we are thus the loci of moral responsibility for at least some of their results; it is in doing this that we are exercising our free will.

We may yet escape moral responsibility for some of our actions and their results then, those which are not free. But we cannot escape *all* responsibility: not all our actions are ones made unfree by ignorance of relevant facts, rushed circumstances or coercion. The inescapability of actions in which we are free and thus for which we have moral responsibility is both a blessing and a curse. A mere object, like a rock, cannot help itself; it undergoes events and causes events in other objects and in agents, but none of the things it ends up doing are its actions. If it ends up being beneficial or harmful to some agent for example, then that can only be for it a matter of luck, the results of events it has undergone and chance. It can neither be properly praised nor properly blamed; when it finally goes out of existence, it is owed no reward; it is due no punishment. But we are not mere objects like rocks: we are agents; if we end up being beneficial or harmful to some agent, the fact that we have been so need not be for us just a matter of luck, the results of events we've undergone and chance; it can be up to us; it can be because we've chosen to help or harm that agent; we've willed that outcome under that description and as a result of that willing brought it about. It is not just that we become good people or bad people as a matter of luck then; by our own choices we make ourselves good people or we make ourselves bad. We can thus be properly praised or properly blamed, rewarded or punished.

We have seen that our later choices are certainly causally affected by our earlier choices and by some of those aspects of our background over which we had no choice at all. Some of our earlier choices result in what we have called self-forming actions. In addition, our background can provide self-forming events and of course is itself in part the result of the actions of others – our parents in the earliest periods of our lives and our friends, partners and colleagues later on. Our prior decisions as well as those of others and mere events have put us where we are now, facing the choices that we are facing; and they have *in toto* caused us to have the capacities, beliefs and characters with which we now approach these decisions. As we have seen, our capacities affect what decisions we can make and our beliefs and characters incline us as to how we exercise our capacities. If I spend time reflecting on the value of honesty at leisure, my moral character will be strengthened. If I reflect now on how badly I would feel were I to lie on a tax form, this moral character will be buttressed by those reflections – presuming that the answer is that I would feel bad (if it's that I'd feel just fine about it, my moral character will perhaps be undermined). That I would feel bad in doing what I know I ought not to do is perhaps something for which, in large part, I cannot properly thank myself; it might well be a strand in my character woven deeply into the tapestry of my psychology by my parents long before I ever started to pattern it for myself. If so, it is them whom I should thank for my having a psychology which makes it easier for me to be honest in the present.[1] But it is a psychology I can choose either to nourish or to starve; suitable decisions now will mean that I will be all the more inclined to do what I ought to do in the future and may thus be in themselves praiseworthy. Unsuitable ones will have the contrary effect and may thus be correspondingly blameworthy. Nature and nurture undoubtedly have an influence on us, but we can build on what nature and nurture have given us or we can tear it down.

As well as making ourselves better or worse, we can also assist others in becoming better people or we can corrupt them and make them worse; we can do our bit to provide for them backgrounds within which good actions are easy or backgrounds within which they are difficult. In doing so, some of the credit for their resultant good actions or some of the discredit for their resultant bad actions may correctly be apportioned to us. (Some, but not all, for our contribution can only have inclined them to act as they did; as we have seen, it cannot have necessitated that they act as they did and thus credit or discredit for their actions will always be theirs.) If, for example, we provide an environment for our children in which they know they are loved, they will naturally incline to love others. And if, conversely, we abuse them, they will find it natural to abuse others. If we educate them and allow them to form for their later lives their own selves, then more of their adult actions will be free than if we keep them in ignorance or coerce them, although of course there are limits to how much parents can keep their children in ignorance or coerce them even in principle. It is no less a truth for being a commonplace that, past their earliest years, one cannot live one's children's lives for them (however much one might wish to do so!). What those we affect ultimately end up doing will be up to them, not us; we can affect them but not *effect* them in anything other than the act of bringing them into existence in the first place. But, from the moment our children are first handed to us, we cannot but affect them. The only issue from then on is how we shall affect them, to what extent by the time they first become agents they will be inclined towards the good and thus find it easy to choose it. And what goes for our children also goes for those who are already agents by the time we first interact with them; we cannot but affect them and it is ultimately up to us whether we do so for good or for ill. This then is the nature of our freedom and the responsibility that comes with it.

GLOSSARY

Agent-Causal Account of Action

The view that as agents we add agent-causal oomph to the world and that this is what makes certain of our bodily movements actions we perform, rather than merely events which we undergo.

Compatibilism

The view that free will is compatible with Determinism.

Consequence Argument

The following argument:

1. We cannot change the past.
2. We cannot change the laws of nature.
3. If Determinism is true, the present, in all its details, is the necessary consequence of the past and the laws of nature.
4. If Determinism is true, we cannot change the present in any detail.

Determinism

The view that given the initial or boundary conditions of the universe and the laws of nature, only one history is physically possible.

Fatalism

The view that we cannot affect the future.

Incompatibilism

The view that Compatibilism is false.

Indeterminism

The view that Determinism is false.

Libertarianism

The view of ourselves as agents comprised of five sub-theses (some of which may be held by non-Libertarians):

1. Sometimes I could do something other than what I actually do.
2. Sometimes I'm morally responsible for what I do.
3. If I couldn't do other than what I actually do, then I wouldn't be morally responsible for what I do.
4. If I wasn't the ultimate author of my actions, then I wouldn't be morally responsible for them.
5. To the extent that I did not will an action under the morally salient description, I am not fully morally responsible for it.

('Libertarianism' is sometimes used – though not in this book – as the name for smaller subsets of 1–4. See note 1.)

The Principle of Alternate Possibilities

The view that more than one future is physically possible for us at moments of choice; this view then is incompatible with Determinism.

('The Principle of Alternate Possibilities', a.k.a. 'The Principle of Alternative Possibilities', is sometimes used – though not in this book – as the name for the principle that for genuine moral responsibility there must be more than one future possible for the agent in question. In that case, it is used as a name for the thesis we have labelled Incompatibilism.)

Ultimate Authorship

The requirement that we be the ultimate authors of those bodily movements of ours that are our actions.

NOTES

CHAPTER TWO: OUR EXPERIENCE OF CHOICE

1 Libertarianism is perhaps more usually defined as the conjunction of the thought which we'll call 'Incompatibilism' and the claim that we do have free will. These two in turn quickly entail Indeterminism, as we'll see, and – with some technicalities pushed to one side – they entail that we're sometimes morally responsible for our actions, which in turn entails that we're not in those cases significantly ignorant, rushed or coerced. See glossary.

2 The image of paths seems inescapable and has guided us in the design of the cover for this volume; a recent 'blog' among contemporary philosophers working on free will takes its name from a story by Borges: 'The Garden of Forking Paths'. Although it has now closed to new comments, it is worth looking through. http://gfp.typepad.com/.

3 God would similarly complicate matters if He miraculously intervened, so let us similarly bracket Him out of our considerations henceforth.

4 Wittgenstein went so far at one stage as to say that freedom of the will just consists in the fact that future actions cannot be known at the moment of choice (in his *Tractatus Logico Philosophicus*, 5.1362).

5 This way of presenting things is perhaps too stark. Knowledge does not entail impossibility of error and thus one might know – to as great an extent as one knows anything – what one will do even prior to doing it. For example, as one is boiling a large pan of water in one's kitchen, with the provisional intention of cooking a ham in it, it might occur to one that one could instead seek to boil one's head in it. But one knows one will not do this even while believing (I would claim knowing) that there is – until the pan has cooled – a physical possibility that one might.

6 According to me then, deliberation implies that the deliberator not believe in Determinism, but not that Determinism not be true. Peter van Inwagen presses the case that without thinking of the world in this way all deliberation would be impossible in his 1983, though contrast Pereboom 2001.

7 The name 'Principle of Alternate Possibilities' goes back to Frankfurt 1969, although it is important to note that he uses it as the name for a different thesis. See glossary.

8 'The man on the Clapham omnibus' is a somewhat archaic, so I am told, way of referring to 'the man in the street' or perhaps 'Joe Public'.

9 A good introduction to the problem of induction may be found at http://plato.stanford.edu/entries/induction-problem/.

10 If you ever visit my College, I suggest you allow your eyes to linger on his portrait as it hangs on the way up the stairs to the dining hall.

11 Though see Honderich 2005.

12 Though there are philosophers who think that mere ability to do otherwise is what grounds freedom. That seems to be van Inwagen's view; the alternative view, called 'Source Incompatibilism' is held by, for example, Pereboom 2001; Hunt 2005; and Timpe 2008.

13 I say this, but the claim that Incompatibilism is the starting point for the man on the Clapham omnibus would be contested by many working in the field of so-called 'experimental philosophy'. I engage with their arguments somewhat obliquely in the main text and rather more in notes below. Tamler Sommers' 'Experimental Philosophy and Free Will' in *Philosophy Compass* takes one further.

14 Though see, for example, Nahmias et al. 2005. It seems to me that one gets the clearest results on the issue of whether or not the majority start as Incompatibilists by simply telling people what the thesis of Determinism is, namely that given the initial conditions of the universe and the laws of nature only one history is physically possible; and then testing people's comprehension of that; then explaining robust moral responsibility, and checking through questioning that they have understood that; and then, finally, asking those who've shown themselves to understand Determinism and robust moral responsibility whether they think that a universe's being deterministic is compatible with any creatures

in it being robustly morally responsible. And asking them to answer that final question without reflecting on whether or not they think ours is a universe with one or both of these features. As I say, that has been the type of experiment that I've conducted over the 15 or so years I've taught this subject and it has yielded the results that I report. The questions preferred by 'experimental philosophers' seem to me in large part to present scenarios from which one would need to *infer* that Determinism is being supposed true of the universes they describe and one cannot, consequently, be sure that the inference was made by the people who respond to the questions then asked, still less that the respondents had a clear understanding of what Determinism is and also a clear understanding of moral responsibility in what I call the 'robust' sense, the one that justifies retributive, not merely consequentially justified, elements. For example, Nahmias et al. 2006, 38, invites people to think about a repeatedly recreated universe which follows the same path each time, in particular follows the same path with respect to Jill's choosing to steal a necklace. The first time I read the scenario as it had been put to people, I thought that he had just described a universe that did in fact follow the exact same path each time – perhaps coincidentally – in which case, of course, someone might have understood that Determinism *wasn't* in fact implied by the scenario and thus the fact that they found Jill morally responsible for her action – even if they had found her robustly so – was no indication at all of their not being incompatibilists. However, on re-reading it, I saw a 'must' in the middle of the description, telling us that the universe was such that it 'must' do exactly the same thing each time it is re-created. But the fact that I missed this in reading it the first time does make me worry that some of his respondents might have done so too. Of course this sort of worry could be assuaged by new surveys. In principle, it is an empirical matter whether or not the majority do start off as incompatibilists or compatibilists. And where each of us starts off will affect where we appropriately judge the burden of proof to lie; this last is a point I make in greater detail in the main text later. See also Vargas 2007, 137ff.
15 Again, the majority spoken of here are from among my students.
16 This is an adaptation of a thought experiment first introduced to the literature by Frankfurt in his 1969 work. Importantly, Frankfurt's original was of a 'counterfactual' intervener; mine is

of an actual one. These sorts of cases have generated much discussion and the original type of case now has many epicycles added to it. We shall come back to look at some of these later. See though Ginet 1996 and Kane 1996b. A good overview is given by Timpe 2008.

17 Although, as a second observation characteristically not made by people who make the first, people find it a lot easier to kill other people if they have ready access to guns.

18 See also later note on Deep Blue.

19 I think that this argument is valid: if Determinism were true, we would be in a situation relevantly similar to that of the Senior Tutor as imagined. Others – some compatibilists to whom we shall come in due course – would reject the validity of this type of argument, which is sometimes called 'the manipulation argument'. There is a good discussion of this – and much else – in Levy and McKenna 2009 – this point at 107f. See also later discussion in the main text.

20 Contrast Kane, for example in his 2005, who thinks that ultimate authorship (ultimate responsibility, as he calls it) is necessary for *free* action, not action per se.

21 The issue of tracing is discussed in Vargas 2005.

22 There is a link to be made here to the problem of acrasia, one pointed out to me by Kevin Timpe. Suppose I know full well that to eat the whole chocolate bar would be greedy, but I give in to my craving for chocolate and eat it anyway. I eat it then not willing it under the description of being greedy, but under the description of getting a chocolate taste (which in itself is a morally blameless description). I am morally responsible though, we would say, for my greediness. This is a complicating factor that I will not refer back to as we go on. But I believe the answer to the problem of acrasia lies in characterizing it as an internal coercion: if one is to be correctly described as morally responsible for one's acratic action (as I am taking it I would be in the case I have just imagined), one must oneself be morally responsible for setting up the psychological structures which later coerced one (a certain sort of self-forming action); we must be supposing if we hold me morally responsible for scoffing the chocolate that I allowed myself to become greedy by developing the vice of gluttony when I could have refrained from doing so rather than, for example, had the vice of gluttony (if it would then

count as a vice) 'brainwashed' into me by some confectionary salesperson.

23 Though again I should refer you to the work of, for example, Nahmias et al. 2006, which calls into doubt whether belief in Incompatibilism really is as widespread as I have suggested.

24 As already mentioned, Libertarianism comes in varieties and I've only given one: see Clarke 2003 for a full discussion.

25 Here they can of course draw support from the findings of 'experimental philosophy' as referred to in previous notes.

26 Compare Vargas 2008 and 2009 and see Nahmias et al. 2006.

CHAPTER THREE: INCOMPATIBILISM

1 We might also wish to consider whether or not it can be properly basic after exposure to the arguments of the compatibilist, which it seems to me it may well not be given that, as I say in the main text, these arguments constitute at least the makings of a good case. As I use the notion of proper basicality hereafter, I do not intend it to carry with it all the meaning that certain people working in the field of Reformed Epistemology might give it. It is also the case that my way of presenting the issue in the main text assumes a sort of Foundationalism, rather than Coherentism, when it comes to justification, which assumption it is only fair to note is controversial. However, the point does not depend on the assumption; I trust that anyone adept enough at Philosophy to notice my assumption will be adept enough to realize that the same point could have been made more laboriously without relying on it.

2 Again though, I must draw attention to the fact that the claim that this is the starting point for the majority would be controversial amongst 'experimental philosophers', several of whom believe that their results suggest Compatibilism is the majority opinion. If they are right in this, the 'dialectical balance', as I put it in the main text, will be different from that I suggest for a larger number of people. If you start off – contrary, if these 'experimental philosophers' are to be believed, to the majority – as an incompatibilist, the balance will be where I suggest it is in the main text. If you start off – as these philosophers would have us believe most start off – as a compatibilist, the balance will be tipped over such that positive arguments for Incompatibilism

are needed. As I say in the main text there is no general truth about where the balance is; there are just particular truths about where it is for particular people with their particular starting points.

3 Proper basicality in religious belief has been a focus for research in this area. One might look to the works of Plantinga and his commentators for discussion.

4 In technical terminology: we need them as defeater defeaters.

5 See, for example, van Inwagen 1983. My discussion draws heavily on Kane 2005.

6 Van Inwagen 1983.

7 Ibid.

8 It is also possible to run a version of the Consequence Argument which employs instead a 'transfer of lack of moral responsibility principle'; this is then sometimes called the direct argument (after van Inwagen). McKenna argues for such a version in his 2001. I think the direct argument sound, but accept that a criticism that may be levelled against it is that it comes closer merely to articulating the incompatibilist intuition (than the Consequence Argument as discussed in the main text), in which case it has less dialectical force.

9 See, however, Slote 1982, as discussed by Bishop in his 1989, 54–60.

10 See Bernstein in Kane 2002 for a full treatment.

11 Or – more precisely – the clock's hands being in a particular position is what constitutes its telling the time that it tells when they are in that position; the rotating shaft to which the hands are most immediately connected is what *causes* the clock to tell whatever time it tells. As we shall not be misled if we do not delve down to this level of horological and terminological precision hereafter, we shall not, speaking instead simply of the hands causing the clock to tell whatever time it tells.

12 In fact, my view is that in a deterministic universe no creature really acts; rather, they merely undergo events (including perhaps events of thinking of themselves – erroneously – as acting). But I agree that to press this point against the compatibilist here would be fairly said to be begging the question, so assume in the main text that even if we are just collections of events, we can still cause ourselves to change, for example, by putting up umbrellas, from people who were starting to get wet to people who are now

staying dry. Later I return to this in the main text as the problem of the 'disappearing' agent.

13 There are lots of such worlds; ones in which I had the extra cup after just a few moments deliberation; ones in which I had it after a longer process; and so on.

14 One might try to maintain a distinction between having a power to do something such that had one done that thing, then the past would have been different and having a power to make the past different. However, for reasons I give in my 2005, 40, I do not believe this can be maintained.

15 Worlds which are 'deterministic except for little miracles' are not then really deterministic.

16 In fact, both aspects of the conclusion which in the main text is called 'ridiculous' are maintained by some compatibilists, though some suggest that local miracles could occur (i.e. that we do not need to change the laws, just violate them) and we could do this without falsifying Determinism. See Fischer's discussion in his 2007, 55ff. The suggestion that we could perform miracles seems to this author the sort of 'ridiculous' result that the compatibilist is best advised to avoid. If Compatibilism is committed to the view that we could all perform miracles, it is no more acceptable than the soul view which we bracketed out earlier.

17 There are many good discussions of the Consequence Argument if you wish to consider it further; two are by Campbell (in his 1997 and 2007). Van Inwagen's 1983 is perhaps the definitive statement.

18 See Taylor and Dennett in Kane 2002. As they say (277, note 35): 'Deep Blue, in spite of its being a deterministic automaton, authored the games of chess that vanquished Kasparov . . . [the creators of Deep Blue] cannot claim credit for those games . . . Deep Blue itself was the originating cause of those magnificent games'. However, several points are relevant here. The credit is not moral credit and Deep Blue was not – if Determinism is true – the originating cause of anything; the Big Bang (or whatever lay ultimately behind that) was. And of course Deep Blue was not an agent, was not the *ultimate* author of the games it authored.

19 Of course this is more a 'could have happened otherwise' sort of 'could have done otherwise' than it is a 'could have acted otherwise' sort, of which more later.

20 Presumably, once he felt he had sufficiently made his point, he did in fact find himself then able to move from it. But that happened later; we are considering Luther at the time he first made this declaration and, let us say, for five minutes or so afterwards.

21 Or perhaps we say that we hold him responsible for his later behaviour, but 'trace' this responsibility back to his earlier actions in drinking.

22 As already mentioned, the first of these was introduced by Frankfurt in his 1969.

23 See discussion of Libet hereafter for reasons to think it might be possible to get them very accurate indeed.

24 For a fuller discussion see Ekstrom in Kane 2002.

25 This term for them was introduced to the discussion by Fischer in his 1994; see also Pereboom 2001 and contrast Mele 2006.

26 See Widerker and McKenna 2002 for good discussion.

27 See my 2005, part I, for a fuller treatment of this conception of God.

CHAPTER FOUR: INDETERMINISM

1 This assuming Incompatibilism was indeed our starting point; again see Lycan 2003 and previous notes on 'experimental philosophy'.

2 We saw in the previous chapter that the classical compatibilist's attempts to make sense of the suggestion that you could have done something other than what you actually did even in a deterministic universe fail.

3 I mean this to be true in the actual world. Of course, there are other possible worlds – ones running to different laws of nature – in which other things happen.

4 There is an argument to be had in this general area, however, to the effect that were Determinism true, we would not really perform actions, merely participate in events, but we shall come to that later.

5 Of course, if they were only statistical, then Determinism would be *ipso facto* false, but the determinist may maintain that appearances here are deceptive; it may be that we can only describe them statistically, but that really there are hidden variables of a deterministic sort that it is physically impossible we discover.

6 The fundamental entity doesn't need to be a particle and the properties don't need to be the 'classical' ones of position, speed etc.

7 Compare Hodgson and Bishop in Kane 2002.

8 Honderich is someone who makes this move.

9 Libet himself tended to view his results as pointing to something along these lines, as suggesting that the readiness potential was an indicator that the subconscious was 'deciding', not when to press the button, but when to present the issue of whether or not to press the button to consciousness and thus he concluded, not that conscious volition had no role to play in whether or not the button was pushed, but rather that it exercised 'the power of veto' (sometimes pleasingly called 'free won't', as opposed to 'free will').

10 In the philosopher's sense of 'sometimes', that a thing happens once is it enough for it to happen sometimes, so one example would in fact suffice.

CHAPTER FIVE: ULTIMATE AUTHORSHIP

1 As Davidson's example of the nervy mountaineer has shown us. This example concerns a mountaineer holding his friend above an abyss by a rope. In the variant relevant here, it occurs to him that he could let go of the rope and let his friend plunge to his death; he forms the intention to do just this in a few moments time; then he reflects on the fact that this is the intention he's just formed and reacts with shock and horror to it; the shock and horror in turn cause him to lose his concentration and let go of the rope, so his friend plunges to his death. This was not, we may say, his freely letting go of the rope. (This is well discussed by Bishop in, for example, his 1989 work.) Although I do not argue for it, the problem of deviant causal chains is, I suggest, best solved by positing agent causation. The nervy mountaineer did not add agent-causal oomph; the events happening in his mental life were all that caused him to let go of the rope. This was not an action he performed. Bishop has his own sophisticated attempt to solve the problem of deviant causal chains using only event causation ontologically, while he would agree with me that agent causation is not conceptually reducible to event causation.

2 Many would agree that agents cause their actions, but contend that this is just agent-involving event causation; they might maintain that this is an alternative to uncaused or caused only by external things. For various reasons, some of which we'll explore as the chapter goes on, I am not myself drawn to this view.

3 On all of this compare Kane in Kane 2002, 426ff.

4 In his chapter in *Four Views on Free Will*, Fischer wrongly contends that 'ultimate sourcehood', as he calls it, requires control over everything that is necessary for free will (so that would include, for example, our own existence). This is obviously not right. Nor is Strawson's similar claim (in his 1986) that ultimate authorship requires one to be the cause of oneself. Perhaps the word 'ultimate' is unfortunate in encouraging this sort of error; 'ultimate' here means simply initiating causal chains; ultimate authors need not be 'unmoved movers'.

5 I might, of course, be indirectly responsible, by way of being responsible for an earlier self-forming action which then caused the reflection to pop up.

6 Perhaps, they sometimes do: we considered Luther as a case that might in fact have met this condition earlier; and me being presented with the 'option' of torturing a puppy to death for the amusement of a sadist might be another such case.

7 I am stipulating that this is what a 'fair die, fairly thrown' entails about the probabilities – that each outcome is in fact equally physically probable. Some – Swinburne in conversation and Clarke in correspondence – doubt that real dice meet this stipulation. So be it, a virtual die might; if you are of Swinburne and Clarke's view, I ask you to imagine seeing a virtual die being rolled on a computer screen.

8 Albeit that, as mentioned in a previous note, we could only do that by stipulating what it was to be a fair die, fairly thrown, namely that it was to make the physical probabilities of each number coming up equal.

9 I take choosing to tell the truth to be an event that is not identical to the event of telling the truth, as it can occur even if the other event does not, due to being 'supplanted' – as I put it when I consider such a case – by the interventions of the right sort of Frankfurt-style-brain-chip operator.

10 For an outcome other than my doing so *was* possible; my background and mental events inclined me towards truthfulness, but

neither they nor anything else necessitated it. In that sense there is no 'contrastive explanation' as O'Connor would put it, no explanation of why this happened rather than that, but that doesn't prevent us explaining why this happened: not all explanations are contrastive. In the main text I use the word 'complete', but 'contrastive' is perhaps better as explanations as complete as the nature of the case allows may be provided.

11 In this case though, given that my intention was to write the truth down and that my failure to provide efficacious causal oomph is hardly my fault, so I would remain as praiseworthy as I would have done had I actually written the truth down on the assumption that if the effects of someone's praiseworthy choice are supplanted in this way then their prior choice does not thereby lose any of its praiseworthiness.

12 Of course, if we talk of the outcome in terms of its being that particular agent's action, then his or her agency will be necessary for it; trivially, nothing and no one other than myself can bring about the outcome of *my* doing such and such. But that is a mere terminological point. Something or someone other than myself could certainly, in principle [in practice the technology may not be available], bring about any outcome that doesn't have built into its description that I bring it about; they could do so by taking control of my body in the right way.

13 *The Stanford Encyclopaedia of Philosophy*'s entry is a good place to start if one wishes to learn more: http://plato.stanford.edu/entries/causation-metaphysics/.

14 Compare Kane 2007, 21.

15 So, on the view argued for, it is not that something or event (x) that causes me (y) to do something (z) is to be understood as causing an effect, me, who then in turn causes another effect – x causes y and y causes z. Rather, x causes merely an event in me, say the event of my vividly realizing myself to have very good reasons to do z, which inclines (but does not necessitate) me to cause z.

16 Compare Pereboom 2001. Again, it might be worth noting that here I part company with Kane, who thinks ultimate authorship not necessary for agency per se, but only for free agency.

17 Here (though not on other issues) I follow Pereboom 2006. The problem is sometimes called the *Mind* objection; see van Inwagen in Kane 2002 for explanation and discussion.

18 Pure event causalists also suffer, I suggest, from a variant of the Consequence Argument that we discussed earlier. If my ending up writing this book is entirely caused by events in the proximate past (roughly, up until the moment I first started writing to the moment I finished), these in turn will be entirely caused by events which preceded them, and so on, back in time to before my birth. The point was first suggested to me by my reading of Bishop's 2003.

19 Compare Pereboom 2007, 101ff., where he too argues that the luck objection cannot be met by the event causalist, but may be met by the agent causalist. Though contrast Kane in, for example, his 2005.

20 I here set myself against van Inwagen 2000, 15f. and Kane 2005, 50f.; my reasons are similar to those given by Griffith in her 2005. The main point to stress is that while it's true that no prior happening explains why it is that I do whatever it is I do, we needn't confine ourselves to prior happenings when looking for things which mean that what I do wasn't lucky; we can – indeed must – look to me. I am not a prior happening.

21 See also Nichols 2004 and contrast Nahmias et al. 2004.

22 Of course, someone might suggest that what is really happening here is just event causation: the mental event that is me thinking 'I don't want to be like Buridan's ass' and the mental event that is me thinking 'I don't want any unnecessary delay in getting my beer' cause – perhaps along with subconscious events – the mental event that is me deciding to ask for a straight glass and that's all there is to it; there's just event-causal oomph, not any agent-causal oomph. But that, I am suggesting, cannot be right. Me deciding to ask for the straight glass cannot be caused by anything but me; that's what makes it *me* deciding to ask for a straight glass, rather than me being caused to think that I'm deciding to ask for a straight glass by mere events or some other agent. Of course, someone might say that I never really do decide anything; it is just that I always get fooled into thinking I decide things by events of this general sort; agents really do disappear when we view the world aright. But my point then would be that we have no reason at all to suppose that this sceptical view *is right*. The mere fact (if it is a fact) that, if it were right, then things would look exactly the same 'from the inside' as they do now is no reason to suppose that it is right, just perhaps reason

to suppose that we cannot know without possibility of error that it is wrong. But there are all sorts of sceptical scenarios that have this feature (brains-in-vats hypotheses of the right sort, for example) and we dismiss them very quickly nevertheless, surely rightly. Contrast Pereboom 2007, 113. Bishop, in conversation, suggests that talk of agents entering the world of events is symptomatic of a sort of 'false consciousness' and there is some weight to this claim, at least for the agent causalist who does not bring in souls (for persons positing souls, it may be true consciousness); for the naturalist agent causalist however, both agents and events are of course in the same – natural – world to begin with.

23 Swinburne and Lowe, for example, are optimistic about substance causation being primary.

24 It is this event's being his or her choosing to do something under some description which explains, by the way, why choices are always in principle morally assessable. They are always in principle morally assessable because they are always choices to perform actions under descriptions – the descriptions held in mind during the choosing to perform them. And the descriptions under which actions are so willed may have moral salience.

25 I take it this is the motive behind, for example, Kane's eschewing what he calls 'extra factor' strategies.

26 I have never been hypnotized, but I am told by those who have been that the same absence can be felt *at the time* by people who do things while hypnotized.

27 In the sense argued for here; as mentioned elsewhere, others – for example, Kane – maintain that we have ultimate authorship but that it involves only event causation.

28 This is not, to repeat, to say that nothing other than agents can cause an agent's actions – events can and usually do.

29 Bishop suggests in correspondence that the relation might be affected by the plurality of the *relata*, but here I side with Clarke in, for example, his 2003.

30 I view it in this regard as rather similar to Leslie's view that the good can cause; people who object to this view don't in my experience object to it because they regard it as incoherent, just false (albeit false of metaphysical necessity).

31 The soul view and the one articulated in the main text, involving a certain type of top-down causation, do not then require

(as Pereboom, suggests, 2001, 79) 'deviations' from the natural laws. They operate within the parameters imposed by the natural laws.

32 On this, see O'Connor esp. 2000b. My own view is that they may be the best candidates, especially when issues of personal identity and the 'qualitative' feel of consciousness are brought in. See my piece on Substance Dualism in James Garvey (ed.) *Companion to the Philosophy of Mind*, Continuum, forthcoming.

33 Indeed it is becoming commonplace in the Philosophy of Mind to assume that the mental supervenes on the physical in a sense that this theory rules out.

34 See Searle 1984, as discussed by O'Connor, 1995.

35 This is controversial; see Davidson's defence of Anomalous Monism in the Philosophy of Mind, for example.

36 Compare Clarke, for example 1993. While agreeing with almost everything Clarke says there, I think, *pace* Clarke, that it is not true that 'we do not introspectively observe agent causation' (199).

37 If we have ever been hypnotized and hypnosis is as it has been described to me, then we will have had experience of a situation in which at the time we noted this absence.

CHAPTER SIX: CONCLUSION

1 See O'Connor in Kane 2002, 351ff.

FURTHER READING

Robert Kane's *A Contemporary Introduction to Free Will* (Oxford: OUP, 2005) is excellent as an overview of the territory which also argues for a similar view to that argued for in this work. Kane is a Libertarian who thinks that one does not need to maintain as I do that agent causation may not be reduced to event causation. His more substantial book arguing for this account is his *The Significance of Free Will* (Oxford: OUP, 1996). The collection of essays he edited, *The Oxford Handbook of Free Will* (Oxford: OUP, 2002), contains contributions from many contemporary philosophers working in this area.

The following works are also recommended.

Almeida, M. and M. Bernstein. 2003. 'Lucky Libertarianism'. *Philosophical Studies*, 113: 93–119.

Augustine. 1993. *On the Free Choice of the Will*, tr. Thomas Williams. Indianapolis: Hackett Publishing.

Ayer, A. J. 1982. 'Freedom and Necessity'. In *Free Will*, ed. G. Watson, 15–23. Oxford: OUP.

Balaguer, M. 1999. 'Libertarianism as a Scientifically Reputable View'. *Philosophical Studies*, 93: 189–211.

— 2004. 'A Coherent, Naturalistic, and Plausible Formulation of Libertarian Free Will'. *Noûs*, 38: 379–406.

Bishop, J. 1983. 'Agent-Causation'. *Mind*, 92: 61–79.

— 1986. 'Is Agent Causality a Conceptual Primitive'. *Synthese*, 67: 225–46.

— 1989. *Natural Agency*. Cambridge: CUP.

— 2003. 'Prospects for a Naturalist Libertarianism'. *Philosophy and Phenomenological Research*, 66: 228–34.

Broad, C. D. 1952. *Ethics and the History of Philosophy*. London: Routledge & Kegan Paul.

Campbell, J. 1997. 'A Compatibilist Theory of Alternative Possibilities'. *Philosophical Studies*, 88: 319–30.

— 2007. 'Free Will and the Necessity of the Past'. *Analysis*, 67: 105–11.

Cartwright, N. 1983. *How the Laws of Physics Lie*. Oxford: OUP.

— 1999. *The Dappled World*. Cambridge: CUP.

Chisholm, R. 1966. 'Freedom and Action'. In *Freedom and Determinism*, ed. K. Lehrer, 11–44. New York: Random House.

— 1976a. 'The Agent as Cause'. In *Action Theory*, ed. M. Brand and D. Walton, 199–211. Dordrecht: D. Reidel.

— 1976b. *Person and Object: A Metaphysical Study*. La Salle: Open Court.

— 1978. 'Comments and Replies'. *Philosophia*, 7: 597–636.

Clarke, R. 1993. 'Toward a Credible Agent-Causal Account of Free Will'. *Noûs*, 27: 191–203.

— 1996. 'Agent Causation and Event Causation in the Production of Free Action'. *Philosophical Topics*, 24 (2): 19–48.

— 2003. 'Freedom of the Will'. In *The Blackwell Guide to Philosophy of Mind*, ed. S. P. Stich and T. A. Warfield, 369–404. Oxford: Blackwell.

— 2003. *Libertarian Accounts of Free Will*. Oxford: OUP.

Davidson, D. 1980. *Essays on Actions and Events*. Oxford: Clarendon.

Dennett, D. C. 1978. 'On Giving Libertarians What They Say They Want', in his *Brainstorms: Philosophical Essays on Mind and Psychology*, 286–99. Montgomery, VT: Bradford Books.

— 1984, *Elbow Room: The Varieties of Free Will Worth Wanting*. Oxford: OUP.

Dilman, I. 1999. *Free Will: An Historical and Philosophical Introduction*. London: Routledge.

Double, R. 1991. *The Non-Reality of Free Will*. New York: OUP.

Dupré, J. 1993. *The Disorder of Things. Metaphysical Foundations of the Disunity of Science*. Cambridge, MA: Harvard University Press.

Ekstrom, L. W. 2000. *Free Will: A Philosophical Study*. Boulder, CO: Westview Press.

— 2003. 'Free Will, Chance, and Mystery'. *Philosophical Studies*, 113: 153–80.

Farrer, A. 1958. *The Freedom of the Will*. London: Adam & Charles Black.

Fischer, J. M. 1994. *The Metaphysics of Free Will*. Oxford: Blackwell.

— 1995. 'Libertarianism and Avoidability: A Reply to Widerker'. *Faith and Philosophy*, 12: 119–25.

— 1998. *Responsibility and Control*. Cambridge: CUP.

— 2007. 'Compatiblism'. In *Four Views on Free Will*, by J. M. Fischer, R. Kane, D. Pereboom and M. Vargas, 44–85. Oxford: Blackwell.

Fischer, J. M. and M. Ravizza. 1992. 'When the Will is Free'. In *Agents, Causes, and Events: Essays on Indeterminism*, ed. T. O'Connor, 239–69. Oxford: OUP.

Frankfurt, H. 1969. 'Alternate Possibilities and Moral Responsibility'. *Journal of Philosophy*, 66: 828–39.

— 1982. 'Freedom of the Will and the Concept of a Person'. In *Free Will*, ed. G. Watson, 81–95. Oxford: OUP.

Ginet, C. 1989. 'Reasons Explanations of Action: An Incompatibilist Account'. *Philosophical Perspectives*, 3: 17–46.

— 1990. *On Action*. Cambridge: CUP.

— 1997. 'Freedom, Responsibility, and Agency'. *The Journal of Ethics*, 1: 85–98.

— 2007. 'An Action Can Be Both Uncaused and up to the Agent'. In *Intentionality, Deliberation and Autonomy: The Action-Theoretic Basis of Practical Philosophy*, eds C. Lumer and S. Nannini, 243–55. Aldershot: Ashgate.

Goetz, S. 1988. 'A Noncausal Theory of Agency'. *Philosophy and Phenomenological Research*, 49: 303–16.
— 1997. 'Libertarian Choice'. *Faith and Philosophy*, 14: 195–211.
— 2000. 'Naturalism and Libertarian Agency'. In *Naturalism: A Critical Analysis*, ed. W. L. Craig and J. P. Moreland, 156–86. London: Routledge.
— 2005. 'Frankfurt-style Compatibilism and Begging the Question'. *Midwest Studies in Philosophy*, 19: 83–105.
Griffith, M. 2005. 'Does Free Will Remain a Mystery? A Response to van Inwagen'. *Philosophical Studies*, 124: 261–9.
— 2007. 'Freedom and Trying: Understanding Agent-Causal Exertions'. *Acta Analytica*, 22: 16–28.
Haji, I. 2000a. 'Libertarianism and the Luck Objection'. *The Journal of Ethics*, 4: 329–37.
— 2000b. 'On the Value of Ultimate Responsibility'. In *Moral Responsibility and Ontology*, ed. Ton van den Beld, 155–70. Dordrecht: Kluwer.
— 2004. 'Active Control, Agent-Causation and Free Action'. *Philosophical Explorations*, 7: 131–48.
Haji, I. and M. McKenna. 2004. 'Dialectical Delicacies in the Debate about Freedom and Alternative Possibilities'. *Journal of Philosophy*, 101: 299–314.
Honderich, I. 1988. *A Theory of Determinism*. Oxford: OUP.
— 2005. *Punishment, the Supposed Justifications Revisited*. London: Pluto Press.
Hume, D. 1984. [1748]. *An Enquiry Concerning Human Understanding*. Oxford: OUP.
Hunt, D. 2005. 'Moral Responsibility and Buffered Alternatives'. *Midwest Studies in Philosophy*, 29: 129–45.
Kane, R. 1985. *Free Will and Values*. Albany, NY: State University of New York Press.
— 1989. 'Two Kinds of Incompatibilism'. *Philosophy and Phenomenological Research*, 50: 219–54.
— 1994. 'Free Will: The Elusive Ideal'. *Philosophical Studies*, 75: 25–60.
— 1996a. 'Freedom, Responsibility, and Will-Setting'. *Philosophical Topics*, 24 (2): 67–90.
— 1996b. *The Significance of Free Will*. Oxford: OUP.
— 1999a. 'On Free Will, Responsibility and Indeterminism'. *Philosophical Explorations*, 2: 105–21.
— 1999b. 'Responsibility, Luck, and Chance: Reflections on Free Will and Indeterminism'. *Journal of Philosophy*, 96: 217–40.
— 2000a. 'The Dual Regress of Free Will and the Role of Alternative Possibilities'. *Philosophical Perspectives*, 14: 57–79.
— 2000b. 'Free Will and Responsibility: Ancient Dispute, New Themes'. *Journal of Ethics*, 4: 315–22.
— 2000c. 'Responses to Bernard Berofsky, John Martin Fischer and Galen Strawson'. *Philosophy and Phenomenological Research*, 60: 157–67.
— 2002. *The Oxford Handbook of Free Will*. Oxford: OUP.
— 2004. 'Agency, Responsibility, and Indeterminism: Reflections on Libertarian Theories of Free Will'. In *Freedom and Determinism*, eds

J. K. Campbell, M. O'Rourke and D. Shier, 70–88. Cambridge, MA: MIT Press.

— 2005. *A Contemporary Introduction to Free Will*. Oxford: OUP.

— 2007. 'Libertarianism'. In *Four Views on Free Will*, by J. M. Fischer, R. Kane, D. Pereboom and M. Vargas, 5–43. Oxford: Blackwell.

Kapitan, T. 2000. 'Autonomy and Manipulated Freedom'. *Philosophical Perspectives*, 14: 81–104.

Levy, N. 2005. 'Libet's Impossible Demand'. *Journal of Consciousness Studies*, 12: 67–76.

— 2009. with M. McKenna. 'Recent Work on Free Will and Moral Responsibility'. *Philosophy Compass*, 4: 96–131.

Libet, B. 2002. 'Do We Have Free Will?' In *The Oxford Handbook of Free Will*, ed. R. Kane, 551–64. Oxford: OUP.

Lowe, E. J. 2008. *Personal Agency*. Oxford: OUP.

Lycan, W. 2003. 'Free Will and the Burden of Proof'. *Royal Institute of Philosophy Supplement*, 53: 7–122.

Mawson, T. J. 2005. *Belief in God*. Oxford: OUP.

McKenna, M. 2001. 'Source Incompatibilism, Ultimacy, and the Transfer of Non-responsibility'. *American Philosophical Quarterly*, 28: 37–51.

Mele, A. R. 1995. *Autonomous Agents: From Self-Control to Autonomy*. New York: OUP.

— 1996. 'Soft Libertarianism and Frankfurt-Style Scenarios'. *Philosophical Topics*, 24 (2): 123–41.

— 1998. Review of *The Significance of Free Will*. *Journal of Philosophy*, 95: 581–4.

— 1999a. 'Kane, Luck, and the Significance of Free Will'. *Philosophical Explorations*, 2: 96–104.

— 1999b. 'Ultimate Responsibility and Dumb Luck'. *Social Philosophy & Policy*, 16: 274–93.

— 2003. *Motivation and Agency*. Oxford: OUP.

— 2005. 'Libertarianism, Luck, and Control'. *Pacific Philosophical Quarterly*, 86: 381–407.

— 2006. *Free Will and Luck*. Oxford: OUP.

Nahmias, E. et al. 2004. 'The Phenomenology of Free Will'. *Journal of Consciousness Studies*, 11 (7–8): 162–79.

— 2005. 'Surveying Freedom: Folk Intuitions about Free Will and Moral Responsibility'. *Philosophical Psychology*, 18 (5): 561–84.

— 2006. 'Is Incompatibilism Intuitive?' *Philosophy and Phenomenological Research*, 73 (1): 28–53, reprinted in *Experimental Philosophy*, eds S. Nichols and J. Knobe (2008). Oxford: OUP.

Nichols, S. 2004. 'Folk Psychology of Free Will: Fits and Starts'. *Mind & Language*, 19: 473–502.

Nozick, R. 1981. *Philosophical Explanations*. Cambridge, MA: Belknap Press.

O'Connor, T. 1993. 'Indeterminism and Free Agency: Three Recent Views'. *Philosophy and Phenomenological Research*, 53: 499–526.

— 1996. 'Why Agent Causation?' *Philosophical Topics*, 24 (2): 143–58.

— 2000a. 'Causality, Mind, and Free Will'. *Philosophical Perspectives*, 14: 105–17.

— 2000b. *Persons and Causes: The Metaphysics of Free Will*. New York: OUP.

— 2002. 'Libertarian Views: Dualist and Agent-Causal Theories'. In *The Oxford Handbook of Free Will*, ed. R. Kane, 337–55. Oxford: OUP.

— 2005. 'Freedom with a Human Face'. *Midwest Studies in Philosophy*, 29: 207–27.

— (ed.). 1995. *Agents, Causes, and Events: Essays on Indeterminism and Free Will*. Oxford: OUP.

O'Connor, T. and J. R. Churchill. 2004. 'Reasons Explanation and Agent Control: In Search of an Integrated Account'. *Philosophical Topics*, 32: 241–53.

Pereboom, D. 2001. *Living without Free Will*. Cambridge: CUP.

— 2006. 'Is Our Conception of Agent-Causation Coherent?' *Philosophical Topics*, 32: 275–86.

— 2007. 'Hard Incompatibilism'. In *Four Views on Free Will*, by J. M. Fischer, R. Kane, D. Pereboom and M. Vargas, 85–125. Oxford: Blackwell.

Pettit, P. 2001. *A Theory of Freedom*. Oxford: OUP.

Pink, T. 2004. *Free Will: A Very Short Introduction*. Oxford: OUP.

Reid, T. 1969 [1788]. *Essays on the Active Powers of the Human Mind*. Cambridge, MA: MIT Press.

Rescher, N. 2009. *Free Will. An Extensive Bibliography*. Frankfurt: Ontas Verlag.

Rowe, W. 1991. *Thomas Reid on Freedom and Morality*. Ithaca, NY: Cornell University Press.

— 2000. 'The Metaphysics of Freedom: Reid's Theory of Agent Causation'. *American Catholic Philosophical Quarterly*, 74: 425–46.

— 2003. 'Alternate Possibilities and Reid's Theory of Agent-Causation'. In *Moral Responsibility and Alternative Possibilities: Essays on the Importance of Alternative Possibilities*, eds D. Widerker and M. McKenna, 219–34. Aldershot: Ashgate.

— 2006. 'Free Will, Moral Responsibility, and the Problem of "Oomph"'. *The Journal of Ethics*, 10: 295–313.

Searle, J. 1994. *Minds, Brains and Science*. Cambridge, MA: Harvard University Press.

Slote, M. 1982. 'Selective Necessity and the Free Will Problem'. *Journal of Philosophy*, 79 (1): 5–24.

Smilansky, S. 2000. *Free Will and Illusion*. Oxford: OUP.

Strawson, G. 1986. *Freedom and Belief*. Oxford: OUP.

— 1994. 'The Impossibility of Moral Responsibility'. *Philosophical Studies*, 75: 5–24.

Stump, E. 1996. 'Persons: Identification and Freedom'. *Philosophical Topics*, 24: 183–214.

— 1997. 'Aquinas's Account of Freedom: Intellect and Will'. *The Monist*, 80: 576–97.

Swinburne, R. 2007. *The Evolution of the Soul* (revised edn). Oxford: OUP.

Taylor, R. 1966. *Action and Purpose*. Englewood Cliffs, NJ: Prentice-Hall.

— 1992. *Metaphysics*, 4th edition. Englewood Cliffs, NJ: Prentice-Hall.

Thalberg, I. 1967. 'Do we cause our own actions?' *Analysis*, 27: 196–201.

Timpe, K. 2008. *Free Will: Sourcehood and Its Alternatives*. London: Continuum.

— Forthcoming. 'The Metaphysics of Free Will'. In *The Continuum Companion to Metaphysics*, eds N. A. Manson and R. Barnard. London and New York: Continuum.

van Inwagen, P. 1983. *An Essay on Free Will*. Oxford: Clarendon Press.

— 1994. 'When the Will is Not Free'. *Philosophical Studies*, 75: 95–113.

— 1995. 'When Is the Will Free?' In *Agents, Causes, and Events: Essays on Indeterminism and Free Will*, ed. T. O'Connor, 219–38. Oxford: OUP.

— 2000. 'Free Will Remains a Mystery'. *Philosophical Perspectives*, 14: 1–19.

Vargas, M. 2005. 'The Trouble with Tracing'. *Midwest Studies in Philosophy*, 29 (1): 269–91.

— 2007. 'Revisionism'. In *Four Views on Free Will*, by J. M. Fischer, R. Kane, D. Pereboom and M. Vargas, 126–65. Oxford: Blackwell.

— 2009. 'Revisionism about Free Will'. *Philosophical Studies*, 144: 45–62.

Watson, G. 1982. *Free Will*. Oxford: OUP.

Wegner, D. 2002. *The Illusion of Conscious Will*. Cambridge, MA: MIT Press.

Widerker, D. 2006. 'Libertarianism and Frankfurt's Attack on the Principle of Alternative Possibilities'. *Philosophical Review*, 104: 247–61.

Widerker, D. and M. McKenna, eds. 2002. *Moral Responsibility and Alternative Possibilities*. Aldershot: Ashgate.

Wiggins, D. 1973. 'Towards a Reasonable Libertarianism'. In *Essays on Freedom of Action*, ed. T. Honderich, 33–61. London: Routledge & Kegan Paul.

Wolf, S. 1990. *Freedom within Reason*. Oxford: OUP.

INDEX

www.ingramcontent.com/pod-product-compliance
Ingram Content Group UK Ltd.
Pitfield, Milton Keynes, MK11 3LW, UK
UKHW020735280225
455688UK00012B/660